THE MASTER MUSICIANS SERIES

WAGNER

by

Robert L. Jacobs

With eight pages of plates and music examples in the text

London
J. M. DENT AND SONS LTD

Made in Great Britain
at
The Pitman Press · Bath
for
J. M. DENT & SONS LTD
Aldine House · Albemarle Street · London
First published 1935
Paperback edition 1974

Hardback ISBN: 0 460 03153 8

Paperback ISBN: 0 460 02150 8

TO MY WIFE

. . . his was a brain of the rarest and subtlest composition, put together cunningly by nature as no musician's brain has been put together before or since. The Muse of Poetry seems to have dipped her wings into the lucid stream of music, disturbing it with suggestions of a world it had never reflected before, deepening its beauty by closer association with the actual world of men. This was the brain of Wagner . . .'

ERNEST NEWMAN.

INTRODUCTION

In this book I attempt to conduct the reader over the threshold of the Wagnerian cosmos and offer a broad clear view—trace the saga of Wagner's life; relate it to his art; survey the music, doing justice to its grandeur yet pointing out its limits; see the limits as all of a piece with the many-sided workings of Wagner's volcanic genius. Though I have done my best not to skimp anything important, a book of this size inevitably contains many topics which might have been further elaborated. Therefore in this opening paragraph I call the reader's attention to the preliminary note on 'recommended reading' attached to the bibliography of Appendix D.

The account of *The Ring* given in Appendix F demands a word of explanation. The plots of the operas have been so often described—and by Ernest Newman in his *Wagner Nights* so supremely well—that to weight this small book with further description seemed superfluous. Yet the workings of Wagner's musical genius are so intimately bound up with his dramas, and the dramas themselves are in their way so rich and subtle, that a detailed paraphrase of at least one of them, endeavouring to catch the flow of the action and the quality of the language, seemed desirable. I chose *The Ring* because it is the richest and most representative.

The reader's attention is also drawn to the Calendar of Appendix A, where he will find various particulars for which there was no space in the text.

It remains to mention that the translated quotations have mostly been taken from standard translations of Wagner's writings and from standard works. Here and there I have turned a sentence into more idiomatic English or given a rendering of my own.

R. L. J.

London, 1965.

NOTE ON THE 1974 EDITION

Although this book was substantially revised when it was reissued in 1965, I have done more than bring this latest edition up to date by revising its bibliography. Originally published in 1935, this youthful work seems to have gratifyingly become a standard introductory study. I have taken the opportunity to give it more polish and precision, and furthermore to reword some rather brashly expressed opinions and in some places to reconsider my judgments and refine upon them.

R. L. J.

CONTENTS

WAGNER'S LIFE

*

ILLUSTRATIONS

CHAPTER I

EARLY YEARS

WILHELM RICHARD WAGNER was born on 22nd May 1813, in Leipzig. He was the ninth child of Frau Karl Friedrich Wilhelm Wagner. Karl Friedrich was an actuary at the town court. Six months later the Napoleonic War broke into Leipzig; the overworked official caught typhoid from the corpses lying unburied in the streets, and died. His widow was left with only the forty pounds of his current quarterly salary.

Less than a year later she was married to, and her seven surviving children were settled and supported by, one Ludwig Geyer, an old friend of the family. Seven months after the marriage she gave birth to Caecilie. In 1870 Richard wrote to Caecilie, who had sent him copies of some letters of her father to their mother:

> . . . it was possible for me . . . to gain a deep insight into the relations of the two in difficult times. I believe I see now with absolute clearness, though naturally I find it most difficult to express myself. . . . It seems to me that our father Geyer felt that by his devotion to the whole family he was atoning for a wrong.

In conversation with his friends afterwards Wagner said that these letters confirmed a suspicion he had long had that Geyer and not Karl Friedrich was his father.

The matter has caused much pother. Evidence of likenesses has been adduced for both sides. Geyer's and Johanna Wagner's comings and goings in the relevant period have been investigated, the result tending to corroborate Wagner's suspicion.[1] But nothing conclusive has ever been nor is ever

[1] See Ernest Newman's *Life of Wagner*, vol. iii, pp. 558–62.

likely to be proved. At one time the problem had a not uninteresting importance, for it was believed that Geyer, the father of the arch-anti-Semite, was a Jew. But now it has been established that Geyer's ancestors were church organists, who married into strictly German families.[1]

Geyer may or may not have been Richard's father, but certainly he had, like Richard, exceptionally versatile artistic gifts. He was painter, dramatist, singer, actor. As actor he had met the Wagners, for Karl Friedrich, whose father had been an excise officer and his grandfathers schoolmasters, had an individual passion for the stage and literature. He named his daughters after Goethe's and Schiller's heroines—Rosalie, Luise, Clara and Ottilie—and rebuked poor Johanna, his wife, for her ignorance of these authors. Her education had been interrupted to marry him when she was fourteen. She was the daughter of a mill-owner, Johann Gottlieb Pätz. She had been sent to a select school by a Weimar prince, who for some reason took an especial interest in her. She was always vague about her extraction, Wagner tells us. She was a droll little person, courageous, harassed, who made up in character and feeling for what she lacked in culture.

> What struck me more particularly about her was the strange enthusiasm and almost pathetic manner in which she spoke of the great and beautiful in art. Under this heading, however, she would never let me suppose that she included dramatic art, but only poetry, music and painting. Consequently she often threatened me with a curse should I ever express a desire to go on the stage.

The threat no doubt had been deliberate. Geyer at that time was a member of the Royal Court Players of Dresden and he was determined that Richard should not follow his footsteps and those of Albert and Rosalie, his eldest stepchildren,

[1] See Ernest Newman, *Wagner as Man and Artist*, p. 334.

into that feckless life. For Richard was intensely susceptible to the theatre. He had been allowed not only to see Geyer act, but to wander among the properties afterwards, where he felt lifted 'from the dull reality of daily routine to that delightful region of spirits.' The tuning of the orchestra seemed to portend the supernatural. Even the humdrum furniture of his bedroom seemed fearfully animate. Nightly he screamed the house down.

He was a tiny, delicate child, whose bright blue eyes radiated the ardent vigour of his imaginative temperament. Geyer felt the glow. He called the voluble, dynamic little boy his 'Cossack.' He was determined to 'make something of him.' He tried to teach him drawing, but failed. Richard wanted at once to paint pictures like his own; the simple studies set him he did reluctantly and badly. When he was seven, Geyer sent him to a village school at Possendorf, a little way out of Dresden (whither the family had moved after Karl Friedrich's death), there to begin a good, solid education under the local pastor. He had been there hardly more than a year, when he was recalled to Dresden to Geyer's death-bed. Geyer's lungs had failed him. To distract the dying man Johanna led the bewildered child into the next room and told him to show how he could play the piano. 'What if he has a talent for music?' Geyer said to Johanna.

To ease the burden thus thrown a second time upon his unfortunate mother, Richard was sent to join his elder brother Julius, who was apprenticed to a brother of Geyer's, a goldsmith, at Eisleben. There his education was continued quietly for about a year, after which he returned to the thrilling theatrical atmosphere of his Dresden home. Johanna was maintaining the family now by letting rooms. Albert had an engagement in Breslau. Luise was being taken charge of and trained for the stage by an actress, Frau Hartwig. Johanna had with her only Rosalie, who as a member of the Royal Court Players was a valuable breadwinner, Clara, who was being trained as a singer, and the children Ottilie and Caecilie.

Johanna need not have worried: Richard's passion for the theatre was not that of the would-be actor, but of the would-be dramatist. He had the dramatist's instinct to seek escape from this world by contriving another. Soon after his return to Dresden he tried to imitate some domestic amateur theatricals with a puppet-show. He rigged up the puppets somehow, clothed them with old rags stolen from his sisters' wardrobe and began to draft the first scene. But they discovered the manuscript and laughed it out of court. At the school to which he had been sent—the Dresden Kreuzschule—the only subject which interested him was Greek tragedy. But he found Greek grammar—like the drawing studies Geyer had set him—a 'bothersome obstacle.' His instinct to create for himself was over-urgent. The only merit of the verses and translations, which he wrote and declaimed with gusto, was that they stimulated him to emulate Greek tragedy in his own language. He had a gift for verse. When the head master ordered a poem to commemorate the death of one of his schoolfellows, his was chosen and published. It looked as if Richard were going to become a poet.

In September 1826 the family moved to Prague and a year later to Leipzig. Left on his own, Richard drifted further and further off the straight path of school work. At first he seems to have done what was required of him, although he could not, he tells us, succeed in bringing his mind seriously to bear upon mathematics. Later he quitted the school friend's family who had lodged him, shut himself in an attic, lived on 'thin Saxon coffee,' wrote verse and began a mighty Shakespearian tragedy. In the summer of 1827 he visited Leipzig, where the sight of the university students swaggering boisterously about in their fantastic clothes, airing their contempt for the dryasdust *bourgeoisie,* made him long to live there. The following December he concocted a story of a 'family summons,' shook the dust of the Dresden Kreuzschule from his heels and went to Leipzig.

At Leipzig the pattern of his life rapidly became complicated. His disgust with the school there—the St. Nicholas School—where he was put into a low form and set to translate simple Greek prose extracts, received an unexpected fillip from his uncle Adolf, Karl Friedrich's brother, a broad-minded scholar, who despised academic pedantry. He enjoyed holding forth to the enthusiastic youngster about the Greek poets, Dante, Shakespeare. This stimulated Richard to carry out his Shakespearian tragedy, a remarkable hotch-potch of vengeful ghosts, fatal lovers, murdering and murdered.[1] He sent it to his uncle with a letter requesting him to announce to the family his resolve to leave school for good and develop himself in his own way. Uncle Adolf had to tell the family, who were horrified. His reply to Richard was reproachful rather than appreciative. 'Nevertheless I was conscious of a wonderful secret solace in the face of the calamity that had befallen me,' Wagner tells us. 'I knew what no one else could know, namely that my work could only first be rightly judged when set to the music I had resolved to write for it, which I intended to start composing immediately.' And forthwith, at the age of fifteen, he began to devote himself to music.

No other great composer began so late. All of them as children showed their genius by the phenomenal ease with which they manipulated musical forms either on paper or on

[1] '. . . two-and-forty human beings died in the course of this piece, and I saw myself compelled, in its working out, to call the greater number back as ghosts, since otherwise I should have been short of characters for my last acts.'

the keyboard and by their delight in them for their own musical, formal sake. Not so Wagner. He took delight less in the symbol than in that which it symbolized—less in music as abstract sound than as a conjurer of fancies and emotions.[1] When he heard the fifths of the violins he beheld ghosts. When he saw Weber conduct, what impressed him was not the music, but Weber's gestures as personification of the music.

He had been brought up in an atmosphere of music-making and musical discussion. Rosalie and Clara both played the piano. The great Weber himself and Sassaroli, a corpulent male soprano, who repelled the child, used to visit the house, and he heard argument about the merits of German and Italian opera. He used to play the *Freischütz* overture by ear. He had, of course, been shown the elements of piano-playing, but not until his twelfth year did he take systematic lessons from one Humann, a tutor at school. And then he only learnt enough to strum through his beloved *Freischütz* at sight. For he valued the music only for the operatic images it evoked.

It was not that he was less musical than the others, but that his goal was and remained—drama. Not until he came to Leipzig in the first flush of adolescence, read a piano-score of Beethoven's *Egmont* and heard the seventh Symphony and Mozart's Requiem did he realize that music was far more than an adjunct to drama; that it symbolized that for which there were no other symbols, expressed his newly awakened, adult, passional self as nothing else could. Then he realized that his Shakespearian drama was neither more nor less than a programme without music; that the creatures of his dramatic

[1] 'I was . . ., chiefly from a perusal of E. T. A. Hoffmann's works, on fire with the maddest mysticism: I had visions by day in semi-slumber in which the "keynote," "third" and "dominant" seemed to take on living form and reveal to me their mighty meaning.'

fancy were shapeless gas-bags, which must be filled and formed by the vital breath of music.

And so, in 1828, he hired Logier's *Methode des Generalbasses* and began to take lessons from one Müller, a violinist in the Leipzig orchestra. But he soon found harmony and counterpoint, like Greek grammar, a 'bothersome obstacle.' Instead of working at them he steeped himself in the score of Mozart's *Don Giovanni* and of a Haydn and a Beethoven quartet, and began to compose a piano Sonata in D minor, a Quartet, an aria for soprano and a pastoral play on the model of Goethe's *Laune des Verliebten,* of which he tells us: 'I scarcely even drafted the libretto, however, but worked it out at the same time as the music and the orchestration, so that, while I was writing out one page of the score, I had not even thought out the words for the next page.'

When in the summer of 1829 a notice came from school that he had not attended for six months, the family wisely bowed to the inevitable. What instrument would he take up? None; he would learn to compose. To that end Müller persuaded him to study the violin for a while. Then he dropped it—and dropped Müller. He spent all his time copying out Beethoven's fifth and ninth Symphonies. The latter, which in those days was regarded as the work of Beethoven's dotage, incomprehensible and unplayable, gripped him as no other music had ever done. He made a piano version of it, which he sent to Schott, who did not publish it, but gave him the score of the *Missa Solennis* as a token of thanks. And it inspired him to an orchestral overture, which was accepted by his friend Heinrich Dorn, the director of the Leipzig theatre, for performance at a Christmas concert. Evidently this overture had tickled Dorn. Wagner had given vent to his musical-mystical fancies by planning to score the brass instruments in black ink, the strings in red and the wind in green. But the performance 'was mainly prejudiced by a *fortissimo* thud on the big drum that recurred throughout the whole overture at regular intervals of four bars; with the result that the audience gradually passed from its initial amazement at the obstinacy of the drum-beater to undisguised displeasure, and finally to a mirthful mood that much disquieted me.'

But in these critical adolescent years his energy needed other outlets than composition. He craved to enter the university, lead the wild, free life of a student and identify himself with the causes of freedom and pan-Germanism which in those days of political upheaval the title of 'student' represented. At Easter 1830 he left school and tried vainly to prepare himself by private study. In June he entered another school—the Thomasschule—where he did no better. Eventually, in February 1831, he contented himself with enrolling as *studiosus musicae*—a second-class student with inferior privileges.

In the summer of 1830 revolution broke out in Paris, Brussels and Warsaw. In Leipzig the students first resisted the authorities, then supported them against the rebellious proletariat. There was hooliganism, in which Wagner took part. He drank with the students. Although diminutive and unskilled he challenged the finest duellers among them; in every case circumstances providentially prevented a fight. He gambled furiously for days and nights on end—and lost. At his wits' end he staked his mother's pension, of which he was the trustee—and won. Overwhelmed with emotion, he swore to abjure gambling for ever (he did not keep the vow), and returned home to confess to his mother and be forgiven. For the time being his appetite for student life was sated.

He felt free now to settle down to discipline his musical development. He had tried to make good the fiasco of his overture at the Leipzig theatre with another, as he thought, better work; it had been refused. And he had written seven compositions to words from Goethe's *Faust.* He realized he must after all study harmony and counterpoint. In February 1831 he began to take lessons from Theodor Weinlig, the cantor of St. Thomas's Church (the post that Bach had held) and a specialist in old Italian vocal counterpoint. It took him only six months to grasp what Weinlig could teach him—the correct handling of the traditional musical organisms. He learnt to appreciate artistry for artistry's sake, the lucid, balanced ordering of varieties in unity. He poured out a spate of works —a piano Sonata, Polonaise and Fantasia, three orchestral Overtures, a Symphony in C major. Thanks to the family's theatrical and musical connections, the Overtures and the Symphony were performed. They were successful. The Overture to Raupach's *König Enzio* and the Symphony were remarkable for the effective competence with which they imitated their models—Mozart's C major Symphony and Beethoven's *Egmont* Overture and seventh Symphony. He was serving, and serving well, that apprenticeship which every creative artist serves; he was binding himself to create with the ready-made symbols of others.

But his term of service had only begun. It was not enough to learn to write shapely instrumental music. He had mastered music, but it had not mastered him. It was still the creature of his will to drama. In the summer of 1832 he began his first opera, *Die Hochzeit* (*The Wedding*).

He began it during a holiday in Prague under the stimulus of a thwarted passion for one Jenny Pachta. She and Auguste were daughters of an aristocratic family, friends of Ottilie, whom Wagner had visited and sighed after in his Dresden schoolboy days. The story of the opera was that of a girl who pushed her importunate lover out of her bedroom window; he fell into the courtyard below and died, and the mystery of his death was revealed by her collapse at his funeral.

The story was crude, but it symbolized emotional conflicts —conflicts between impulse and obligation, love and morality— which were to haunt Wagner all his life and occasion some of his greatest music. At his present immature stage he could but envisage their musical expression. Nor was there a model to imitate; Beethoven's *Fidelio* was inimitable. Therefore, probably, and not merely because Rosalie disliked the gruesomeness of the libretto, he dropped the work, after having written an orchestral introduction, a chorus, a recitative and a septet (of which Weinlig commended the 'clarity and singableness').

In 1833 he moved to Würzburg and spent a year there as choirmaster and *Chorrepetitor* at the theatre, where his brother Albert, who was the tenor and stage-manager, had procured him the post. He earned necessary money (hitherto he had been entirely dependent on his mother and Rosalie), steeped himself in the various current operas, gained invaluable insight into the realities of production and wrote his second opera, *Die Feen* (*The Fairies*). With this work he consciously imitated the operas of Weber and Marschner—operas of which the music did not, like Beethoven's, express deep emotions, but rather conjured scenes and images to transport the hearer to a romantic fairy-world in which the call of an Oberon's horn solves all problems. The imitation was again remarkably competent. Extracts from it were successfully performed at Würzburg, and Rosalie was actually able to get it accepted for production at the Leipzig theatre. He returned to Leipzig in January 1834 in high spirits. He had learnt to write music for the stage; and in doing so he had at last won the esteem of his sister Rosalie and of his mother, to both of whom he was devotedly attached. The success of *Die Feen* would finally wipe out the sins of his feckless boyhood.

But it did not succeed. The director, Hauser, could not bring himself to produce it. Not because it was a palpable imitation, but because he did not admire the models imitated. The classics were his gods: the works of Weber and Marschner—the leaders of modern German romantic opera—seemed to him to be a futile degradation of a glorious heritage for the sake of stage effect—futile because they did not obtain the stage effect with the ease and certainty of the Italians Rossini, Bellini and Paer, and the Frenchmen Hérold and Auber, whose operas he was compelled to produce because they were so popular.

Before long Wagner himself was holding this view. But he drew a different conclusion. In the summer of 1834 he wrote an article exalting that superior stage-effectiveness of the French and the Italians—their facile 'catchy' melodies, their lighter, more flexible orchestration—and condemning the Germans as 'too learned and too intellectual to create warm human figures.' And he sat down to sketch the libretto of a new work to be based on the models of the French and the Italian operas.

There were several reasons for this surprising *volte-face.* One was the influence of Laube, the editor of the *Zeitung für die elegante Welt,* who in 1832 had praised his Symphony and who now published his article. Laube was an 'advanced' spirit. The gay, sensuous hedonism of Latin opera symbolized for him freedom from the rusty fetters of German pedantry, Puritanism and political tyranny. This standpoint impressed the ex-student of Leipzig University.

Another far deeper influence was the performance of the celebrated dramatic soprano, Wilhelmine Schröder-Devrient, as Romeo in Bellini's *I Capuletti ed i Montecchi.* He had already in 1829 been carried away by this wonderful woman in *Fidelio.* She had been a revelation. She had swept the infinitely deep emotions which Beethoven's music evoked into a personal dramatic utterance. She had embodied the concepts of his imagination. Wagner's impulse had been to compose a work for her on the spot; but at that time he could not. Now he could. But it would not be in the style of Beethoven. He had recently heard an indifferent performance of the ninth Symphony. Beethoven, he agreed with Laube, was too recondite, too 'classic,' too super-sensual. Nor would it be in the style of Weber. 'Our modern romantic grimaces are foolish phantoms,' he wrote. 'Away with them—lay hold of real passion.' He would compose for Schröder-Devrient in the style of Bellini, in which she would express warmly, easily and joyfully what at that time he conceived to be 'real passion.'

Not long ago he had had a taste of this 'real passion.' In Würzburg he had had two callow love affairs: with Therese Ringelmann, a member of the chorus with whom he had to practise daily, and an 'infinitely more genuine' one with Friederike Galvani, the fiancée of the oboist. He was no longer in the mood to dramatize his thwarted passions as he had tried to do in *Die Hochzeit,* or indulge romantic fancies as he had done in *Die Feen.* He was in the mood brazenly to enjoy life as he found it. In May 1834 he spent a riotous holiday with his friend Theodor Apel, the son of a distinguished Greek metrist. Theodor was a versatile, ambitious, 'advanced' young artist like himself. They drove about Bohemia in their own carriage sightseeing, arguing and drinking. At Teplitz Wagner stole away one morning to sketch the draft of the libretto of his new opera, *Das Liebesverbot* (*The Love Ban*). He adapted it from Shakespeare's *Measure for Measure,* and made it an attack upon the hypocrisy of Puritanism and a glorification of sensuality.

Then they visited the Pachta family in Prague, and Wagner

took revenge on Jenny for her former treatment of him by behaving with studied frivolousness. He felt frivolous. One night in a fit of crazy bravado he incited a drinking party in their hotel to shout out the forbidden, revolutionary *Marseillaise,* and then exuberantly 'clambered on to the outer ledges of the windows from one room to the other on the second floor.'

He returned home to find he had been offered the musical directorship of the Magdeburg theatrical company. Stegmayer, the conductor of the Leipzig theatre, whom Wagner had been pestering to perform his *Die Feen,* had recommended him in order to get rid of him and at the same time put him under an obligation. Wagner went to look at the company at Lauchstädt, a small watering-place where it was having a summer season. He found a set of lazy, dilapidated people. He would have refused to join them had he not at his lodging met Minna Planer, the leading juvenile actress. She attracted him violently. 'I engaged a room on the spot . . . regretted greatly that I had not brought my luggage with me from Leipzig and hastened to return thither as quickly as possible in order to get back to Lauchstädt all the sooner. The die was cast. The important experiences of serious life confronted me.'

His return to Lauchstädt marks the end of the first stage of Wagner's apprenticeship to his art. He had learnt technique by imitating the current models. He could write the German opera of romantic illusion, the Latin opera of sensuous artifice. In the stage now beginning he learnt to express himself in opera. And he learnt this, not by turning outwards to the ready-made symbols of others, but inwards, discovering himself in the struggles and passions of 'serious life'—then framing his own new symbols.

CHAPTER II

MAGDEBURG—KÖNIGSBERG—RIGA—PARIS

WAGNER made his début at Lauchstädt in August by conducting *Don Giovanni.* Although it was the first time he had conducted an opera, the performance was a success. For he had the born conductor's power to grasp the composer's intention and force it upon others, 'above all . . . the . . . dash and aplomb that gives confidence to players and singers who are none too intelligent or too industrious and hides from the dazzled audience the thinness of the ice over which the performance has been skating.'[1] He needed all his dash and aplomb in Magdeburg. His manager, Bethmann, was a penurious old toper, who subsisted on a pension from the King of Prussia, the lover of his late wife, a famous actress. Bethmann had neither artistic principles nor power to manage. Wagner had to content himself with the doubtful pleasure of making the most of his resources.

If only he had been compelled to make the most of his resources in other matters! He was—and he remained all his life—a wanton, incorrigible spendthrift. He was the victim of his imperious will to drama, which was not content to seek escape from this world by conjuring his musical instinct to create for him another, but must dramatize his daily life in this. The world, it seemed, was a stage and its goods properties at his, Richard Wagner's, disposal. He needed many properties—comfortable furniture, showy clothes, rich food, drink, women. His needs were exaggerated in the limelight

[1] Ernest Newman, *Life of Richard Wagner,* p. 173.

of his self-contemplation. The daylight world that must supply them he disregarded.

Thus his very first season ended in a fiasco. The wonderful Schröder-Devrient had given a couple of guest performances under his baton. She had been so delighted with him that she promised to appear at a benefit concert he planned to give in May 1835, at the end of the season, to mend his shattered finances. He advertised strenuously, but few believed so famous a singer would visit their unimportant town again so soon. They thought the advertisement a trick. Thus Schröder-Devrient had the unusual experience of singing to a half-empty hall, and Wagner an experience which was to become, alas! only too usual—that of being at the mercy of his creditors.

'I have been so ill a judge of my own affairs and got myself into such a slough of debt by all kinds of foolishness that the very thought of it makes my hair stand on end,' Wagner had written to his friend Apel in December 1834. There had, however, been an especial reason for the 'foolishness' at that time. Minna Planer had rebuffed him. It had, of course, never seemed possible to win her in the ordinary facile way. What had attracted him so much at that first encounter was not merely her prettiness, but her 'majesty and grave assurance,' her 'scrupulously clean and tidy dress.' She seemed to have that 'pure and dignified womanliness' he tells us he admired in Rosalie. She stood out from her sordid, trivial environment. In September he had written to Apel: 'For the moment I am pretty free of any love-affairs—I have no time for them—but I keep up with Toni a little. *Ach du lieber Gott,* that 's all there is to it.' But his need for Minna grew. She became the sisterly recipient of his confidences, his stand-by. She was kind, practical, sympathetic. When he had one of his chronic bouts of erysipelas, she tended him repeatedly.

One evening, to assure him his swollen features did not repel her, she gave him a kiss, 'with a friendly serenity and composure that had something almost motherly about it.'

She was not taking him too seriously then, however. For she was an exceptionally clear-headed young woman. She came of humble stock: her father had been a mechanic. At the age of seventeen she had been seduced; she had a daughter whom she passed off as her sister. Thus her knowledge of the perils of life was vivid. She had chosen her profession in order to avoid them. Acting to her was a business, not an art. Her values were exclusively material. She could cold-bloodedly reciprocate the advances of wealthy admirers without a pang of self-reproach. This had maddened Wagner. She seemed to violate that which he most valued in her—'her pure and dignified womanliness.' He violently abused her and she coldly rebuffed him. There was a rupture. Partly from despair, partly in order to arouse her pity and perhaps her jealousy, he had plunged into 'all kinds of foolishnesses.'

In the end these tactics—in so far as they were tactics—succeeded. Her better judgment yielded to her pity for the abject, brilliant, urgent little man. They became lovers.

After the fiasco of the benefit concert he returned to Leipzig. The company having gone bankrupt, he received no salary. He placated his creditors by talk of 'opulent connections' in Leipzig, and spent an unhappy summer there, living on his relatives and pestering them for money. Eventually he decided to rejoin the Magdeburg company, which had been reinstated by its patron, the King of Prussia. Minna would be there. He undertook a tour to engage new singers. He was determined to raise the standard of the performances. He increased the orchestra—at the unwilling Bethmann's expense. He obtained the services of the local regimental band and chorus, 'in return for free passes to the gallery granted to their relatives.' He took endless trouble rehearsing the singers.

He returned to Magdeburg in September 1835 and lived there with Minna and her mother. He worked not only at the theatre but at the composition of *Das Liebesverbot,* which he planned to give next March at the end of the season at the benefit concert due to him for the defraying of the expenses of his tour to engage singers. He anticipated a sweeping success that would enable him to pay off his creditors. For last season three works of his had been successfully performed in Magdeburg—the Overture to *Die Feen,* an Overture to *Columbus* (a play by Apel which the company had produced) and a New Year Cantata. And he hoped that the work would be taken up, if not in Leipzig, then in Berlin or even Paris. It deliberately imitated the popular Franco-Italian operas. He would get it translated.

'Our epicureanism is pure and strong—it is not a vulgar amour. We love each other and trust each other and leave the rest to Fate,' Wagner wrote to Apel from Magdeburg in October. And Fate willed that he and Minna should marry. Her position at the theatre had been made so intolerable by a Madame Grabowsky, her rival, whose husband was the stage-manager, that in November she accepted an engagement at the Königstädt Theatre in Berlin. Her absence unhinged Wagner. His urgent temporary need of her compelled him to demand marriage of a woman who had little mental affinity with him, whose values were materialistic, whose culture inferior, whose imagination limited—and to demand it passionately, insistently in letter upon letter. He attacked the stage-manager at a theatre-committee so vehemently that he agreed to take Minna back on fair terms. And Minna agreed to marry him. Triumphant, in tears, he welcomed her home.

He plunged again into the composition of *Das Liebesverbot,* on which now all their hopes were staked. The season ended prematurely, for the company had gone bankrupt again, but Wagner's directorship had been so effective, so popular, that the singers promised to stay on for his sake—for ten days. In that short time, however, they could not properly learn the long, elaborate opera. By shouting directions and singing with them he managed to galvanize the rehearsals; on the night itself he had to leave them—stranded. The tenor eked out his part 'by means of routine work in *Fra Diavolo* and *Zampa,* and especially by the aid of an enormously thick, brightly coloured and fluttering plume of feathers.' The proceeds of the first night went to cover the cost of the production, only those of the second to Wagner's benefit. On the second night there was no audience. And no performance. The husband of the *prima donna* took the opportunity to assault the second tenor, of whom he was jealous. The *prima donna* 'rushed despairingly to her raging spouse, only to be so soundly cuffed by him that she went into convulsions.' General pandemonium ensued.

So Magdeburg ended. This time Wagner's creditors took legal action. A summons was nailed on his door. In May 1836 he departed for Berlin, to get *Das Liebesverbot* taken up there, and Minna for Königsberg, where she had accepted an engagement. Wagner hoped to join her soon, for the conductor, Schubert, was only there temporarily during the rebuilding of the theatre at Riga to which he was permanently attached; Wagner was offered the post as soon as he would leave. But Schubert was in love with the *prima donna* at Königsberg. And the Riga theatre delayed and delayed reopening.

After two months Wagner travelled to Königsberg, unable to endure the separation any longer. Minna persuaded the manager to give him a small retaining fee until Schubert's departure. In September they were both offered engagements in Danzig; the fear of losing Minna made the manager definitely promise him the conductorship for next April. On the strength of this, in November they married. Wagner gave a series of orchestral concerts during the winter, composed the *Rule, Britannia* and the *Polonia* Overtures and wrote the libretto of a light pot-boiler, *Die glückliche Bärenfamilie,* the music of which, however, he broke off in disgust.

It was a wretched time. He had arrived to find Minna a tower of strength and comfort in the flat, dreary town where he must hang round for so long waiting. But they soon quarrelled. She detested his ruthless extravagance, he her cold-blooded improprieties. His jealousy hounded him on to marry her, to possess her at all costs—despite their poverty, despite their incompatibility. Ill-omen shadowed every incident of their marriage. He had to contract new debts to furnish their new home. 'In rainy, cold November weather' they walked to the parsonage to arrange the wedding; they were kept waiting over-long and bickered so violently that they were on the point of separating when the parson at last appeared. The congregation in the church the next day was frivolous and indifferent. 'There was not one real friend.' When the preacher bade them invoke the help of 'an unknown friend,' Wagner 'glanced up inquiringly for further particulars of this mysterious and influential patron who chose so strange a way of announcing himself. Reproachfully and with peculiar emphasis the pastor then pronounced the name of this unknown friend: Jesus.'

Marriage only exacerbated their differences. How must Minna have felt when the very morning after the wedding her husband was summoned by the magistrate to answer the demands of his Magdeburg creditors! Meanwhile the theatre was going bankrupt. In an atmosphere of unpopularity worked up by his predecessor, whom he had ousted, Wagner struggled desperately to save the situation by demanding sacrifices and tightening discipline. And then his Königsberg creditors—furniture-dealers and others—began to threaten him.

Minna could not stand it. She made friends with one Dietrich, a wealthy Königsberg merchant. When Wagner heard of this, he vented his rage upon her with such dire effect that his sole concern afterwards was to restore her shattered nerves. Then, one evening in May, he came home after a hard day's battle at the theatre to find neither Minna nor her daughter Natalie (who had been living with them) at home. 'I waited patiently, sinking down exhausted at the work-table, which I absent-mindedly opened. To my intense astonishment it was empty. Horror-struck, I sprang up and went to the wardrobe, and realized at once that Minna had left the house.' She had, in fact, fled—with Dietrich.

It is unnecessary to follow the details of the distressing aftermath of the catastrophe. Wagner tried and failed, through lack of funds, to pursue her. Then he learnt she had gone to her parents in Dresden, that Dietrich had only accompanied her part of the way. 'I succeeded in assuring myself that she really only wished to get away from a position that had filled her with desperation.' He left Königsberg for Dresden, where he found her in a pitiable, distracted state. His remorse, and his hope of obtaining the conductorship at Riga, for which he had been negotiating and which he now travelled back to Berlin to confirm, induced her to try life with him again. But after a few weeks together in the neighbourhood of Dresden she left him a second time—again with Dietrich. And this time he could not find her.

He took refuge in Dresden with his sister Ottilie and her husband, Hermann Brockhaus, an expert in Oriental languages. In the kindly, cultured atmosphere of their home he found rehabilitation. Here a germ that had been planted in him during his two months' stay in Berlin last year bore fruit. He had been so deeply impressed by a brilliantly efficient performance of Spontini's grand opera, *Fernand Cortez,* that he had conceived a desire to compose a work in this genre himself. Now, at Ottilie's, he read Bulwer Lytton's *Rienzi* and saw in it an ideal libretto for a grand opera. He resolved to compose it in Riga.

It would be very different from *Das Liebesverbot.* That work had been conceived in a spirit of youthful hedonism, which he had outgrown. Minna had revealed to him his craving for love, real love—she had both inspired and thwarted it. But this at least *Rienzi* had in common with *Das Liebesverbot* and *Die Feen*—it aimed to conquer the world by giving it what it wanted. His experiences of the last three years had made him aware of the difficulty of that conquest. The only work of his that had been performed outside Magdeburg and Königsberg was the *Columbus* Overture, in Leipzig in 1835 —and it had failed. *Die Feen* had been turned down in Leipzig and *Das Liebesverbot* in both Leipzig and Berlin. He decided that it was futile for him, an obscure young German, to compete with the foreign commodity merely by imitating it—a commodity whose success was largely due to the snobbery which acclaimed its foreignness. He must, like Meyerbeer, outdo it—unite German sincerity with Latin brilliance, write a grand opera on the scale of *Robert le Diable* and *Les Huguenots,* which, like these works, would defeat the enemy in his own camp, conquer Paris. Then, like Meyerbeer, he could impose himself on his countrymen as a unique universal genius.

He had for some time past hankered after Paris. *Fernand Cortez* had already stimulated him to sketch a libretto for a grand opera, based on a novel by Heinrich König, *Die hohe*

Braut; he had had it translated and sent to Scribe, the celebrated Parisian librettist, suggesting boldly that Scribe should procure him a commission to compose the work for the Paris Opera and on that condition put it into verse. Having received no reply, in the spring of 1837 he had sent Scribe the score of *Das Liebesverbot,* for which, as we know, he had also contemplated Paris.

But these had been merely projects of a restless, desperate ambition. *Rienzi* was more than a project: it was a wish-fulfilment. It has been said of his model, the grand opera of Spontini and Meyerbeer: 'The gestures are those of demi-gods rather than of men, the rhythm . . . is based on the march, now in hymn-like guise, now in broad flow of choral song, now in pathetic monologue.'[1] In this style Wagner would marshal all the resources of orchestra, chorus, ballet and scenery pompously, bombastically to apotheosize Rienzi, the deliverer of the Romans from their corrupt patriciate, the noble, lonely, doomed tribune—to apotheosize himself, that is to say, embodied in Rienzi—himself gloriously at war in the cause of his art in a hostile, corrupt world.

He went to Riga in September 1837. A month later Minna rejoined him. She too, poor thing, had found rehabilitation. Dietrich had deserted her, and she had written Wagner a 'positively heart-rending letter,' in which she confessed her guilt, begged his forgiveness and assured him that 'in spite of all she had now become fully aware of her love' for him. No doubt she had told herself she must take Wagner as God made him. She was twenty-eight, near the end of her career as juvenile actress. He had brilliant virtues as well as faults. He loved her honourably. And he was earning money again.

Although not long ago he had been planning to divorce her, he took her at her word, welcomed her warmly and

[1] Paul Bekker, *Richard Wagner,* p. 91.

promised never to mention the name of Dietrich. She, for her part, gave up the stage and all it involved and devoted her splendid common sense and energy faithfully to his welfare. Their relationship became stable. They learnt what to expect of, and how to adapt themselves to, each other. They became trusty comrades in the struggle for existence.

Not until the spring of 1839, when Wagner was suddenly dismissed from his post, did that struggle become urgent again. It had, of course, always been difficult to make both ends meet on his small salary alone. He piled up debts as usual. In 1838 they moved into more expensive lodgings, in which were an ante-chamber, a *salon* and a study. The study contained a divan, a desk and a hired grand piano, on which he composed *Rienzi.*

He incurred the enmity of his manager, Holtei, a clever, unprincipled creature with a passion for vaudeville and light opera. At first Wagner had made 'the best of a bad bargain,' he tells us, and indulged him. He wrote an additional bass aria to Holtei's words for a *Singspiel.* He unearthed *Die glückliche Bärenfamilie*—only to throw it away a second time. He could not conceal the repulsion which he, the creator of *Rienzi,* must feel for the provincial, frivolous, vicious atmosphere of the theatre. He could interest himself only in the serious operas in the repertory. This infuriated Holtei. He called it 'pedantic nonsense' and resisted Wagner's demands for an increased orchestra and strenuous rehearsal.

Wagner was too absorbed in serious composition to allow this to worry him. He wrote the two acts of the first part of *Rienzi,* 'Rienzi's Might,' and one or two minor serious works —a bass aria for *Die Schweizerfamilie,* Weigl's 'faded old opera,'[1] and a *National Hymn,* which was performed annually for several years.

[1] Ernest Newman, *Life of Richard Wagner,* p. 191.

His seriousness had been deepened by the death of his sister Rosalie shortly after Minna's arrival. He was determined to extricate himself as soon as possible from this shoddy, unworthy environment. He pinned all his hopes on *Rienzi.* It would soon wing out into a new world—Paris—and gather fortune for him there.

His dismissal surprised and enraged Wagner. He believed it to be the result of an intrigue between Holtei and his 'false friend,' Dorn, his successor, who had been the cantor and director of the municipal music (that same Dorn who years ago in Leipzig had performed that disastrous Overture, written in multi-coloured ink). According to Dorn it was the inevitable result of his debts, which had become appalling. The theatre could not keep on a conductor whom his creditors might at any moment compel to fly from the town.

He was offered compensation in lessons and concerts, all of which he refused. For he had resolved to make a virtue of the necessity of his escape from Riga—not to wait, as common sense demanded, till *Rienzi* was accepted for performance in Paris, but to go there now himself and enact in real life the dream which had haunted him for the last two years—play Rienzi to Paris's Rome and conquer as Rienzi conquered.

He persuaded Minna against her better judgment. He had just heard from Caecilie's husband, Eduard Avenarius, the Paris agent of the Brockhaus publishing firm, who had on his behalf called on the celebrated Scribe, that the latter 'had some recollection of the subject of the libretto' he had sent him and had taken the trouble to have 'portions' of *Das Liebesverbot* 'played to him.' He had also written to Meyerbeer, 'informing him of my plans and begging him to support me.' True, he had received no reply, but at any rate he could tell Minna he was at last 'in communication with Paris.'

There was one excellent reason, however, for going to Paris —there he would be out of the range of his creditors.

They left Russia in June 1839, took ship at Pillau, near Königsberg, to London and from there travelled to Boulogne, where they landed on 28th August. They had several hair-raising adventures. Because of his insolvency, Wagner's passport had been impounded in Riga: thus they had to smuggle themselves across the frontier behind the backs of the sentries who stood on guard a thousand paces apart. Their flight was arranged by their trusty friend Möller, of Königsberg. For Minna's sake he concealed from them the danger. They were conducted to the frontier by devious ways, made to shelter in the hut of a sentry out on duty—he had been bribed—and there await the 'relief of the watch during which the sentries were elsewhere engaged.' Then they had to dash for the ditch that bounded the frontier, scramble across it, tear over the open ground until at last they were out of the range of the rifles of the other sentries who had *not* been bribed.

'I was simply at a loss to convey to my poor, exhausted wife how extremely I regretted the whole affair,' Wagner writes.

This was only the beginning of their adventures. They had chosen to travel by sea, partly because it was cheaper than by land, partly because it was easier to take 'Robber,' their huge, beloved Newfoundland dog, that way. Not that it was easy A bark from him might have ended their lives at the frontier —or caused their arrest when they had him hauled on board 'up the steep side of the vessel' to avoid 'attracting attention.' The vessel was a tiny merchant ship manned only by seven men. The journey, which should have lasted eight days, lasted three and a half weeks. First they were becalmed, then driven by storms to take refuge in a Norwegian fishing village up a fiord. The captain put out again too soon, the ship struck a reef with shocking violence. There was no damage, and before long they were under way again. They met worse storms than ever; there was thunder and lightning; they thought their last hour had come.

Eventually they were piloted through dangerous sandbanks (on which, Wagner was informed, four hundred ships foundered every year), down the English coast to the murky Thames, of which the red lights and the fog-bells terrified Minna, who kept pointing them out to the sailors lest they should miss them. They stayed at the King's Arms boarding-house, Old Compton Street, for a week. It was too expensive, but the bustle and size and variety of London fascinated Wagner, and Minna needed a rest. He looked up Sir George Smart, the conductor of the Philharmonic Society, to whom he had sent the *Rule, Britannia* Overture he had written in Königsberg. Smart was out of town. Then he looked up Bulwer Lytton at the House of Commons to have a chat with him about *Rienzi.* None of the officials understood what he wanted. 'I was sent step by step to one high dignitary after another, until at last introduced to a distinguished-looking man . . . as an entirely unintelligible individual.' This gentleman politely informed him that Bulwer Lytton was out of town. Perhaps he was tickled by the odd, lively, urgent little foreigner, for he took the trouble to get him into the House of Lords, where he heard a debate, and the House of Commons and 'gave . . . such careful details of various things' that Wagner felt he 'knew all there was to know about the capital of Great Britain.'

On the Channel Wagner got into conversation with a lady who gave him an introduction to Meyerbeer, who was staying at Boulogne. And so at once Wagner met the great man, who treated him with the stereotyped amiability celebrities often assume, listened to his reading of the libretto of his *Rienzi,* asked to keep the score of the first part to look over, assured him of his interest when he called a second time, complimented him on his handwriting and gave him introductions to Duponchel, the manager, and Habeneck, the conductor of the Paris Opéra. He was, in fact, considerably impressed, and several times in the years ahead went out of his way to help Wagner.

The letter to Duponchel came to nothing. The manager of the most celebrated opera house in Europe was a business man out to make money by exploiting whatever means he could. (His predecessor had not scrupled 'to give intimate suppers at which the great attraction was the ladies of the ballet.'[1]) His plans were carefully laid; that they could be altered for the sake of obscure young Richard Wagner from despised, provincial Germany was out of the question.

Habeneck, the conductor, however, was kind enough to run through his *Columbus* Overture at a Conservatoire rehearsal soon after his arrival—a futile kindness, for the work, Wagner realized later, was 'queer' and 'superficial.' A year later it was actually performed—the only work of his he ever heard during this stay in Paris.

His pennilessness reduced him to one expedient after another. He wrote light songs to French texts, an aria in the style of Bellini, a setting of Heine's *Two Grenadiers,* and hawked them round to various famous singers. They received him amiably enough; Madame Pauline Viardot, for instance, '. . . praised them, but did not see why *she* should sing them.' He and Minna had to pawn all their trinkets, wedding presents, even their wedding-rings. Towards Easter 1840 Meyerbeer's agent, Gouin, promised to get *Das Liebesverbot* produced at the

[1] Ernest Newman, *Life of Richard Wagner*, p. 255.

Renaissance Theatre. On the strength of this they moved into better rooms in the Rue de Helder and bought furniture. They had just settled in when they heard that the Renaissance Theatre had gone bankrupt. 'Face to face with unheard-of misery I shuddered at the smiling aspect which Paris presented in the bright sunshine of May.'

They were forced to take in lodgers—a dreary, miserly old spinster and a German commercial traveller, a decent fellow who 'in his leisure hours zealously played the flute.' In July Wagner began to write articles for the *Gazette Musicale* of a musical publisher, Schlesinger, to whom Meyerbeer had introduced him.[1] And Schlesinger commissioned him to work out a new 'Method' for the *cornet-à-pistons* from five existing methods. He followed this up with an order to write fourteen suites for this instrument based on popular arias from current operas. Fortunately, when Wagner was 'in the midst of this work,' the first cornet player in Paris, Schiltz, took it over.

In September Wagner was in danger of being committed to a debtors' prison. He wrote a desperate letter of appeal to his old friend Apel, who time and again had helped him in the Magdeburg days. Other sources of help were exhausted. The family in Dresden evidently regarded him as a pretentious, talented adventurer, to whom hardship might teach sense; Avenarius, Laube, Schletter, an art patron of Leipzig, Schlesinger and others had all done what they could. A month later a still more desperate letter stated—probably falsely

[1] Wagner had urged Schlesinger to publish his songs; Schlesinger had refused. Then Wagner decided to take over the financial responsibility of the publication of *The Two Grenadiers* himself. But no copies were sold; he owed Schlesinger fifty francs, whereupon Schlesinger suggested that he should pay off his debt by writing articles.

—that he actually was in prison.[1] The danger impended again in December, but somehow it was staved off. They were on the verge of starvation when one morning Schlesinger burst in upon them in high good humour, called for pen and ink and wrote out the following commission: '*La Favorita* [2]—complete arrangement for pianoforte, arrangement without words for solo; ditto for duet; complete arrangement for quartet; the same for two violins; ditto for a *cornet-à-pistons*. Total fee, francs 1,100. Immediate advance in cash, frcs. 500.'

At those rehearsals of the Conservatoire orchestra at which Haberneck had so kindly run through his *Columbus* Overture soon after his arrival, Wagner heard Beethoven's ninth Symphony worthily performed for the first time in his life. The effect upon him was comparable only to that caused by Schröder-Devrient in his early youth—it was a revelation.

'Where formerly I had only seen mystic constellations and weird shapes without meaning, I now found, flowing from innumerable sources, a stream of the most touching and heavenly melodies which delighted my heart.' But that indifferent performance of 1834 had not been the sole cause of his repudiation of Beethoven, and neither was this performance now the sole cause of his return to the true faith. He had repudiated Beethoven then because he had—to put it crudely—no further use for him. He had taught him the symphony and the overture; but already in 1834 his aim was musico-dramatic expression, which he could achieve only by the imitation of operas which were the expressions of experience within his range—the opera of romantic illusion, the frivolous,

[1] That Wagner in his extremity was probably lying is convincingly argued by Strobel & Wolf (*Sämtliche Briefe,* Vol. I, pp. 414–416).

[2] Donizetti's opera.

sensuous Latin opera, the grand opera of self-apotheosis. The experience which Beethoven's *Fidelio* and his ninth Symphony expressed was beyond him.

Not so now. 'I have to learn to *renounce*,' he wrote to Apel, under the shadow of the debtors' prison—to renounce the dreams of his *Rienzi*. He had to learn to lose the world, to gain his own soul. And he gained it now—through Beethoven.

The experience that Beethoven's music uttered to him he too would utter. In February 1840 he completed *Eine Faust Ouvertüre,* in which he endeavoured to express the spirit of Goethe's wonderful words:

> Und so ist mir das Dasein eine Last,[1]
> Der Tod erwünscht, das Leben mir verhasst.

But now, as ever, his urge to self-expression could not find fulfilment in instrumental music alone. During that dreadful journey to London he had been haunted by an image of himself as the hero of an ancient saga he had read of at Riga in a story of Heine's—as the Flying Dutchman, condemned to perpetual lonely voyaging until redeemed by the love of a woman. He conceived this as the subject of an opera embodying the emotions expressed in Beethoven's music.

The conception grew in him slowly. In the summer of 1840 he offered *The Flying Dutchman,* in the form of a one-act libretto, to Pillet, the new director of the Paris Opéra. He intended it as a curtain-raiser before an evening of ballet, believing that he would more easily obtain a commission to compose such a work than a full grand opera. In the meantime he worked steadily throughout the year at the last three acts of *Rienzi,* appropriately entitled 'Rienzi's Fall.' Although it conformed to the original design, yet here and there, in the

[1] This doth my being so with grief oppress,
I long for death, my life is heaviness.

greater weight and pathos of the solo writing, it bore the imprint of his deepening sensibility. In December he sent the finished score not to the Paris Opéra—he knew too well what to expect there—but to Dresden, with elaborate letters of self-recommendation to the King of Saxony and to Baron von Lüttichau, the intendant of the royal theatre.

He did this not only from expediency, but because he was home-sick for Germany. The whole trend of his artistic development was leading him back there—to the classical tradition which culminated in Beethoven, even to the romantic opera of Weber. For Weber had blazed the trail he was about to follow. Whereas a Bellini or Spontini grand opera was conceived with an eye to the sensational effect of *coloratura* arias and grandiose choruses, Weber's *Euryanthe* (ruined, alas, by its libretto) contained music which not only evoked a faery world, as in *Oberon,* and the atmosphere of landscape, as in *Der Freischütz,* but was beginning to capture the flow of drama and the clash of personality.

Wagner had glimpsed the way past Weber. He expressed his vision in a short story that he wrote for Schlesinger's *Gazette Musicale* in the latter part of 1840—*A Pilgrimage to Beethoven.* He portrayed Beethoven himself pointing the way: why had he felt impelled to set the last movement of his ninth Symphony to the words of Schiller's *Ode to Joy*? Because the music was the expression of an emotion so overwhelming that it burst the bonds of conventional symphonic pattern and demanded words to define its object. Not that the pattern of the music was not self-sufficient as music—Wagner was elsewhere at pains to emphasize this—but because Beethoven realized that music was of its nature incapable of defining the emotions it expressed and envisaged the creation of a new art work in which music would be 'fertilized by poetry'—by the flesh-and-blood dramatic elucidation, that is to say, of the emotions implicit in the music. This new music-drama would be neither a string of set musical forms, nor a loose tone-painting of stage effects, but an endless stream of expressive melody, the emotional significance of which would be revealed in a genuine human drama.

In July 1841 Wagner took the first step of the long, tremendous journey he had begun to map out—he started the composition of *The Flying Dutchman.* But not in the form of a curtain-raiser. Pillet had eventually accepted the one-act libretto which Wagner had offered him last year, only in order to hand it over for composition to one of the several composers with whom he had contracted to supply librettos. Wagner's first indignant impulse had been to withdraw the work altogether. But an offer of five hundred francs in the summer of 1841 persuaded him to part with it. Let them do with the curtain-raiser what they would; five hundred francs gave him the leisure to convert it into a three-act romantic opera for Germany.

But he sat down to the composition in July in fear and trepidation. The piano he had hired he 'did not dare touch for a whole day.' Could he still compose? Since the end of last winter he had been without a piano; he had neither touched nor written a note—only words. He had sent, in all, eight pieces to Schlesinger's *Gazette Musicale.* In the spring he had begun to send unpaid 'reports' to the Dresden *Abend-Zeitung,* in order to bribe the editor, Hofrat Winkler, who was the secretary of the Dresden theatre, for information about the fate of *Rienzi.* He had also written a couple of articles for Lewald's quarterly, *Europa,* entitled *Parisian Amusements* and *Parisian Fatalities for Germans.*

The money for these had helped to eke out those eleven hundred francs for the work on *La Favorita* and the sum Apel had sent in response to Minna's appeal. These writings (of which the finest is the quasi-autobiographical short story, 'An End in Paris') reflect on the one hand the romantic idealism and phantasy of E. T. A. Hoffmann and on the other the piquantly ironic humorous journalism of Heine—whom Wagner had in fact met in Paris through Laube.

The latter style came quite naturally to him. His sufferings had daunted neither his sense of humour nor his self-confidence. He could post off *Rienzi* to Dresden in that dreadful winter of 1840 full of hope that it would be accepted. He could throw aside 'the confounded *Favorita*' and enter 'enthusiastically into the fun' unexpectedly provided by his comrades in misfortune, Anders, the musical bibliophile, Lehrs, the philologist, Kietz and Pecht, the painters, who on New Year's Eve burst in upon him armed with provisions for a riotous supper. They got very drunk. Wagner mounted the table, denounced life in general and eulogized the South American Free States. 'My charmed listeners broke into such fits of song and laughter and were so overcome that we had to give them all shelter for the night. . . . On New Year's Day I was again busy with my *Favorita*.'

In the early months of 1841 he had needed all his self-confidence and humour. They had planned to quit their expensive lodgings in the Rue de Helder and sell the furniture, but because they gave notice two days too late, 'owing to . . ignorance of the Paris customs,' they found they would have to keep them on another year. They managed to let them, at least for the summer. On 24th April they moved out to Meudon, in the outskirts of Paris. This move Wagner calls 'a flight from the impossible into the incomprehensible.' They had no money at all.

The five hundred francs for *The Flying Dutchman* rescued them. And in June his self-confidence was brilliantly justified: *Rienzi* was accepted at Dresden. This gave him just the stimulus he needed to compose *The Flying Dutchman* for Germany. He began it, as we have seen, in July. The inhibition which had gripped him was quickly broken. Many of the themes he had already conceived. Now new themes welled within him so spontaneously, so inevitably, that he had the sensation of having composed them also before. In seven weeks the entire conception was complete.

The composition of *The Flying Dutchman* was a turning-point in his artistic development; the acceptance of *Rienzi* was a turning-point in his career. He had banked on *Rienzi*, and won, as he knew in the end he would win. It was a truly grand grand opera. Meyerbeer, Winkler, Schröder-Devrient had recommended it. It contained a fine part for Schröder-Devrient and a still finer one for Tichatschek, the famous Dresden tenor.

The victory marked the end of Wagner's stay in Paris, to all intents and purposes. His intents and purposes were in Dresden, his return there for the production, which was to be 'at the beginning of next year at the latest,'[1] a foregone conclusion. He bombarded Wilhelm Fischer, the stage-manager and chorus master, and Ferdinand Heine, the costume designer, with letters about details of performance; he begged them to speed up the preparations, to make sure of Devrient. In November she dismayed him by insisting on performing Gluck's *Armida.* Now *Rienzi* must be postponed till the Easter of 1842.

And so for several months longer they had to drag on the weary struggle for existence in Paris. Not only had they exhausted the five hundred francs at Meudon, but the family to which they had let their lodgings in the Rue de Helder had suddenly departed, and they had to sell their furniture in order to pay their landlord rent for lodgings they could not occupy.

[1] Ernest Newman, *Life of Richard Wagner*, p. 304.

Kietz had to finance their return to Paris and support them in a miserable, cold apartment in the Rue Jacob. Wagner remained indoors—his shoes were soleless—and orchestrated *The Flying Dutchman* and wrote the overture to it. In November he posted the finished score to Count Redern, the director of the Opera at Berlin. Now he was free to support himself again by journalism and by transcribing another opera for Schlesinger, Halévy's *La Reine de Chypre.* He also earned two hundred francs by working up a libretto from Hoffmann's *Bergwerke von Falun,* to be composed by one Dessauer, a Jewish musician of Prague, for the Paris Opéra. On Christmas Day he received proof of the family's changed attitude towards him since the acceptance of *Rienzi*—five hundred francs from his sister Luise. In February, thanks again to Meyerbeer's recommendation, *The Flying Dutchman* was accepted in Berlin. At Easter Friedrich Brockhaus, Luise's husband, lent him money for the journey to Germany. On 7th April they took sad leave of Caecilie and Eduard Avenarius, who had borne with them through all their miseries, of Lehrs and Anders, who were so old and delicate they might well fear never to see them again, and Kietz, the cheerful, faithful, unfortunate painter Kietz, who painted so slowly that he 'even complained because some of his sitters died before their portraits were completed.' Minna 'never stopped crying all through the journey,' Wagner wrote to Caecilie. 'Even when she began to get a little calmer her only answer to the attempts at consolation I felt I ought to make was: "May I cry again now?"'

CHAPTER III

DRESDEN

Rienzi was produced in Dresden on 20th October 1842. Fischer and Heine had done their utmost to carry out Wagner's instructions; Schröder-Devrient was enthusiastic; Tichatschek still more so. After each rehearsal of a certain ensemble passage he handed round a collection-plate for Wagner, to which the soloists, moved no doubt by the sensational achievement of the obscure, needy young composer, willingly contributed. They talked about him all over the town. The first night was crowded and eager. 'You and the other Paris friends of Wagner should have seen him,' Heine wrote to Kietz. 'He looked like a spectre; he laughed and wept at the same time and embraced every one who came near him, while all the while cold perspiration ran down his forehead.'

His success was stupendous. He became a celebrity overnight.

One result was that the management acquired *The Flying Dutchman* from the Berlin Opera and performed it in January, three months later. Although Schröder-Devrient sang Senta, it was a failure. It only ran four nights. Wächter as the Dutchman was inadequate; the scenic effects did not come off; after *Rienzi* the music seemed gloomy and dull.

Another result was the offer to Wagner of the post of musical director at the theatre. This he refused, for he would be subordinate to the two royal *Kapellmeister.* But one of the latter posts had also fallen vacant; it too was offered him and he accepted it. The customary trial service for a year in the subordinate position was waived, so highly did they think of him.

He was appointed on 2nd February 1843. At last he had the money—fifteen hundred thaler a year—the fame, the power for which he had struggled through so many years: yet he accepted the post with misgiving. For the Dresden theatre was a typical hide-bound, bureaucratic court institution. The intendant, Baron von Lüttichau, was an authority not on art, but on forestry—until 1824 he had been Saxon Master of Forests. Like the director of the Paris Opéra, he was an *entrepreneur* who had to cater for all tastes. The repertory was a medley of operas, plays and farces.

Wagner's misgiving was soon justified. A member of the orchestra died and he tried to break the custom according to which each player, no matter how old or incompetent, succeeded to the post of another in order of seniority, by inviting a new, good player from Darmstadt to fill the vacancy. The whole orchestra was against him; he had to withdraw the invitation. Then, in April, there was trouble when he tried to apply the principles he had been evolving in Paris to Mozart's *Don Giovanni*—to present the music not as an abstract conventional pattern, but making each phrase a spontaneous, expressive declamation. He had achieved this in Gluck's *Armida* in March. But in Mozart traditions of performance were more set. The critics attacked his 'Paris tempos.' Lipinski, the vain and brilliant first violin, who literally 'led' the others in that he played ahead of them, headed the opposition at a meeting before Lüttichau. Wagner lost his temper. He had to promise—in the words of his letter to Lüttichau the following day—'to alter nothing in the hitherto accepted interpretation of tempo, etc., when conducting older operas, even when it goes against my artistic judgment, leaving myself nevertheless free, when studying newer operas, to exercise my best judgment with the object of getting as perfect an interpretation as possible.'

There had been another reason for the misgiving with which he had accepted his appointment—his urge to compose a new opera that would follow, not the path of *Rienzi,* but the lonely path of *The Flying Dutchman.* In that last winter in Paris his longing for his homeland had found vent in the reading of German medieval history and legend. He had been captivated by an old version of the Tannhäuser legend in a German *Volksbuch.* He laid aside the libretto he had been drafting of a historical grand opera on the lines of *Rienzi, The Saracen.*[1] In June 1842, during a holiday at Teplitz from the worries of the forthcoming production of *Rienzi,* he had conceived both the scenario and the themes of the new opera.

He had accepted his appointment reluctantly—but he had accepted it. He could not, he tells us, resist the 'instinct that urges every man to take life as he finds it.'[2] His triumph dazzled him. He was lionized by society. He was elected conductor of the Dresden Choral Society. He wrote for it *The Love Feast of the Apostles,* which was sung by all the choirs of Saxony at a festival in July 1843. He wrote also—in his official capacity as royal *Kapellmeister*—a chorus for male voices to celebrate the unveiling of the statue of the late King Friedrich August I in June. He spent a short holiday afterwards at Teplitz in an overworked, excited state. In October he moved to a comfortable, expensive apartment in the Ostra Allee and furnished it as if he were settling there for life. He even formed a library.

All this time the music of *Tannhäuser* had been fermenting

[1] *The Saracen* was based on an episode in the life of Manfred, the son of the Hohenstaufen Frederick II.

[2] *A Communication to my Friends,* p. 322.

within him. He had completed the poem in April 1843. He began the composition in August, and by the end of January 1844 had finished the first act. He wrote it, he says, 'in a state of burning exaltation that held my blood and every nerve in fevered throbbing.' It was a more original, more subtle conception than *The Flying Dutchman.* The latter still held to the design of conventional opera; it was divided into 'numbers,' some of which even had cadenzas. 'The joining of the situations,' Wagner himself says, was 'imperfect,' the verse and diction 'bare of individual stamp.' In *Tannhäuser* he would try to shake off the cramping bonds of habit. He would do away with 'operatic diffuseness'; he would expand 'numbers' to 'scenes'; he would humanize the issue—present his hero as suffering under the compulsion not of an external curse, but of an inward psychological conflict—the conflict between the desire of the flesh for pleasure and of the spirit for redemption.

In doing all this he would of course demand more of his singers and of his audience than he had done in *The Flying Dutchman*; and in the latter it seemed he had already demanded too much. It had failed in Dresden mainly because the singer of the title part could not act—the music had not been to him, as it had been to the composer, an expression of emotion. In Berlin, where it had been given in January 1844, the singers on the whole realized Wagner's effect, but that effect had proved too compelling, too strange, unsuitable to the routine of opera repertory. Again the work had been withdrawn after four nights.

He did not finish the score of *Tannhäuser* until the spring of 1845. He was distracted from it not only by his professional duties but by two enterprises in 1844, which he carried out with characteristic gusto. One was the composition of a choral and orchestral paean of welcome to the King of Saxony on his return from England in August, and the organization of its surprise performance one morning at his country seat in Pillnitz. The other, later in the year, was the arranging of the removal of Weber's remains from London to Dresden and their appropriate reception. He wrote and delivered, with great effect, a funeral oration, after which a male choir sang words and music of his composition.

The production of *Tannhäuser* was fixed for the autumn of 1845. Its success would bring him not only artistic but also financial salvation, of which he stood in desperate need. For after the triumph of *Rienzi* all his old German creditors had swooped upon him. Schröder-Devrient had generously lent him a thousand thaler, but still he was helpless, for half the money had to be sent to pay off his debts in Paris, and in Magdeburg alone he owed 657 thaler. This had not deterred him, however, from living comfortably above his income in the Ostra Allee, for he had anticipated that his operas would be taken up all over Germany. But as yet *The Flying Dutchman* had been given only in Berlin, Riga and Cassel, and *Rienzi* only in Hamburg. Elsewhere the latter had been rejected as too costly, too elaborate and too dependent for success upon the tenor. Wagner had decided that the operas would be accepted more quickly if they were published. In June 1844, with sublime self-confidence, he arranged with one Meser to publish them at his own expense, that is to say, at the expense of those in Dresden whom he had persuaded to lend him the money. Thus he had mortgaged his dubious artistic future.

The rehearsals of *Tannhäuser* were trying. Wagner could not make the good, simple, hearty Tichatschek understand the despair and self-pity of Tannhäuser, nor his youthful niece Johanna—Albert's daughter—the exalted self-abnegation of Elisabeth. Schröder-Devrient was depressed with her part, Venus. It was sketchy, incoherent; she was not beautiful enough. 'What on earth am I to wear as Venus?' she exclaimed, with 'a despairing smile.' 'I can't just put on a girdle.' The special scenery ordered from Paris did not arrive in time. After the first performance, which was a failure, Tichatschek fell hoarse for a week, during which the critics, who were linked with the conservative elements in the theatre and therefore hostile, attacked the opera 'as ravens attack carrion thrown out to them.' The rumour was spread that it was Catholic propaganda.

The second performance went better. Tichatschek's part had been cut, the scenery had arrived. The house was small but select, capable of grasping the finer points. The third performance was packed; thereafter the work settled into the repertory. But it owed its popularity not to those 'finer points,' which only the cultured few grasped, but to the several conventional operatic effects Wagner had not yet schooled himself to avoid—to the procession in Act II, to Wolfram's lyric 'O Star of Eve,' to Elisabeth's 'Greeting.'

It was imperative that the work should be given outside Dresden—above all in Berlin, where royalties were paid, not a single inadequate fee as in Dresden and other provincial towns, and where a success would cause it to be taken up everywhere. In December 1845, therefore, he visited Berlin—fruitlessly. The director, Küstner, considered the opera 'too epic.' Wagner returned to Dresden to face a horrible financial crisis. Various usurers, from whom he had borrowed to pay his swelling account with Meser, were threatening action. Breitkopf & Härtel were demanding payment for the grand piano which he had installed in the Ostra Allee when he had moved there. Schröder-Devrient, unhinged by jealousy of Johanna Wagner and by an unhappy love-affair, handed her lawyer Wagner's IOU for the thousand thaler she had lent him in 1842. His affairs were the talk of the town. His last resource was to appeal to Lüttichau, who showed his esteem for Wagner's talents by arranging for a loan of five thousand thaler to be granted him from the Theatre Pension Fund at a rate of five per cent interest.

All this time he had been itching to begin a new opera—*Lohengrin.* He could not, for sheer worry. He had discovered the subject in the winter of 1841–2 in Paris, in that same book which contained the Tannhäuser legend. The opera first took shape in his mind during a holiday in July 1845 at Marienbad. He had overworked; his doctor had ordered him to 'take the waters' and rest. He could only resist the temptation to sketch out the new opera by sketching something else instead, the scenario of a comedy, *The Mastersingers of Nuremberg,* the material for which he had come across in a recent reading of Gervinus's *History of German Literature.* But even this did not free him from 'the thrall of the idea of Lohengrin.' One morning he jumped out of his bath before the prescribed hour and, 'barely giving myself time to dress, ran home to write out what I had in my mind.' He completed the poem in the winter of 1845 and drafted a sketch for the music in the summer of 1846 at Gross-Graupe, a village to which he had retired to recuperate after yet another exhausting season.

Two undertakings had absorbed his energy. One was a performance of Beethoven's ninth Symphony at the Palm Sunday concert in April. He took immense pains to execute his principles of interpretation. He rehearsed the cellos and basses no less than twelve times in their recitative passage introducing the last movement. He lashed the choir into a state of exaltation. He wrote a programme note, into which he inserted passages from Goethe's *Faust* to illumine the work's spiritual meaning. He had a wonderful success.

The other undertaking was the drafting of a long, elaborate report, *Concerning the Royal Orchestra,* in the early months of

1846. It was 'the quintessence of practical common sense.'[1] He suggested, for instance, that the orchestra should be increased so that good players need not waste their energy on trivial operas, vaudevilles and the like; that old, inefficient players should be pensioned off; that there should be a series of orchestral concerts every winter.

He turned to the music of *Lohengrin* in the summer as he had turned to compose *Rienzi* in Riga—to forget the alien world. He was feeling ever more isolated in Dresden. The court esteemed his talent, but resented his presumptuous reforming zeal. His colleague, Reissiger, the senior royal *Kapellmeister,* was—not unnaturally—jealous of him. Among important musicians only Liszt and Spohr had praised him unreservedly. To Mendelssohn and Schumann, the two great representatives of the classic tradition, he was antipathetic. *Tannhäuser* had given him the entrée into a circle of writers and artists from which he had derived stimulus; but he was the last person to enjoy for long a society in which, as he puts it, 'after all no one thought much of anybody else's talents.' He wanted adherents, not colleagues—adherents like Fischer; Heine; Röckel, the subordinate musical director; Pusinelli, his doctor and generous creditor; Uhlig, a violinist in the Dresden orchestra; Carl Gaillard, the editor of a Berlin musical journal; Alwine Fromann, the reader to the Princess Augusta of Prussia.

He felt isolated. He had the understanding of friends, but not of the public. He had been 'able to make a complete success of' the ninth Symphony. 'Yet,' he says, 'as often as it was put on the stage, my *Tannhäuser* taught me that the possibilities of its success had yet to be discovered. How was this to be done? This was . . . the secret question which

[1] Ernest Newman, *Life of Richard Wagner,* p. 442.

influenced all my subsequent development.' In *Lohengrin* he made a big step towards answering it. He devised a music that would not only express powerfully the emotions of each character, but express also the interactions of the characters in dramatic conflict. He elaborated the technique of the *Leitmotiv*: he did not merely take a *motif* from its original context to recall for a particular dramatic purpose that original context, but made several *motifs* recur constantly throughout the opera, embodying the chief dramatic issues. Thus the conventional operatic forms, which in *The Flying Dutchman*, and still more in *Tannhäuser*, had been blended together, tended further to disappear. The characters, which had hitherto been more or less isolated units, expressing themselves in 'numbers' and 'scenes,' became actors in a realistic dramatic situation, which determined the pattern of the opera.

And this situation was that in which Wagner now found himself. Like Lohengrin he came from another world—the Montsalvat of his art; like Lohengrin he demanded of this world the love that accepts without questioning; like Lohengrin he must submit to the torture of being doubted even by his own wife.

In the winter of 1846–7 he interrupted the composition of *Lohengrin* to devote himself to another stimulating problem of interpretation, a production of Gluck's *Iphigenia in Aulis*. He dovetailed arias and choruses, revised the German text for the sake of the declamation, coached the singers. In the spring of 1847 he heard that his report, *Concerning the Royal Orchestra*, had been rejected—nearly a year after he had presented it. He could hardly have been surprised. Shortly after he turned his back on Dresden, moved to an outlying suburb and took rooms in the secluded old Marcolini Palace, in the lovely garden of which he spent many happy hours composing *Lohengrin* and studying his old favourites, the Greek dramatists, and the fascinating Scandinavian mythology. He continued to fulfil his wearisome duties as conductor at the theatre, but absented himself more and more from the committee meetings, where matters of policy and administration were arranged. On one occasion he turned up only to talk about totally irrelevant aesthetic questions, in order to show how he despised their petty affairs, in order to exasperate Lüttichau. For he was exasperated by Lüttichau. 'Whom ought one to pity,' he wrote to Spohr, 'these Junkers, who are set like foxes to herd the geese and make themselves laughing-stocks at every step—or the artists who suffer under their errors of taste?' Lüttichau's last unpardonable 'error of taste' had been to allow Gutzkow, the dramatic manager, to produce an opera, Halévy's *Les Mousquetaires de la Reine*—Gutzkow, Wagner's *bête noire,* unmusical, dogmatic, interfering, an intriguer against him in the theatre, in the press. . . .

Wagner was so furious that he wrote demanding that unless 'the conduct of the opera' was confided to him 'more unreservedly than has hitherto been the case,' he should be released from his official duties altogether and his 'proved capacity as dramatic composer and conductor' be 'utilized in such a way' that an honorarium could be granted him. The demand was refused, but that Wagner was able to make it at all shows what prestige he must have had in Dresden. If he had had money too he would have broken there and then with the theatre. *Rienzi* and *Tannhäuser* were confirmed successes, but only in Dresden: there they stuck obstinately.

In Berlin that October, however, *Rienzi* would at last be produced. Wagner travelled there full of optimism—he was a born optimist—determined at all costs to secure a success that would bring him economic and with it spiritual independence. He failed. The public was appreciative, but the tenor who sang Rienzi was inadequate and the critics were hostile. Nor could he find opportunity to read *Lohengrin* to the vacillating Friedrich Wilhelm IV, who had had passing enthusiasms for *Rienzi* and *Tannhäuser* in Dresden, and of whose patronage and support therefore he had had hopes. On top of this Küstner denied that he was under obligation to pay Wagner's expenses during the two months he had spent in Berlin rehearsing, since his co-operation, valuable though it was, had not been invited. Wagner received royalties only for the three performances he had conducted. Next year there were five performances. And then no more till 1865.

No wonder he returned to Dresden in a 'hideous state of mind.' Again he had to humiliate himself by appealing to Lüttichau—to raise his salary to that of Reissiger, two thousand thaler. Lüttichau put the matter before the king: he acknowledged Wagner's talents, but censured his extravagance and pretentiousness; he recommended that the appeal should be granted but that Wagner should be 'threatened with instant dismissal' unless he mended his ways. The king wrote to Wagner accordingly. Lüttichau handed him the letter. It stupefied him. Yet there was nothing for it but to swallow his pride, accept the increased salary and continue to perform his duties. In the early months of 1848 he conducted a series of orchestral concerts—the series he had advocated in his report. This was the one item in it that had been adopted.

In the meantime Wagner had been stirred by two events—the death of his mother in January and the outbreak of revolution in Paris in February. The revolution quickly spread to Berlin and Vienna. The Frankfort Parliament was inaugurated to legislate for a new united Germany. In Saxony there was a change of ministry. After he had finished *Lohengrin* in March, Wagner drafted a comprehensive *Plan for the Organization of a German National Theatre for the Kingdom of*

Saxony, of which the basis was the emancipation of the theatre from the court and its reorganization under a 'national union of composers and dramatists.' He expounded it to Oberländer, the Minister of the Interior, who was sympathetic and suggested that Wagner should try to get private members of the Chamber of Deputies to further it. Wagner did so; he was disgusted to find them impervious to the claims of art in the reformed society.

Wagner had been profoundly stirred by the revolution. It seemed that his solitary struggle was to be merged in a great popular uprising—that in a new, reformed society the theatre would be reformed—that in this new society his artistic goal would be reached.

He had for some time past been gradually working towards a new, clearer perception of his artistic goal and of the means of attaining it. In *Lohengrin*, for the sake of dramatic expression, he had broken the conventional design of opera. Dramatic expression, it seemed then, was his aim; therefore he resolved henceforward to write drama pure and simple, not opera—but a new kind of drama, stripped of the artificial trappings of modernity, reaching back to the great elemental figures of medieval history, saga and myth, which since that last winter in Paris he had perpetually been studying—figures like Frederick Barbarossa and Siegfried. Such figures he termed 'purely human' (*rein-menschlich*): in them ultimate emotional realities were revealed. The revolution appeared to him as a manifestation of these realities, to which a new drama—his drama—would give artistic utterance.

In 1848 he returned to a play about Barbarossa, sketched two years previously. It dissatisfied him. He found his dramatic purpose—the expression of the universal 'purely-human' emotions that underlay action in all its appearances—entangled in a network of irrelevant issues and 'relations.' To alter these would be to violate history. He turned therefore from refractory history to the simpler, more plastic myth—to the figure of Siegfried.

In doing so he attained a far clearer vision of his goal. He 'became aware of the bearings of true poetic stuff in general.' He decided that poetry was of its nature incapable of expressing the 'purely-human,' for it was a 'mere organ of the intellect.' Only music, after all, could express it—music, the language *par excellence* of elemental emotion. Not, of course, the cut-and-dried music of conventional opera, but the music he had envisaged in Paris, the endless stream of expressive melody. The function of the 'true poetic stuff in general' would be none other than to define the otherwise indefinite emotions which this melody would express. In the new drama, in other words, music would supply the dynamic power of expression; poetry would fulfil its function in directing this power.

He realized that he had turned to myth instinctively because it was the ideal 'poetic stuff' to his purpose. The myth dealt in universals, not particulars. Since it was common property there would be no need to compel music to violate its nature by narration. It could at once identify itself with the situations and develop concurrently with them. The situations, stripped of non-essentials, would be few, plastic, weighty; the music would make articulate the unconscious universal emotions implicit in them.

Wagner's belief that he had turned from the spoken drama to the music drama for drama's sake was, of course, a delusion. His dramatic purpose was valid only for himself, who had at his command a language uniquely capable of expressing those emotional essences which he termed the 'purely-human.' He mistook the laws of his own being for those of art in general. He rationalized on a grand scale. He even supposed that 'with the disappearance of the historico-political subject must necessarily vanish in the future the spoken form of play as inadequate to meet the novel subject'!

He was, in fact, realizing the implications of the vision he had formulated in Paris eight years before in that short story, *A Pilgrimage to Beethoven,* published in the *Gazette Musicale.* He had conceived music as a language of emotion and music drama as a continuous melody 'fertilized by poetry.' Now he was discovering the subject and the technique of that music drama.

He turned to Barbarossa in revolutionary 1848 because the great-hearted medieval Emperor seemed topical. Wagner was revolted by the philistinism and hypocrisy of the politicians and was on worse terms than ever with the court. In June he addressed a political union, the *Vaterlandsverein,* on the subject of 'Republic or Constitutional Monarchy?' and, with Barbarossa in mind, upheld monarchy—but monarchy unhampered by obsolete courts and constitutions, monarchy that meant leadership. The speech caused an uproar in the court and the orchestra. If Lüttichau had not stood by him, he might have been dismissed.

His debts, too, were worse than ever. He owed at least five thousand thaler. Desperately, unsuccessfully, he appealed to Pusinelli, Schletter—and Liszt. For Liszt by now had won the expensive privilege of friendship with Wagner. They had first met in Paris. Wagner had disliked the triumphant virtuoso. But since then Liszt had devoted himself more and more to making Weimar, where he had settled, a centre of musical culture. They found they were kindred spirits. In March 1848, for instance, Liszt had looked up Wagner unexpectedly; they had visited Schumann and argued about Mendelssohn and Meyerbeer (Wagner's one-time hero and patron now embodied all that was detestable to him in contemporary opera), till Schumann, 'completely losing his temper, retired in a fury to his bedroom for quite a long time'; this gave them 'a most amusing topic of conversation on the way home.'

It was in the summer of 1848 that Wagner shelved the Barbarossa project. Instead he wrote *The Wibelungs,* a quasi-historical essay, and then another prose-work, *The Nibelung Myth as a Sketch for a Drama,*[1] which began by outlining the framework of the epic of *The Ring* from Wotan's theft to Brynhilda's awakening and ended as a detailed scenario of the drama of *The Dusk of the Gods.* Then in the autumn of that year Wagner wrote that drama. He entitled it *Siegfried's Death* and incorporated the epic he had outlined in the form of narratives. Like *Lohengrin, Siegfried's Death* presented a lonely hero in an alien world; Lohengrin was misunderstood, Siegfried annihilated. In December he presented this situation in yet another form in a sketch based on the life of Jesus of Nazareth. He abandoned it afterwards, however, as unfit for dramatic representation.

In the meanwhile his situation in Dresden had been growing ever more intolerable. Emboldened by the successes of the reaction in Vienna and Berlin in the autumn of 1848, the court did all it could to muzzle the popular composer of *Rienzi* and *Tannhäuser,* whom they considered a dangerous revolutionary. *Lohengrin* was rejected—despite Lüttichau's efforts to produce it; a revival of *The Flying Dutchman* was cancelled; the series of orchestral concerts was conducted by Reissiger.

This had the effect of driving Wagner into the revolutionary

[1] Wagner's so-called 'Nibelung Myth' was very much a personal creation. His manipulation of his sources in Icelandic saga and German legend is described in Jessie Weston's *Legends of the Wagner Drama.*

movement. He had long since given up his hope that the revolution might 'come from Above, from the standpoint of erudite intellect'—from deputies, from liberal ministers, from a purified monarchy. He believed now that it could come 'only from Below, from the urgence of true human need.' He contributed articles in February and April 1849 to the revolutionary *Volksblätter,* of which his friend Röckel was the editor. He renewed his agitation for a national theatre. Rumours reached the court. He went so far as to expound the plan to a meeting of the orchestral political union. He was summoned by Lüttichau to a conference to hear a memorandum wildly abusing him—to hear such phrases as 'all the time he has been here he has been no use whatever,' 'slovenly performances of church and operatic music, noted with displeasure in the highest quarter.' Perhaps Lüttichau's fury was pardonable. The man whom time and again he had befriended had behind his back been advocating a plan of which the essence was that for the sake of the theatre he, Lüttichau, should be dismissed! How could Lüttichau realize that Wagner's ingratitude was no ordinary callousness, but the effect of a devotion to an artistic ideal which inevitably overrode all other obligations?

In the spring revolution actually broke out in Dresden. The Saxon government, under the influence of Prussia, had rejected the Imperial Constitution drawn up by the Frankfort Parliament; the reactionary Beust, who had been appointed Foreign Minister, had dissolved the Chamber, prohibited a public demonstration and summoned Prussian troops to his aid. The rebels formed a 'Committee of Safety' and attacked the guard in the arsenal. The king and the government withdrew to the fortress of Königstein, to await the inevitable victory of the advancing Prussian troops. For a few days there was civil war. Then the rebel provisional government retreated to Freiberg and thence to Chemnitz—accompanied by Wagner. But they arrived separately at Chemnitz; Wagner went to an inn, the others to an hotel, where they were captured. Wagner escaped.

The civil war had fascinated Wagner. He threw pamphlets to the guard outside the arsenal: 'Are you with us against foreign[1] troops?' He wound his way through the street-fighters in the barricaded streets to the tower of the Kreuzkirche and there spent the day and the night watching the fray. He lost all sense of reality. 'With a delight that was full of despair' he embraced the idea of a retreat to the Erzgebirge, there to concentrate the reinforcements that were pouring in and 'inaugurate a German war.' He conveyed Minna out of danger to Chemnitz, where his sister Clara and her husband Wolfram lived. Then he returned to Dresden, reported to the provisional government the fatigue of the reinforcements he had passed, set out to Freiberg to requisition horses and carts for them, turned back to Dresden a second time and on the way met Bakunin, the Russian nihilist—his friend—and two other members of the provisional government in a 'smart hired carriage,' and with them their army—in retreat. He joined them. His excited voice, we are told, drowned the rattling of muskets and the clattering of feet beside the carriage. And so to Chemnitz.

Wolfram had to persuade him to take refuge in Weimar, for in the 'dreamy unreality' of his 'state of mind' he could not decide whether he was guilty of treason or not. Before long he heard from Minna that a warrant was out for his arrest. Liszt proved a friend in need. He spirited him to a village, Magdala, where Minna visited him; procured him the passport of a Dr. Widmann; gave him money. It was decided that he should go to Paris, through Switzerland.

[1] i.e. Prussian.

He took a last farewell of Minna at Jena. On 28th May he entered Switzerland, safe, free, exhilarated.

And Minna? She had listened to him, urging revolution for the sake of the theatre, as she had listened to him in Riga, urging that crazy trip to Paris. This time, however, she was not persuaded against her better judgment. Then he had had little to lose and everything to gain; now, it seemed, he was wantonly throwing away that which he had gained for another gain, beyond her comprehension—beyond every one's comprehension at that time, perhaps, save Wagner's own.

No wonder she came coldly, reproachfully to the refugee at Magdala, hungry for her embrace, for her consolation; no wonder she spoke thus: 'Well, I am come, as you were so determined on it. Now perhaps you will be satisfied. You may start on your journey at once. In any case I shall go back to-night.'

CHAPTER IV

SWITZERLAND

WAGNER'S feeling of exhilaration as he crossed the Swiss frontier on his way to Paris soon passed. He was free, his soul was his own—but the ownership was lonely. Minna could not share it.

For years she had not shared it. As his long, tense pursuit of his artistic goal had led him into conflict with his environment —with the stereotyped, the corrupt, the trivial—so it had led him into conflict with her. In Riga, in Paris, they had been trusty comrades in the struggle for existence: their interests were united. In Dresden they clashed. Minna's interest was security; Wagner's jeopardized security. 'When I came home deeply depressed and agitated by some new trouble, some new insult, some new failure, what did this wife of mine produce instead of consolation and inspiring sympathy? Reproaches, more reproaches, nothing but reproaches!'

But he could not live without her. He needed her care; he loved her physically. From Paris he wrote to her imploring her to rejoin him. She replied that she would do so only if he were in the position to earn enough to keep her somewhere abroad, for after he had so suddenly thrown up a post and broken off connections such as he could never hope to establish again, it was hardly to be expected that a woman should again entrust her future to him. Whereupon he persuaded Liszt to finance his return to quiet, congenial Zürich, which he had visited on the way to Paris, and Minna's journey there from Dresden. In Zürich, with Minna beside him, he could 'gaily' work at the librettos for operas he had in mind for

Paris—*Wayland the Smith* and *Achilles.* And to Minna he painted a bright picture of the future he would build for her there.

But Wagner was deceiving himself and them. The fashionable, vulgar, corrupt Parisian Opéra was the epitome of everything in contemporary art that he detested. He had only gone to Paris from a sense of duty to Liszt, who, like Minna, was anxious to further his career. Besides lending him money, Liszt had produced *Tannhäuser* at Weimar early in 1849; he had written a glowing article about it in the *Journal des Débats*; he had given him a letter to Belloni, his influential Paris secretary.

Wagner returned to Zürich in July. In September Minna rejoined him, bringing with her their pets, Papo the parrot and Peps the dog, and various other household gods. Minna was annoyed to find that he had not been sketching opera librettos for Paris, but finishing his essay, *The Wibelungs,* and writing a lengthy pamphlet, *Art and Revolution,* concerning those ideas which had led him to ruin in Dresden. In November and December he wrote a similar, still lengthier pamphlet, *The Art Work of the Future.* She nagged at him until, 'merely to have a little peace,' he worked at *Wayland the Smith* and, in January 1850, returned with it to Paris. The effort made him ill. He could do nothing. Belloni was away in Weimar. *Wayland the Smith* was, after all, quite unsuitable. A performance of the *Tannhäuser* overture had to be cancelled because the orchestral parts were missing. . . . He grew desperate. He seemed to stand at the end of a blind alley. Germany was closed to him and the other path to success, Paris, he could not follow. And Liszt could not help him on indefinitely, for he himself was in financial straits. He told Liszt that in the last resort he would sacrifice *Lohengrin* to Paris. Meanwhile he would await Belloni's return with the orchestral parts of the *Tannhäuser* overture, which Liszt possessed.

Wagner was saved unexpectedly by two admirers—Frau Julie Ritter of Dresden, an elderly widow who had heard of his predicament from his friend Uhlig, with whom he had been corresponding, and Jessie Laussot, *née* Taylor, a young, charming, wealthy Englishwoman. Jessie Taylor had studied music in Dresden, become friendly with Frau Ritter and her son Karl, and with the latter met Wagner. (Frau Ritter had never met him.) Since then she had married a business man, Laussot, of Bordeaux. The two women arranged to give Wagner an income of two thousand francs for two years. In March Wagner accepted with alacrity an invitation to visit the Laussots in Bordeaux. Jessie's homage balmed his spirit, smarting from Minna's reproaches. She was artistic, sensitive, understanding. He confided to her all his misery. She too was unhappily married. They fell violently in love.

Wagner wrote to Minna disingenuously. He tried to overcome her aversion to 'accepting alms' by representing Jessie's action as one of high-minded friendship. But rumours of their love reached Minna. She angrily insisted that he should return to his business in Paris. Her letter decided Wagner to break with her. After three or four weeks he left Bordeaux for Montmorency, near Paris, there to await Jessie, with whom he intended to tour Greece and the Near East and forget detestable Europe. He communicated to Minna his decision to break with her, his intention to travel—but not his expectation that Jessie would accompany him and finance the tour. Minna, in despair, travelled to Paris to find him. Wagner avoided her by going to Geneva, where he awaited news of Jessie from Frau Ritter, in whom, it seems, the lovers had confided. Then he heard from Jessie that she had been obliged to confess their affair to her mother, who was living with her, and her husband, who swore to shoot him. Whereupon Wagner set out for Bordeaux. He found the Laussots' flat empty. He returned to Geneva distraught, and there met for the first time the devoted Frau Ritter, who had travelled all the way from Dresden to give him advice and consolation.

Jessie, it appears, had not the strength of mind to resist her mother and husband, who regarded Wagner as an unscrupulous adventurer. They intercepted his letters to her; they maligned him. Karl Ritter, with whom Frau Ritter had left Wagner to recuperate in the lovely country of the Valais, shortly received word from Bordeaux that Wagner's letters would be burnt unread. Meanwhile the Laussots had informed Minna that Wagner had seduced Jessie. When Wagner heard this he longed to deny it to Minna. He ached with pity for her. Her pathetic journey to Paris had proved the depth of her love for him—a love that cast pride to the winds in seeking its object. Karl now went to Zürich and reported her grief, her courage; she had taken a small house by the lake and furnished it according to Wagner's wishes in the hope that he would one day return to her.

On 27th July he rejoined her. The shock of his flight, like the shock of Minna's flight from Königsberg in 1837, had a cathartic effect upon their marriage. Again they adapted themselves to, again they realized what to expect of, each other—to expect now still less—indeed tragically little. 'I can no longer blind myself to the fact that for me there is henceforth no happiness in life . . . youth has left me,' he wrote later to Frau Ritter; and to Liszt:

Not a year . . . has passed recently without bringing me *once* to the very verge of a decision to make an end of my life. Everything in it seems so lost and astray. A too hasty marriage with a woman estimable but totally unsuited to me has made me an outlaw for life. For a long time the ordinary pressure of circumstances and ambitious plans . . . could conceal from me my inner emptiness of heart. The truth is that I reached my thirty-sixth year [the year 1849] before I completely realized that terrible emptiness.

During those weeks of anxious waiting for Jessie at Montmorency Wagner had perused the score of his *Lohengrin.* 'A great longing,' he wrote to Liszt, 'has flamed up in me to have this work performed. Get my *Lohengrin* produced!' Liszt took him at his word. A month after Wagner's return to Minna, he conducted *Lohengrin* at Weimar before a distinguished audience. The performance established Wagner's European reputation. Liszt himself wrote an eloquent tribute. Journalists from all parts of Germany and even from Paris praised the opera.

Liszt now eagerly awaited a new composition from Wagner. For he had identified his cause with Wagner's. He meant to make Weimar the rallying-point of a new school of music—of music like Wagner's, like his own—subjective, romantic music that burst the bonds of classical form. He was undeterred by jealousy of a greater man. He liked effacing himself and serving others; he felt that Wagner, by reason of his greatness, had a unique claim on his devotion.

But Wagner at this time had no desire to compose a work for Weimar. He wrote instead his notorious article *Judaism in Music,* which was published in the *Neue Zeitschrift* in September. He then began an article on *The Nature of Opera,* and extended it into a massive treatise, *Opera and Drama,* which occupied him until February 1851.

Why this persistent disinclination to compose and this mania for what Liszt rudely called 'political platitudes and socialist gibberish'? We have seen how after shelving the historic Barbarossa subject Wagner had turned to myth as the material for a new kind of music drama, because it lent itself to cogent, plastic, musical treatment, because it embodied the 'purely human' emotions inherent in music. He had regarded the revolution as a manifestation of these emotions and his music drama as the organ of expression of a regenerated community. The triumph of the reaction in 1849 had not shaken his belief in the revolution. Because he was in a state of upheaval, therefore the world must be. New artistic ideas sprouted from the churned soil of his emotions, and these ideas he would graft upon society. . . . And so, instead of composing, he raked vast fields of history, sociology and aesthetics for theories. He had been reading Feuerbach, the popular philosopher of the revolution, and had been deeply impressed by his exalting of the value of subjective feeling and knowledge at the expense of theological and political dogma. In Zürich in 1849 Wagner wrote *Art and Revolution* to arraign contemporary culture and exhort revolution. He cited the Greeks: their art had not been cultivated for the profit or pleasure of individuals, for it had been a solemn act of communal expression — a great drama gathering to itself all the separate arts — music, literature, dance, painting, sculpture, architecture — to form one 'unified art work,' mirroring the whole nature of the community. Only in a regenerated society, purged, as the Greek had been, of materialism, was such an art possible. Hence the need for revolution.

Then Wagner went on to write *The Art Work of the Future* to elaborate his conception of this 'unified art work.' It would mirror the whole nature of the community, that is to say, of the 'folk,' 'the sum of all those who feel a common need'; it would attract all the senses simultaneously and by doing so achieve a concrete, dynamic, synthetic embodiment of truth. The arts singly could not achieve this. For the substance, but not the meaning, of music was concrete; and of poetry the meaning but not the substance, for poetry was the product of thought, 'that mere phantom of reality.' And painting and sculpture were static, not dynamic. The arts could fulfil themselves only in the 'unified art work.' Here music and poetry would lend each other substance and meaning; here painting, which had hitherto attempted to fulfil its purpose—the representation of nature—in 'the narrow frames of panel-pictures,' would have the 'ample framework of the tragic stage'; here its purpose would be fulfilled, for here the nature which it represented would acquire its real significance—it would become a background to man.

By the 'folk' Wagner meant the German folk. Like the Greeks, the Germans had a common heritage of myth and legend; like the Greeks they were, as he put it later, 'a nation of high-souled dreamers and deep-brained thinkers.' Therefore he must arraign the Jews, who did not share this heritage, who were alien to the 'folk' among which they lived and themselves disintegrated as a 'folk.' Their art was necessarily imitative, superficial, baneful.

Let it be emphasized here that Wagner's anti-Semitism, which aroused so much hostility to him, was a principle rather than a practice. By attributing those forces in contemporary Germany which he detested to some agent demonstrably non-German, he was able to keep intact his fetishistic belief in the potentialities of the German 'folk.' He detested the meretricious, Frenchified, Italianized opera of Meyerbeer, a Jew; he detested the pseudo-Beethovenian, decadent instrumental music of Mendelssohn, a Jew; he detested the press, scabrous, corrupt, ignorant—the press was largely in the hands of Jews.

After *Judaism in Music* Wagner wrote *Opera and Drama,* in which he applied himself less to 'The Art Work of the Future' and more to Richard Wagner's new music drama. He did not cease, however, to rationalize his intentions. He expounded, for instance, an elaborate theory of speech-origins, in which he distinguished what he termed 'tone-speech' from 'word-speech.' 'Tone-speech' was the wordless outcry of primal man, the 'purely human' pristine melody; 'word-speech' was the product of civilization, which to frame intellectual concepts had formed words by grafting consonants upon the vowels of 'tone-speech.' In so doing it had suffocated the vowel, the outlet of emotion. Language as a medium of emotional, artistic expression needed to be revivified by the melody from which it sprang. Then it would live again as 'word-tone-speech'—the 'word-tone-speech' of Wagner's music drama.

This 'word-tone-speech' would be an endless wave of melody, for the emotions it expressed streamed endlessly. But in this music drama not only the wave but the impelling currents, the underlying issues, would be presented—by means of the orchestra. As in *Lohengrin,* these issues would be embodied in instrumental *Leitmotive.* But they would not merely recur at points of climax; they would permeate the entire orchestral tissue of the music drama. The orchestra would no longer merely focus itself upon the uttered word, but upon the unutterable feeling behind the word—the mood, the presentiment, the memory. These latent feelings would inhere in the subject of the drama. Their dramatic development would be reflected in the harmonic, rhythmic transformations of the themes embodying them. This music would spin itself out into a vast Beethovenian, dramatic-symphonic pattern, organic and immutable, like those ultimate psychological realities which it embodied.

There would be no chorus, no 'scene,' no 'number,' no kind of stylized musical form. The drama would have the ebb and flow of reality; in revealing the forces beneath that ebb and flow the music would find a new and greater fulfilment.

In *Opera and Drama* Wagner finally elucidated the aims and the technique of his music drama. Yet still he hesitated to compose a work for Liszt, for the good reason that this new music drama of his postulated a theatre that would spare no cost on constructing special scenery and on specially training and rehearsing picked soloists and a picked orchestra. Such a theatre existed neither in Weimar nor anywhere else.

Yet sheer economic necessity forced Wagner to consider composing a work for Weimar. After his disastrous affair with Jessie, Frau Ritter had continued to support him by herself, inadequately. In the spring of 1851 Liszt answered an appeal of his for money by commissioning him to compose *Siegfried's Death* for fifteen hundred marks. In May he offered to compose for Liszt not *Siegfried's Death* but a prelude to it, a lighter, more producible music drama, *Young Siegfried.* In June he wrote the libretto and conceived themes for the new work. After this he wrote a lengthy introduction to his long-planned publication of the poems of *The Flying Dutchman, Tannhäuser* and *Lohengrin,* entitled *A Communication to My Friends,* in which he traced his artistic evolution through these operas and related it to the conception of music drama expounded in *Opera and Drama.* In the autumn he went to Alpisbrunnen to undergo a drastic 'water cure' to relieve his nerviness and a certain chronic gastric disorder and thus get strength to compose *Young Siegfried.*

At Alpisbrunnen Wagner heard from Frau Ritter that a legacy now enabled her to allow him an annuity of 2,400 marks. This made him independent of Weimar. He borrowed 600 marks from Karl Ritter to pay back the 600 marks Liszt had advanced him for the composition of *Young Siegfried.* And he informed Liszt and Uhlig of a great new plan: to expand and dramatize the narrative passages in the two Siegfried poems dealing with the epic outlined in *The Nibelung*

Myth as a Sketch for a Drama. Abortive attempts to compose *Siegfried's Death* had revealed the necessity of converting its narratives of Siegfried's youth into *Young Siegfried.* 'But the more the whole took shape the more did I perceive that I had only increased the necessity for a clearer presentation of the whole story to the senses.' So, as he had felt compelled to preface *Siegfried's Death* with *Young Siegfried,* he must now preface *Young Siegfried* with *The Valkyrie.* These three would form a trilogy, *The Nibelung's Ring,* to be prefaced by yet another drama, *The Rhinegold.* The four dramas, since they were the four parts of a great organism, must be performed on four successive days at a specially instituted festival. Such a performance was conceivable only in a society purged by that revolution which Wagner still anticipated. But his immediate concern was the composition of the work, which, he wrote, 'if I am to have any regard for my health will occupy me three years at least.'

In turning from *Siegfried's Death* to the earlier portion of the myth, Wagner had been actuated by far more than a motive of artistic expediency. *Siegfried's Death* had presented a lonely hero in an alien world, and perhaps, too, the repressed depths of Wagner's nature had found expression in its story of a hero who unwittingly plays the role of a sinister tyrant towards his wife. But in the *Nibelungen* myth a tragedy greater than Siegfried's death is presented—the tragedy of the world that destroyed him. Now that he had written *Opera and Drama* he could begin to set to music this greater tragedy, to link the particular with the universal, convey the myth's emotional philosophy, if one may so term it. And not only because he had written *Opera and Drama* could he do this, but because since 1848 he had had a new, deep, tragic experience of life. He had freed himself from the conventions that had frustrated him in Dresden; he had thrown up his career, broken with Minna. He had experienced Siegmund's love, Siegfried's freedom, Wotan's reluctant obedience to convention and Alberich's forswearing of love. And so he could tell Liszt: 'It was no mere cold reflection, but veritable inspiration that gave me this plan of mine!'

But the experience had been too fleeting, too shattering. It left him a sick, unhappy man, able to conceive, to project, but scarcely to execute. 'This everlasting life of the imagination, without any satisfying reality, is so injurious to mind and nerves that I dare only work with lengthy pauses . . . if I am to avoid falling into a permanently invalid condition.' He had hoped to finish *The Ring* in three years. Two years passed before he could begin the composition—two distracted years.

In November 1851 Wagner returned to Zürich, to live in the town in a small flat which Minna, during his absence, had arranged. He was enfeebled by the water cure and over-excited by his new plans. He was certain that next year's elections in France would be the starting-point of a great social upheaval. Thus the Paris *coup d'état* of 2nd December, by which the Second Empire was established, shocked, perplexed and deeply depressed him.

He turned—as in Dresden he had so often turned—to public musical enterprise in order to distract and to encourage himself. Early in 1852 he conducted three subscription concerts in Zürich. He gave the *Tannhäuser* overture with electrifying effect. He was induced to superintend three performances of *The Flying Dutchman.* In May, exhausted, he went to the Rinderknecht estate by Lake Zürich to recuperate. There he wrote the poem of and conceived music for *The Valkyrie.* In July he went for a long, dangerous tour across the Alps to Lugano. On his return he was heartened, yet worried, to find requests from theatres all over Germany for the rights to perform *Tannhäuser*—worried because he had no means of controlling the performances. He refused the rights to the Berlin Opera, unless Liszt, to whose discipleship at Weimar these demands were due, was allowed to conduct. He was not allowed. There was a lengthy, irritating correspondence. For the other theatres Wagner wrote a pamphlet of instructions for performance, which he printed, bound and dispatched at his own expense.

Meanwhile he wrote the poem of *The Rhinegold* and then made revisions to *Young Siegfried* and especially to *Siegfried's Death*. In 1848 he had believed in revolution; thus although Siegfried died because he cruelly betrayed Brynhilda, his death had redeemed Wotan and signified the dawn of a new era. Now Valhalla would perish in Siegfried's funeral pyre. (It was in 1856, after his discovery of Schopenhauer's philosophy brought home the tragic implications of *The Ring* that *Siegfried's Death* was re-entitled *The Dusk of the Gods*.)

If only he were in the mood to compose the work! He needed some new stimulus, he told Liszt. He needed to hear his *Lohengrin*. If only Liszt could get the Weimar court to influence the King of Saxony to permit him to re-enter Germany! Zürich was a 'desert.' 'I shall rot away here soon and everything will come too late, too late!'

The thought that *The Ring* would be unproducible tormented him. And yet the repeated triumphs of *Tannhäuser* could not shake his resolve to compose *The Ring*, 'as if the present operatic stage did not exist.' Perhaps, after all, he might find the stage he needed in Zürich. For in this 'desert,' this provincial, boring Zürich, he was an honoured exile; he had influence, friends—Jacob Sulzer, a liberal-minded government official; François Wille, a retired radical Hamburg journalist and his clever, sympathetic wife Eliza; Georg Herwegh, the poet; Otto Wesendonck, a wealthy Rhenish silk merchant and patron of the arts and his wife Mathilde, who, like Jessie Laussot, was young and lovely and artistic and intelligent. . . . In February 1853 Wagner read the completed poem, fifty *de luxe* copies of which he had had printed at his own expense, to a select gathering of friends and admirers at the Hôtel Baur au Lac. 'The verdict seemed altogether favourable.' He wrote a pamphlet, *The Theatre in Zürich,* setting forth his principles of theatre reform. But the wary Zürichers did not take his hint. In May, however, the Zürich Musical Society organized a festival of fragments from his operas. Nine thousand francs were subscribed. Three triumphant concerts were given by a picked orchestra. Wagner heard his *Lohengrin* music at last. He was banqueted. Invitations to repeat the concerts poured in from all over Switzerland.

In July Liszt came to spend eight joyful days with him. Wagner went afterwards to St. Moritz for a 'cure,' then travelled to Italy—to Genoa, Turin and Spezia. The novelty of it all soon wore off. He caught dysentery. One day he returned to his room in Spezia after a dreary country walk and sank down exhausted, utterly relaxed. He fell into a doze. He seemed to be 'sinking in swiftly flowing water. The rushing sound formed itself in my brain into a musical sound, the chord of E flat major, which continually re-echoed in broken forms.' It was the music of the prelude to *The Rhinegold.*

At last the long-desired mood had come! He returned to Zürich and would have begun to compose at once had he not kept an engagement to meet Liszt in Basle in October. He met also the fascinating, formidable Princess Carolyne Sayn-Wittgenstein, Liszt's friend and lover, and a bevy of young Wagnerians, among whom was Hans von Bülow, whose prodigious musical talent Wagner himself had moulded in Dresden and Zürich. They had a riotous time. Liszt diffused 'magnificent unconventionality.' Wagner accompanied him to Paris, where Liszt introduced him to his daughters, Blandine and Cosima, who were then in their teens.

Wagner returned to Zürich at the end of the month and plunged into the music of *The Rhinegold.* In composition he forgot his ill-health and depression. He worked passionately, rapidly. By 14th January 1854 he had finished the draft of the entire work, by May of that year the instrumentation. A month later he began the draft of *The Valkyrie* and by the end of the year had completed it.

Whence this sudden return of his creative powers? Was it because that experience had been growing into his life the denial of which had been the root cause of all his nervous debility? He had first met Mathilde Wesendonck and her husband at the concerts he had given after his return from Alpisbrunnen early in 1852. His genius had thrilled them. He became their constant guest. It was Otto Wesendonck who had been mainly responsible for financing the festival of Wagner's music in 1853. 'I laid the whole festival at the feet of one beautiful woman,' Wagner wrote. This woman was Otto Wesendonck's wife.

At first the relationship with Mathilde had been that of master and pupil. It had delighted him to initiate her into his art and his theories. She was a 'white page' upon which he 'had undertaken to write.' But in 1854 she became the beloved 'wish-child' who divined his secret thoughts—Brynhilda to his Wotan. He dedicated the prelude of *The Valkyrie* to her. In September and October, during Minna's absence on a visit to Germany, he would come in the late afternoon to play on her piano what he had composed in the morning. 'He called . . . himself the "twilight man,"' Mathilde wrote. 'Dreariness was unknown to him. He supplied the stimulus where it was needed. If he happened to come into the room obviously tired and strained, it was beautiful to see how after a short rest and some refreshment, his face would clear and a gleam light up his features as he seated himself at the piano.'

It was impossible that she should bring him that 'satisfying reality' which he craved, but she brought him reality indeed—the bitter reality of a love enjoining renunciation. His life was no longer an 'everlasting life of the imagination,' a life of 'terrible emptiness,' of dreaming, conceiving, projecting.

In the latter part of the year he read Schopenhauer and was thereby fortified in his renunciation. In the doctrine of the negation of the will to live he found philosophic justification of his doubts about the original happy ending of *Siegfried's Death.* Schopenhauer interpreted to him the meaning of his work and of his life. 'I now take delight in living for my wife,' he told Liszt. It was in this mood that he conceived *Tristan*: 'As I have never in my life tasted the true joy of love, I will set up a memorial to this most lovely of all dreams, in which from first to last this love shall for once be satisfied utterly.'

In December 1854, while under the stress of these emotions he was finishing the draft of the last act of *The Valkyrie* (the act of Wotan's wonderful, poignant farewell to Brynhilda) he received a startling invitation—to conduct the coming season of the London Philharmonic Society's concerts. He accepted it, partly because he needed every penny of the £200 offered him. Since the beginning of the year he had been in financial straits. The royalties from the performances of *Tannhäuser* had, contrary to hopes, failed to cover the expenses of the larger flat into which he had moved in 1853, of the *de luxe* publication of the *Ring* poem and of other typical extravagances. He had had to interrupt the composition of *The Rhinegold* early in the year to conduct concerts in Zürich. In the summer Minna had developed symptoms of heart-disease —precipitated, no doubt, by the agitations of their married life—and to enable her to take a cure at Seelisberg he had had to borrow money, it seems, from Sulzer or Otto Wesendonck. Later in the year he had even had to withdraw his condition that Liszt should conduct *Tannhäuser* in Berlin. A mediocre production was accordingly brought out in 1856.

He accepted the London offer also because he longed to live again in a great musical centre and conduct a first-class orchestra. And he hoped to get *The Ring* taken up at Covent Garden.

He went to London in March 1855. His anticipations were disappointed. Covent Garden was devoted only to Italian opera. And the eight concerts which he conducted were exasperating. Only for the second of them was he allowed, as a special favour, more than a single rehearsal. The programmes were enormous jumbles; they made him feel, he said, like the London omnibus-conductor who cried: 'Full inside!' The audiences' indiscriminate, tepid applause of every item disgusted him. Mendelssohn was the rage in the London of those days, and so the critics, notably Davison of *The Times*, reviled Wagner. Wagner believed that Davison was in the pay of Meyerbeer and called the press a gang of Jews.

As the season drew on the orchestra and the public warmed to him. The *Tannhäuser* overture was given at the fifth concert with striking success. At the seventh it was repeated by request of Queen Victoria, who attended with the Prince Consort. Afterwards she received Wagner. 'The question arose of putting my operas on the stage, and Prince Albert objected that Italian singers would never be able to interpret my music. I was amused when the queen met this objection by saying that, after all, a great many Italian singers were really Germans.'

As usual he made friends, notably Sainton, the leader of the orchestra, at whose suggestion he had been invited to

London, Klindworth, a brilliant Liszt pupil, who began forthwith to make a piano arrangement of *The Valkyrie*, and Berlioz, who was in London conducting the New Philharmonic. Wagner had known Berlioz in his early, impressionable Paris days and been fascinated and influenced by his music. Now they discussed the 'problems of art, philosophy and life at a five hours' sitting . . . we suddenly discovered each other as companions in suffering and I thought myself on the whole happier than Berlioz.'

Wagner returned to Zürich in June. His uncongenial exertions in the foggy London climate had brought on his old malady, erysipelas, which delayed the completion of the scoring of *The Valkyrie* until March 1856. The following May a birthday present from Liszt of a thousand francs enabled him to take a cure at Mornex, where the doctor rightly treated the illness as a symptom of nervous trouble. The great work upon which he had been engaged in the last years had been that of an unhappy man, in which he poured out his unhappiness. It had strained him. 'Despair alone was creative,' Wagner said of *The Valkyrie*—the despair of Wotan's renunciation.

Wagner gave up all work at Mornex, lived very quietly, followed a strict diet and returned to Zürich cured. He must have undergone a profound emotional reaction after completing Wotan's tragedy, for the music which he wrote to the first act of *Siegfried* that autumn and winter radiates youth and hope and happiness.

At Mornex plans for the future had occupied him. He had brooded over the idea of *Tristan* and of a subject culled from Burnouf's *History of Buddhism,* which he called *The Victors.* And he had planned to purchase a country property where he could not hear 'the abominable tinkle of pianos' with which his neighbours in Zürich plagued him. To this end he wrote to Breitkopf & Härtel, the publishers of *Lohengrin*, proposing that they should buy *The Ring* for ten thousand thaler and advance him money. Meanwhile Liszt had been hounding on the Grand Duke of Weimar to procure his amnesty. Liszt hoped that if the grand duke succeeded Wagner would be invited to complete *The Ring* in Weimar, and that eventually the cycle would be performed there.

In October Wagner's work on *Siegfried* was interrupted by a long-wished-for visit from Liszt, accompanied by the Princess Wittgenstein, who wasted their valuable time together by drawing them into the social gatherings which were her passion. And throughout, the composition was interrupted by the noise of five pianos, a flute and a tinker who lived opposite. Wagner was so maddened that he gave notice, although as yet no project for a future home had materialized. He wrote bewailing his plight and appealing for help to the Wesendoncks, who were spending the winter in Paris. During their absence they were having built for them a handsome mansion in the Enge, a suburb on the left bank of Lake Zürich. In January Wesendonck offered to lease Wagner at a low rent a small house and garden adjoining this mansion. Wagner joyfully accepted the offer. The house was altered for him according to his wishes. He superintended, spurred on the workers. In April 1857 he moved into it.

Shortly after, he decided to abandon *The Ring* for the present and compose a new opera—*Tristan and Isolde*. Breitkopf & Härtel had finally refused to publish *The Ring*; the Grand Duke of Weimar had not yet procured his amnesty and demurred at the costliness and difficulty of a *Ring* production. The sight of his huge, dumb, impotent score depressed Wagner. He would write a new, 'thoroughly practicable,' lucrative work—a work on the scale of *Tannhäuser*, which at that time was bringing in good royalties from Berlin and Vienna.

There was another, deeper cause for his decision. The current of emotion which had borne him through *The Rhinegold, The Valkyrie* and the first act of *Siegfried* had begun to flow out of the pre-ordained course and debouch into *Tristan.* In *The Ring,* it seems, he had been obsessed by the fatality of desire. The ring, the talisman of world-power, is desirable and therefore accursed. Nature alone has wisdom and permanence, for nature alone is innocent: to the Rhine-maidens the talisman is but a toy; Erda, the Spirit of Earth, knows and sleeps and wants not; Loge, the Spirit of Fire, serves man's ends without desiring them. But Alberich, Siegmund and Wotan all desire and are frustrated. Wotan in his despair determines to raise a new, free, guiltless humanity. He raises Siegfried, the innocent, ignorant *dumme Knabe,* the child of nature who would unwittingly gain the Ring and inherit the world.

But upon Siegfried too the curse of desire descends. As the forest bird guides him to penetrate the fire—the barrier of inhibition—which encircles the sleeping Valkyrie, the child of nature desires with terrible intensity. He ceases to be Siegfried the liberator and becomes another, greater Siegmund, another guilty lover, in whose tragedy the great background upon which it is played is blotted out—Tristan, whose doom is his consummation, who abjures the world and yearns for death as the only aftermath to love.

Wagner spent the summer at the Asyl, as his little house was appropriately called, composing the second act of *Siegfried* —the act in which the forest bird sings to the hero of the Valkyrie whom he is destined to love. In July Mathilde came to live in the mansion next door. On 18th September he brought her the finished poem of *Tristan and Isolde.* 'On this day, at this hour, I was born again,' Wagner wrote. '. . . A lovely woman . . . threw herself into the sea of pains and troubles so that she might create for me this glorious moment, might say: "I love you." . . . At last the spell of my yearning was broken.'

Mathilde had persuaded Otto to offer Wagner the Asyl—to curb his jealousy, to acknowledge the necessity of their love. Wesendonck, in Wagner's words, 'in the last resort wished to keep the mother of his children and for their sake he accepted his renunciatory position.'

The months that followed were perhaps the most exquisitely happy of Wagner's life. We have but to hear the songs, the *Five Poems,* which he wrote to Mathilde's words, to feel their unique pulsating atmosphere. Into the two loveliest of them Wagner distilled some of the magical essences of the music of *Tristan,* which poured from him that autumn and winter.

Like Tristan, Wagner loved a woman who was plighted to his friend. Tristan relinquished her in death. Wagner, too, had to relinquish Mathilde. Early in 1858 he wrote to Liszt: 'I am at the end of a conflict in which everything a man holds sacred is involved.' Should he unite with Mathilde for ever and betray Otto, Otto's children and his own wife, or should he separate from her? Either alternative seemed too cruel. . . . He fled to Paris; after three weeks he returned, so utterly resigned to the impossibility of betraying those others that now he could come to Mathilde in peace of mind. 'The last trace of egoism vanished from my heart, and my resolve to visit you both again now represented the triumph of the purest humanity over final stirrings of selfish longing.'

Mathilde had explained this to Otto, but Wagner had not done so to Minna, for he feared, rightly, that she would misunderstand him. Minna was shocked, therefore, by a letter of Wagner's to Mathilde which she intercepted early in April. Evidently 'selfish longing' had been stirring the lovers again. The letter was full of jealous anguish.

I felt in that mood all night. When morning came, I became sensible again and managed to send a heartfelt prayer to my angel. . . . and that prayer is love, all love. How my spirit rejoices in that love! Thence comes my salvation. The day dawned and brought bad weather. The joy of seeing you was denied me; I made no progress with my work. And so the day went by in a struggle between ill-humour and the longing for you.

Naturally all this confirmed Minna's worst suspicions. She was beside herself with fury. She refused to believe Wagner's eloquent assurances that he had not betrayed her and never would, that he had renounced possession of the woman he loved so desperately. 'I told him that I would not have this deception practised on that poor man, that I would go away, but that he must call this woman his for ever.'

The excitement aggravated her heart-disease. 'Minna, you are very ill,' Wagner said. He persuaded her to go to Brestenburg, a health resort three hours away. He hoped gradually to 'convince' her that their marriage was 'not in jeopardy' and that therefore 'she should show herself wise, sensible and noble, renounce all foolish revenge and avoid . . . sensation.' Before going away, however, Minna insisted on speaking to Mathilde, 'to straighten out the whole affair.' Wagner forbade this. Minna disobeyed. 'If I were an ordinary woman I would go to your husband with this letter,' she said to Mathilde. Mathilde treated her politely and Minna left her with the feeling that she had achieved her object.

But Mathilde in reality was furious—furious with Minna and furious with Wagner for having denied to his wife the understanding which existed between herself and Otto. Minna's coarse suspicions polluted the atmosphere of fine feeling in which they had been living. During a short visit Minna paid to the Asyl from Brestenburg Wagner tried in vain to make her comprehend the necessity of his love for

Mathilde and its compatibility with loyalty and affection to herself. He merely hurt her. In her pain she struck back and then, instead of soothing her as he had intended to do, he lacerated her with abuse—according to Minna 'until two in the morning.'

A few weeks later Minna returned for good from Brestenburg, where she had been dangerously ill; her manservant had erected a 'flower-trimmed' arch of welcome and Minna insisted that it should remain for several days, to advertise to her neighbours her dignity as Wagner's wife. Naturally the sight of this arch in honour of the woman who, she considered, had insulted her, further infuriated Mathilde.

Interesting visitors came and went that summer: Hans von Bülow and his wife Cosima, Liszt's daughter; Tichatschek and Albert Niemann, the famous tenors; the Countess Marie d'Agoult, Liszt's one-time mistress and Cosima's mother; Klindworth, Karl Ritter and Karl Tausig, the pianist, then a boy of sixteen. They could not but feel the tension and unhappiness in the Asyl. Cosima and Bülow actually arrived in the middle of a painful scene between the Wagners.

The situation became impossible. Mathilde could not endure the proximity of Minna. Neither could Wagner. She agreed to go to Dresden to be cared for by their faithful Dr. Pusinelli; then, when she had recovered health and peace of mind and overcome her jealousy, Wagner would rejoin her.

Wagner too would leave the Asyl. Minna's intervention, it seems, had brought Mathilde down to earth. She realized that their renunciation of each other could be genuine only if they separated. She lacked the courage to desert her husband and children and dare all for Wagner's sake. . . . And so Wagner had to leave. At first Mathilde cut off all correspondence with him. They heard news of each other through their confidante, Frau Wille, and expressed their feelings in diaries, which later in the year they exchanged.

On 17th August 1858 Wagner abandoned the Asyl, which he had entered so joyfully little over a year ago. He awoke that day before dawn. 'Red with shame the sun crept up from behind the mountains. Then I took one more lingering glance at the house opposite. . . .' He was beyond tears. He set forth with Minna to the station, his eyes fixed upon the 'house opposite,' not upon her. She turned him gently towards her and said: 'Do look at me, Richard.'

Wagner went to Geneva, where he met Karl Ritter, with whom he travelled to Venice. There he remained in solitude until March 1859, composing the second act of *Tristan.* It was as if all that had happened at the Asyl had happened just for this, that he should compose a masterpiece. He had loved and lost. The loss would have broken another man. It inspired him.

For Wagner, it seems, love involved the renunciation of love. He was, he had always been, torn by that conflict which in one form or another has torn the life of every man since the beginning of civilization, the conflict between the compulsion of desire and that of morality—of morality, civilization's creation. We have observed its marks in his very first libretto, *The Wedding,* and in all his librettos since *The Flying Dutchman.* It was because they were telling expressions of this conflict that Wagner had been attracted to the symbols of primitive mythology.

Tristan resolved it by denying life altogether. He fulfilled his desire and appeased the morality he outraged by his death. For Tristan, 'death-devoted Tristan,' Wagner could write that marvellous music, which expresses, as nothing else he ever wrote does, the excruciating ecstasy of the greatest desire, swelling with the immense strength of its yearning until at last it bursts and swoons into blissful Nirvana.

CHAPTER V

UNSETTLED YEARS

WAGNER left Venice in March 1859. The Saxon authorities had been agitating for his expulsion. In any case he could not endure the unhealthy summer there. He recrossed the Alps and settled in Lucerne, where again he lived alone, absorbed in the composition of *Tristan*. Early in August he had the whole work ready for publication.

He had arranged with the director of the Karlsruhe Opera, Eduard Devrient, the dramatic historian, who had been his friend in Dresden, to have the work produced in Karlsruhe that autumn. Wagner hoped that the production would inaugurate a new period of material prosperity for him. In the meantime he resolved to continue his exile in Paris. He longed to live again in a great musical centre, where he could hear first-class orchestras and quartets, and perhaps, since he was now a composer of European reputation, engineer worthy performances of his own works. But he would not let himself be distracted from his quiet mode of life, 'with no social fuss,' for he must preserve his strength for future composition.

He decided also that Minna should rejoin him in Paris. He needed a housekeeper. And he earnestly wished to do the right thing by Minna. Since their separation he had written her many affectionate letters to soothe her sense of injury, which provincial tittle-tattle in Dresden had inflamed. The worst interpretation had been put upon a visit which he had paid to the Wesendoncks from Lucerne (he had been invited by Otto in order to give the lie to certain rumours about the Wagners' hasty departure from Zürich last year). 'Having me always at her side, a thousand occasions for anxiety and troubled fancy will be removed from her,' he wrote to Dr. Pusinelli, who opposed their reunion. Perhaps the doctor knew that Wagner was setting himself a programme of conduct which he would be unable to carry out. He could be kind enough to Minna on paper, but 'at her side' her 'anxiety' and 'troubled fancy' infuriated him.

To Mathilde also Wagner could express his feelings now only on paper. 'When we are there we do not see ourselves, only when we are not there can we gaze lingeringly at each other.'

Yet he preserved his friendship with the man who divided them. Wesendonck could afford to be generous now, and Wagner sorely needed his help. Since he had begun *Tristan* he had spent far more than the occasional royalties from his early works had brought him. He had no one to turn to save Wesendonck. Liszt's power in Weimar had been undermined by jealous intrigues, and their friendship by the Princess Wittgenstein, who disliked Wagner and feared that he would eclipse her lover. Thus, although Wagner had begged him to visit him at the Asyl, at Geneva, at Venice, Liszt had not come. They did not meet again until 1861, in Paris, where Liszt plunged into a social whirl and saw little of Wagner.

When Wagner had finished *Tristan,* Wesendonck gave him the help he so sorely needed. He bought the completed portions of *The Ring* for twenty-four thousand francs. With this sum Wagner was able to execute his decision to settle with Minna in Paris.

He went there in September 1859. The very next month he heard from Devrient that the Karlsruhe Opera was cavilling at *Tristan,* because it was too difficult. In December Devrient abandoned its production. Wagner was indignant and disappointed, of course, but he could hardly have been surprised.

At times the originality and complexity of this opera, which was to have been so producible and lucrative, had appalled even while it delighted him. 'Child, this Tristan will be dreadful!' he had written to Mathilde from Lucerne.

Once again Wagner was thrown upon his resources in Paris. Although he had run through Wesendonck's money (he had taken and repaired an expensive house near the Champs-Elysées, paid rent for three years in advance, had his furniture transported from Switzerland, hired a companion for Minna and a liveried servant for himself), he boldly resolved to organize a cycle of his operas, including *Tristan,* with a specially engaged cast of German singers. Funds were unexpectedly provided by the publisher Schott, of Mainz, who paid ten thousand francs for the copyright of *The Rhinegold,* which of his own accord he undertook to publish. (This money was by rights due to Wesendonck; afterwards he accepted as compensation the ownership of the as yet unwritten *Dusk of the Gods.*)

And so, to popularize his music and pave the way for *Tristan,* Wagner was able to give three grand concerts early in 1860. He performed the prelude to *Tristan.*

As though scales had fallen from my eyes, I saw how immeasurably far I have travelled from the world during the last eight years [he wrote to Mathilde]. This little overture was so incomprehensibly *new* to the musicians that I had to lead them from note to note as if searching for precious stones in a mine. . . . But don't ask me *how* I did it. Enough that I see now that I must not dream of further creative work till I have bridged this terrible gulf. I *must* perform my works first. *And what does that mean?*

Child, it means plunging me into an ocean of sacrifice and suffering in which I shall probably perish. This concert and the lack of sufficient time for preparation have shown me that I must become *rich*. . . . I must let my earlier operas be given here in

French and with the considerable profits derived therefrom set free my new works to the world. That is what lies before me—I have no other choice. . . . I look forward to nothing but the terrible pangs of bringing my last works into the world.

To become rich, then, Wagner must give up all idea of a quiet life, 'with no social fuss,' for future creative work and bend his energies upon a production, not of *Tristan*—that was out of the question—but of *Tannhäuser*. Since his arrival in Paris he had been negotiating intermittently with Carvalho, the manager of the Théâtre-Lyrique, who for years had been hankering after this opera. But now Wagner turned to the Opéra. The imperial major-domo who controlled it was an intimate friend of the detested Meyerbeer. Wagner, however, had powerful allies at the court—Count Pourtalès, the Prussian Ambassador, and his attaché, Count Paul Hatzfeld, Marshal Magnan and, above all, Princess Metternich, the wife of the Austrian Ambassador. At her instigation the emperor commanded the production of *Tannhäuser* at the Opéra.

While the libretto was being translated in the spring and summer of 1860 Wagner lived in 'brilliant misery.' The three concerts which he had given early in the year had been both disastrous and triumphant; he had been left with a deficit of eleven thousand francs and the admiration of some of the most brilliant spirits in Paris—Baudelaire, Champfleury, Gustave Doré, Berlioz,[1] Villot, the warden of the Louvre, and many others. Evidently he was in his element. But Minna was not in hers. She could not cope with all these distinguished people. Wagner kept her at a

[1] Berlioz' admiration was not whole-hearted. His troubles had embittered him; he could not but be jealous of Wagner's triumph. In 1860 he attacked him in the *Journal des Débats*, and Wagner retaliated. That was the end of their friendship.

distance, for he could not endure her philistinism and perpetual harping on the past. She had grounds for suspecting that he was carrying on an affair with the amusing, intelligent Blandine, Liszt's elder daughter.

In March Wagner had tried and failed to retrieve his financial losses by giving concerts in Brussels. The help of various individuals pulled him through the summer—of Frau Szemere, a Jewish admirer, of the Frau von Kalergis, a beautiful, talented friend of Liszt's, of Baron Erlanger, a banker. In July, thanks to the efforts of his patrons at the court, he received his longed-for amnesty at last: he was allowed to re-enter every state in Germany except Saxony.

In September the rehearsals for *Tannhäuser* began. They delighted Wagner. The Paris Opéra committed many crimes in the name of art, but it committed them with French thoroughness. Such superbly meticulous organization was unknown in Germany. . . . He spent himself in preparations. To a publication of his librettos in French prose he wrote an introduction expounding his theories. And he employed the technique he had acquired in composing *Tristan* to work up the ballet of the first act to a veritable orgy of passion and to create a new, far more significant Venus.

But fatal difficulties confronted him. Again and again he was pestered by the management to transfer the ballet to the second act: the most important subscribers to the Opéra, the young aristocrats of the Jockey Club, always arrived in their boxes late after dinner and they liked to see their mistresses dance. But a ballet after the dramatic climax in the second act was out of the question. Wagner was obdurate. And so, deprived of its ballet, the Jockey Club staged a demonstration which wrecked the performances in March 1861.

The demonstration was aimed not only against Wagner, but against his unpopular Austrian patrons, the Metternichs.

The corrupt, reactionary, anti-German press, who had attacked Wagner's concerts last year, naturally took full advantage of the outrage; and so, no doubt, did the powerful *claque,* which Wagner had offended by disdaining its services. It was one of the most spectacular scandals in the history of the stage. The music was drowned by the yells, cat-calls, whistles and derisive laughter of the Jockey Club and by the protests of the majority of the audience. After the third performance Wagner withdrew his opera.

Wagner would have minded more if he himself and not the incompetent conductor Dietsch had directed the performances. He had tried in vain to have the rule which forbade a composer to conduct his own work revoked. In the end he had lost interest in the whole affair; under Dietsch it could have no artistic worth. On the third night he stayed at home with Minna drinking tea and smoking.

And if the opera had been *Tristan* Wagner would have minded more. . . . In April he left Paris for Karlsruhe to arrange, if possible, to direct *Tristan* there and convince them that the work was not too difficult. He was warmly welcomed. The next month he went to Vienna to pick singers for the Karlsruhe production. He found the conductor of the Vienna Opera, Heinrich Esser, eager to perform his music. In Wagner's honour he now conducted *Lohengrin*; the performance was so beautiful that Wagner was moved to tears. (It was the first time he had ever heard *Lohengrin.*) The enthusiasm was unbounded. Wagner arranged to produce *Tristan* next autumn in Vienna—not in Karlsruhe.

He returned to Paris at the end of May to wind up his affairs there. It was decided that Minna should repeat the cure she had taken at Bad Soden last year and then settle in Dresden until Wagner could find the wherewithal for a stable existence. He attributed their failure to live peaceably together to his misfortunes. Worry had unnerved him and made him unable to give her the calm, sympathetic treatment her delicate health required.

At present he had no money. From the *Tannhäuser* fiasco he had drawn precisely 750 francs—the royalties for the three performances. His patrons at the embassies came to the rescue: they put him up and gave him money to pay off his debts, store his furniture and send Minna off to Soden. In August he went to attend a musical festival at Weimar, where he met Liszt and many friends and admirers—too many. 'Everywhere little talent, much foolery,' he wrote bitterly to Mathilde. Liszt was amiable, but unapproachable. They soon departed—Liszt to join the princess in Rome and Wagner to Vienna, where he stayed at first with Dr. Standhartner, a 'kindly enthusiast.' 'The people here are good to me, but not one of them knows the danger I bring them into with my *Tristan*.'

Rehearsals were delayed by a throat affection of the tenor, Ander. Once again Wagner was condemned to 'brilliant misery.' He was lionized; he had warm friends—Peter Cornelius, the gifted composer; Karl Tausig, the brilliant young pianist, who had been his guest at the Asyl. But until *Tristan* was produced he was without a livelihood. 'All my little future hangs . . . on the vocal cords of a tired tenor.' Now Ander recovered; now he relapsed. Wagner tried in vain to get hold of Tichatschek or the highly-spoken-of young tenor Ludwig Schnorr: both were engaged. Meanwhile the press said the work was unsingable. And this intimidated the management.

Towards the end of the year he escaped for a few days from this 'ocean of sacrifice and suffering' to meet the Wesendoncks in Venice. He found Otto and Mathilde completely reconciled and happy. He realized bitterly that his longing for her, which separation had never stilled, was utterly futile.

He spoke of his trials in Vienna. But he also spoke of a fresh hope: a comic opera, *The Mastersingers of Nuremberg*, concerning which he had just written to Schott, based on that sketch of his written in Marienbad in 1845 after he had finished Tannhäuser. The sketch was in Mathilde's possession; she returned it. Meanwhile the overture was ringing in his ears, 'transparent, yet pithy music,' he told Schott. The delighted publisher bought the publication rights for ten thousand francs, Wagner undertaking to complete the work by October next year.

Since *Tristan* in Vienna was cancelled for the time being, Wagner went to Paris, where Prince Metternich had again offered him refuge at the embassy. He arrived in December to find that for unforeseen cogent family reasons the Metternichs could not accommodate him. He took rooms at a dingy inn on the Quai Voltaire, lived on money Schott had advanced him for *The Mastersingers,* steeped himself in the libretto and 'forgot that he was alive.' 'I see nothing but mental images clamouring only for music.'

What had stimulated Wagner thus to alter the course of his life in order to embark upon a new great comic work?

Perhaps the work itself is the explanation. He had originally conceived it in a mood of reaction from his passionate outpouring in *Tannhäuser*. He had poured himself out in *Tannhäuser* again in Paris—with the tones of *Tristan*. Again he underwent a reaction, a far profounder one. In 1845 he had only entered the outskirts of the Venusberg; now he had probed its depths. And so now—and not till now—could he be inspired to music by *The Mastersingers.*

When in 1861 he redrafted the sketch, he gave new significance to the figure of Hans Sachs. Hans Sachs, the mature philosopher, renounces passion; he sees it as

. . . the ancient madness
That runs through all our striving,
To folly ever driving.

So Wagner must have regarded his passion for Mathilde when in Venice he realized its futility. He detached himself from it and contemplated it as Sachs contemplated Walther's passion—as a remembered dream, a sweet folly, a youthful idyll.

And having renounced passion, having freed himself from the curse of desire, Wagner could win as Sachs the power denied to him as Wotan. He could defeat Beckmesser-Alberich and educate Walther-Siegfried. He would write not a music drama dealing with the tragic fundamentals of human nature, but a music-dramatic-operatic comedy, celebrating holy Art, 'die heilige Kunst,' with himself, Wagner-Sachs, as its supreme exponent, a comedy combining music drama with conventional opera, reconciling the personal with the impersonal.

In Switzerland, to fulfil himself as an artist, he had had to renounce the theatre of his day as the characteristic institution of a society that he detested, and compose for a stage 'that did not exist.' He had left Switzerland and re-entered society to create that stage and dominate it. In *The Mastersingers* he would dramatize this domination; he would present a vision of the world-mastery to which his compositions in Switzerland gave him the right. From the pinnacle of mastery he would lovingly contemplate, playfully castigate, satirize, instruct his fellows; for there he was detached from them, there their follies could not injure him.

But he must find someone to share that pinnacle. Hans Sachs was sad and bereaved. His renunciation was, after all, only a passing mood of reaction from Tristan's outburst. Wagner could not go through life a widower.

He still hoped against hope that one day, when his livelihood was secure, he would live with Minna. At present, however, while engaged on the libretto of *The Mastersingers* in Paris, he looked only to find a comfortable 'nest' in Germany 'in which to hatch out musically the egg he had laid.' He sounded the Bülows, Caecilie Avenarius, Cornelius and others. Eventually he decided to settle in Biebrich on the Rhine, near his protector Schott in Mainz. He went there in February 1862. Minna appeared unexpectedly, to help him with the removal. She stayed for ten days—ten dreadful days. A letter and a parcel from Mathilde arrived. Minna stormed in the old way; Wagner lost his self-control; Minna had a heart attack. He realized that he must steel himself to cut the ties that bound him to his old comrade. He would provide her with a home in Dresden and visit her from time to time for the sake of appearances. . . . He poured out his soul in a letter to Cornelius. He would never have the heart to divorce her, he wrote. He must spend the rest of his days unmated. 'And so, I think, all my wife's sorrows are avenged.'

The first act of *The Mastersingers* progressed slowly. Wagner struggled to find the happiness he needed. At times he found it —in Mathilde Maier, a well-bred, serious-minded, devoted girl, whom, it seems, he would have married if he could;[1] in Friederike Meyer, a lively actress, with whom he carried on an affair; in a circle of admirers: Hans and Cosima von Bülow; the tenor Ludwig Schnorr (whom, when he heard his Lohengrin in Karlsruhe that spring, Wagner hailed as the male equivalent of Schröder-Devrient); Schnorr's wife, the soprano Malvina Garrigues; Weissheimer, a young conductor and composer of Mainz.

The summer ended disastrously. Schott refused to continue to advance money for *The Mastersingers,* since Wagner

[1] Minna wrote to him so insultingly of this relationship that he hardened himself to ask her for a divorce. She refused. And Mathilde would not consent to marry him, because she suffered from a hereditary deafness.

had not kept his promise to finish it that October. Wagner was forced to borrow from whom he could—from Weiss-heimer, Pusinelli, Wesendonck and others. He hoped that from concerts of selections from his operas and from the production of *Tristan* in Vienna, which was to be attempted again that autumn, he could scrape together the means to return to Biebrich next year and finish *The Mastersingers.*

But his hope was vain. It would be both painful and unprofitable to recount in detail Wagner's doings in the next eighteen months. Desperate efforts to earn a living kept him from the composition of *The Mastersingers,* the royalties from which he relied upon to secure the future. And those efforts were foredoomed to failure. We have seen how at the very outset of his career he had regarded himself as a unique being, for whose needs it was the business of society to cater. Now he had proved himself to be a unique being, and his needs had multiplied. He was a master, and he must live like one —tip liberally, travel first-class, wear silk underclothes, upholster his rooms with silks and velvets. For the sake of his art he must so live, he had declared: 'Mine is a highly susceptible, intense, voracious sensuality, which must somehow or other be flattered if my mind is to accomplish the agonizing labour of calling a non-existent world into being.'

During this period Wagner made Vienna his headquarters. He went there in November 1862, having just given in Leipzig an unsuccessful concert arranged by Weissheimer. (Minna had persuaded the authorities to permit him to re-enter Saxony.) After the concert he spent a few embarrassed days with Minna in Dresden. He never saw her again.

He travelled to Vienna with Friederike Meyer, who was the sister of the Vienna Isolde, Frau Dustmann-Meyer, whose capacity and enthusiasm he had had every reason to trust. But now her enthusiasm cooled, for she disapproved of the liaison with Friederike. Ander fell ill again. Wagner read the libretto of *The Mastersingers* at a party, to which Hanslick, the famous anti-Wagnerian critic, had been invited. Hanslick rightly took Beckmesser to be a caricature of himself and left the party in dudgeon. And so the production was still further prejudiced.

It was the same old lamentable story. Again Wagner negotiated in vain for Schnorr. Again he had to fall back on the help of personages at the court and the embassies. Again he gave brilliant, disastrously expensive concerts.

In February 1863, however, he gave a concert in Prague from which, thanks to the extraordinary efforts of the friends who arranged it, he actually drew a profit. Then he went to Russia (in Paris three years ago he had refused a tempting invitation to give concerts there; but now he dared not refuse), conducted in St. Petersburg and Moscow and returned home with five thousand thaler, a fifth of which he at once remitted to Minna. The rest he squandered on fitting up a new, luxurious household in Penzing, a suburb of Vienna.

He could only work fitfully at the instrumentation of the first act of *The Mastersingers* that summer. He was too lonely; the future was too dark. *Tristan* seemed less likely than ever to be produced in Vienna. In July 1863 he conducted in Budapest and in the autumn in Prague, Karlsruhe, Breslau and Löwenberg. At Löwenberg he met a wealthy widow, Henriette von Bissing, a sister of Eliza Wille, who promised to pay off his debts (he was in debt again) and provide for his future. Thus at Christmas he gave a party, at which he presented Cornelius with an overcoat, a dressing-gown, a scarf, a cigar-case and match-box, silk handkerchiefs, gold shirt-studs, *Struwwelpeter,* pen-wipers, cravats, an initialled meerschaum cigar-holder. . . . All this for Cornelius alone! [1]

[1] For further details of this party, see Ernest Newman's *Wagner as Man and Artist*, p. 132.

Frau von Bissing did not keep her promise, and now Wagner was ruined. He borrowed from usurers at a 'sacrificial' rate of interest, on the strength of concerts he had arranged to give in Russia in 1864 (he had evidently exhausted his friends; no doubt they had all by now come to feel, with Bülow, that Wagner 'could not be helped'). Early in 1864 the concerts fell through. Wagner was now at the mercy of his creditors; under Austrian law they could have him arrested and put into jail. In March his friends gave him the means to flee to Switzerland. He applied to the Wesendoncks for shelter; but they refused to house this feckless, dangerously fascinating genius. He was received instead by his old friend and confidante, Eliza Wille, whose husband was away at the time.

Wagner was near the end of his tether. '*Some* light must show itself,' he wrote to Cornelius, '*someone* must arrive to give me vigorous *help now*, and *then* I shall have strength to recompense that help—but *later* I shall not. I feel it.' Frau Wille has vividly described his gloom, his sudden outbursts. In his gloom he spoke of Minna: everything might have been all right; he had spoilt her; she had denied him his due. Another time, when Frau Wille tried to cheer him by speaking of a brighter future, he burst out: 'What 's the good of talking of the future, when my scores are lying locked in the cupboard?' . . . He paced the room excitedly. Suddenly he stopped and said: 'I 'm not made like other people. I have finer nerves—I must have beauty and brilliance and light. The world owes me what I need. I can't live on a miserable organist's post, like your master Bach! . . .'

After a few weeks Dr. Wille returned. Wagner felt that he must leave. He betook himself to Stuttgart in the hope that his friend Eckert, the conductor of the opera there, might do something for him—produce *Tristan,* or get the court to give him funds to compose *The Mastersingers.* But his hope was vain. He telegraphed to Weissheimer to come to him. Weissheimer came. He found Wagner in despair. 'I am at the end—I can't do any more—I must disappear from the world.' Weissheimer offered to accompany him into the mountains near by and help him to find a quiet spot where he could compose. Then Weissheimer would go to Mainz and try to get some money out of Schott.

The evening before their departure Wagner spent at Eckert's house. A card was handed to him—the card of no less a person than the private secretary of the King of Bavaria, Herr Pfistermeister. Astounded and alarmed (was he not wanted by the Austrian police?), Wagner refused to see the gentleman. On returning to his hotel he heard that the King of Bavaria's secretary had called there too and desired urgently to meet him. Wagner then arranged an interview at ten o'clock next morning. He slept badly that night, for he anticipated some new calamity.

The King of Bavaria was a boy of nineteen—Ludwig II. He had just come to the throne. Wagner's music was the passion of his life. When he had read the preface to the edition of the *Ring* poem, which Wagner had had published in 1862—the preface in which Wagner had set forth the idea of a production of his cycle at a great festival, to be financed by some liberal-minded prince, closing with the words: 'Will such a prince appear?'—Ludwig had known that *he* was that prince. He had longed for the day when as King of Bavaria he could 'appear' and devote his power to serve Wagner. Now that day had come.

Thus at ten o'clock in the morning of 3rd May 1864 Pfistermeister handed Wagner the king's signet-ring and the king's portrait, bidding him come to Munich and grant the king the privilege of knowing him and caring for him for ever

> He wants me to stay with him always to work, to rest, to produce: he will give me all I need for that [Wagner wrote to Frau Wille from Munich the next day]. I am to be my own absolute master, not a *Kapellmeister*, nothing but myself and his friend. And he means all this seriously and literally, just as if we two, you and I, were talking together. What do you say to that?—What do you say?—Is it not fabulous?—Can it be anything but a dream? . . . My happiness is so great that I am quite overwhelmed by it. . . .

It was not a dream; it was sober reality. That had happened which had to happen if Wagner's transcendent artistic visions were to be materialized and his mastery established—he was made economically independent.

'I should never be obliged to make merchandise of my works,' he had written in 1859. Inevitably there was no demand for his 'merchandise,' for until it was sold and used there could be no conception of its nature. In the last resort, surely, Wagner's failure to produce *Tristan* was due to the reluctance of the average German court intendant to risk money and prestige for a work that he could not visualize—moreover, a dreadfully big, elaborate, expensive work, offered to him by a man notorious as a rabid, cranky aesthetician, Anti-Semite and ex-revolutionary.

But for Ludwig II Wagner might have been irretrievably ruined and his later works unwritten. One is tempted to attribute his salvation to providence or to call it, with Paul Bekker, 'the supreme triumph of his prophetic will'; but it was nothing of the sort. It was pure chance—the chance that a neurotic youth, who had found in Wagner's music an outlet for his pent-up emotions, should have been born the heir to a throne. But it was not a chance—far from it—that Wagner's music should have had that significance for Ludwig. Many artists have ruined themselves as he ruined himself. But perhaps only Wagner could have been delivered thus.

CHAPTER VI

MUNICH AND TRIEBSCHEN

After that rapturous meeting with the king in Munich, Wagner hurried off to Vienna, his pockets full of money, to pay off his creditors and settle his affairs. Then he returned to Lake Starnberg, where the king was spending the summer. A villa was found for him ten minutes by carriage from the royal castle. 'He sends once or twice daily and then I always hasten as to a sweetheart. . . . I have never known such lovely impetuosity in the impulse to seek instruction, such quiver and glow!'

This intercourse, ecstatically delightful though it was, could not assuage a feeling of intolerable loneliness. The king was a 'dear lad'—but he was a lad. In June Wagner wrote to Bülow beseeching him to come with his wife, children and maid and stay with him for as long as he could. He told Bülow not to take this request 'as the sudden fruit of a passing whim, but as an important paragraph in the last will and testament of a dying man.'

The Bülows came. And now there was granted to Wagner that without which he was lost and impotent, Ludwig's help notwithstanding. A woman gave herself to him, uniquely capable of serving him, understanding him, loving him—a woman of affairs, a diplomatist, a thinker, a musician—Liszt's daughter, Cosima von Bülow.

Wagner knew that Cosima loved him. Years ago in the Asyl he had sensed a strange tenseness in her behaviour towards him. During his concert tour in Germany in the previous autumn he had visited the Bülows in Berlin, and then—in Wagner's words—'a violent craving for acknowledged truth compelled us to the admission, for which no words were needed, of an incalculable disaster that had befallen us.' A disaster certainly for Bülow, perhaps for Cosima, but not for Wagner. Once again he must possess his friend's wife; he needed her for his life, and his life was more valuable than other men's, even his friends'. The creator of *Tristan* could not think otherwise.

That Cosima and Bülow's marriage was unhappy no doubt made it easier for Wagner to take her from his friend. Bülow had a difficult, irritable nature; his inferiority to his masters, Liszt and Wagner, whom he served and honoured, galled him. And Cosima, the illegitimate child of an adored, wonderful father, whom she seldom saw, longed to devote herself to a genius and only to a genius. Thus secretly she had consecrated herself to Wagner—had preferred devotion to this man old enough to be her father than to her husband who relied upon it implicitly.

To have the Bülows with him, Wagner made the king appoint Bülow court pianist; in November they settled in Munich. They found Wagner installed in a sumptuous villa, and there henceforward Cosima spent most of her time, running the house, dealing with Wagner's correspondence and generally taking charge of his affairs.

Meanwhile Wagner's affairs had become very complicated. Royal favourites are seldom popular; the clerical reactionary government of Bavaria detested this one—this North German, free-thinking Protestant, this 'barricade man'—this arrogant artistic Sybarite. When the king proclaimed his intention to spend public money on building a magnificent theatre and founding a school of music for Wagner, the taxpayers grumbled. In February 1865 attempts were made by the clerical party and by the Jesuits to bribe Wagner to further their rival political intrigues—the former offered to further *his* cause, the latter offered him shares in a bank. But Wagner refused them both; his concern was art, not politics. Since he now proved himself to be useless as well as detestable, both parties determined to get rid of him. To this end they stirred up a ferocious anti-Wagner campaign in the press.

In the spring of 1865 Wagner forgot the exasperation of all this in the joy of producing *Tristan*. He had already produced *The Flying Dutchman* and *Tannhäuser* in Munich, the latter with the marvellous Schnorr in the title part. And now at last *Tristan*. . . . Three performances would be given in May. 'They will be wonderful, like *nothing* ever known before,' he told Frau Wille. No expense, no trouble would be spared. Schnorr, of course, would sing Tristan and Schnorr's wife Isolde.

But the production of *Tristan*, it seemed, was still accursed. At the last moment Frau Schnorr fell ill; the performances had to be postponed and many who had come from abroad to hear them could not await her recovery. The work was given in June. Bülow conducted. To Wagner this longed-for consummation was a supreme delight. The audience was perhaps less delighted than impressed by the novel, overwhelming power of the opera. The singers dispersed tired and happy, Wagner's praise ringing in their ears. But the insatiable king demanded a fourth performance; it took place on 1st July. Then the curse fulfilled itself. Three weeks later Schnorr—the one and only Schnorr, the Wagnerian hero incarnate—died of rheumatic fever.

In the autumn plans to raise the Wagnerian kingdom of heaven in Munich were pressed forward. Wagner's old friend Gottfried Semper, the Dresden architect, with whom last year the building of a theatre had been discussed, now arrived to discuss the building also of a new splendid street and bridge

(Ludwig had inherited the Wittelsbach passion for extravagant architecture). Bülow busied himself with the organization of the school of music; Schnorr, alas! was no longer there to rear a new race of singers, but Cornelius and Heinrich Porges, the conductor and journalist, had been paid to leave Vienna and work for Wagner. Porges would not only teach in the school; he would sub-edit a Wagnerian journal, which a Dr Grandauer would edit and to which Wagner would contribute.

All this was grist to the mill of Wagner's enemies. They were utterly unscrupulous. The reactionary ministry had behaved unconstitutionally; it cleverly made Wagner the scapegoat of offended public opinion by attributing its actions to his influence over the king. Dreadful things were said of that influence: it was hypnotic, erotic; Wagner was another Lola Montez,[1] an evil genius, an anti-Christ. He was betraying Bavaria to Bismarck. He was draining the royal treasury to pay his debts.

In November Wagner, with Cosima's help, wrote a newspaper article defending himself and advocating the 'removal of two or three persons' from the ministry, who, he declared, were responsible for the agitation. Thus he put the king, who loathed governing as much as he loved Wagner, into the agonizing position of having to exert himself to choose between the ministers, whom he relied upon to govern for him, and Wagner. The 'persons' indicated, Pfistermeister and Pfordten, the minister-president, proceeded to put the weak, inexperienced youth on the rack. They skilfully engineered appeals, deputations, demonstrations to convey the impression that the agitation against Wagner was national, not partisan. They convinced Ludwig that for the sake of Bavaria, even for the sake of his throne, he must banish Wagner.

[1] The notorious mistress of Ludwig I.

Early in December the king wrote Wagner a pathetic letter asking him to leave the country for the time being. 'Believe me, I had to do it, never doubt the loyalty of your best friend.' Wagner did not doubt his loyalty, but, he replied, it pained him that the king should suffer when he had merely to use his royal power to relieve himself.

Wagner went to Switzerland and rented a country house near Geneva for three months. He made his return to Munich conditional upon the king's dismissal of his ministers. In the meantime he resumed work upon the first act of *The Mastersingers.* In Munich he had scored the second act of *Siegfried* and begun to sketch the third act, for he had anticipated the production of *The Ring* in Munich. But now that prospect was remote.

In January 1866 Wagner was saddened by the news of Minna's death. In March Cosima visited him—with the consent of Bülow, who was engaged on a concert tour. Wagner desired now only to find some quiet spot in Switzerland where he could live beside Cosima and finish *The Mastersingers.* Together they scoured German Switzerland. They settled upon Triebschen, on the Lake of Lucerne, a large, white house built upon a tiny peninsula studded with poplars. It was an isolated, enchanting place.

Wagner forthwith arranged for the removal of his luxurious household goods from Munich to Triebschen. The king was deeply distressed. On 22nd May he paid Wagner a surprise birthday visit and besought him to return. But the king's feelings—like Bülow's—had to be sacrificed to Wagner's art. Wagner encouraged him to put his house in order: then he would return.

The sacrifice required of him had by this time been revealed also to Bülow. How it was revealed is not known—probably, as Bülow had a strong sense of guilt towards Cosima for the unhappiness of their marriage, and fully realized how indispensable she was to Wagner, some understanding between the three had been reached since Cosima's fateful visit to Lake Starnberg. At any rate Bülow was under no illusions when Wagner wrote to him in April, again begging him to come with Cosima and his family and gladden his life. He complied, sending Cosima and the children on ahead.[1]

Not that Bülow's situation was not an exceedingly painful one. Since his future was bound up with the performance of Wagner's operas at Munich self-interest as well as pride—and he was very proud—compelled him to endure, silencing it as best he could, the gossip to which Cosima's sojourn at Triebschen gave rise. So obstinate was this gossip that Cosima went to the length of addressing the king: 'My august friend, who came into our life like a divine apparition, do not, do not permit us, *the innocent ones*, to be driven out.' She implored him to vindicate her honour in a public epistle to Bülow, a copy of which she enclosed for him to autograph. The king, who disbelieved and resented these rumours about his dearest friends, of course did what she asked.

In an atmosphere of tranquil domestic bliss such as he had never known before Wagner spent the winter of 1866–7 composing *The Mastersingers*. By March 1867 he had it ready for scoring. The time had come to arrange for a Munich production. The condition upon which his return to Munich depended had been fulfilled: Pfordten's misconduct of Bavaria's policy during the Prusso-Austrian War had

[1] Mr. Ernest Newman in *The Life of Richard Wagner*, vol. iii, pp. 490–505, tears to shreds the hitherto accepted story that Wagner and Cosima had managed to deceive Bülow throughout the whole of the Munich period, and that Bülow discovered the truth by accidentally opening a love-letter from Wagner to Cosima, shortly after the latter's departure for Triebschen.

caused his downfall; his ministry had been replaced by that of Prince Hohenlohe, who was sympathetic to Wagner. Hohenlohe reversed the ultramontane separatist policy of his predecessor and threw in his lot with victorious Prussia.

Bülow, who had spent the winter in Basle, returned to Munich in April, where he was appointed *Hofkapellmeister* Extraordinary and decorated. For the sake of appearances, which, in view of the forthcoming production of *The Mastersingers*, were all-important, Cosima rejoined him. They took a house, in which two rooms were set aside for Wagner, who occupied them frequently in the course of the next twelve months. The plans for a school of music and for a journal were revived. Both were founded in the autumn, the school under the directorship of Bülow and the journal in the form of a musical and dramatic supplement of the new state-supported *Süddeutsche Presse* under the editorship of Julius Fröbel, who shared Hohenlohe's views. Extracts from a lengthy article which Wagner had written that summer were published in this supplement.

By the autumn Wagner had finished the scoring of *The Mastersingers*. Early in 1868 rehearsals began and thenceforward till the first performance in June Wagner was constantly in Munich dealing with one complication after another —difficulties of casting, dissensions with Perfall, the new intendant, who on Wagner's recommendation had been chosen to replace the reactionary Lachner, and with Fröbel, who was more concerned with political self-advancement than Wagnerian propaganda.

The orchestra was directed by Bülow and the choir by Hans Richter, a young Viennese musician who had spent many months at Triebschen copying the score. Wagner attended only the main rehearsals. The first performance attracted an even greater concourse of visitors than that of

Tristan and was a still more brilliant success. The king made Wagner sit with him in the royal box—an unheard-of breach of etiquette. Afterwards the several vested interests Wagner had offended in Munich—the musical profession (by his outspoken criticisms, by his founding of a rival school, by his attracting to Munich superior talent from other countries); the clerical party; the Jesuits—united in objurgating his opera. Wagner withdrew ill and exhausted to Triebschen and there swore never again to return to 'my hell,' Munich.

The hostile press did not scruple to insinuate that Bülow owed his position as *Hofkapellmeister* to his complaisance as a husband. The slander was intolerable—but not so intolerable as the loneliness Wagner had endured these last twelve months in order to silence slander. But now *The Mastersingers* had been produced; now, come what may, Wagner would no longer live without Cosima. In November 1868 she fled to him, never to leave him again. 'They will drag us through the mud,' she wrote in her diary. 'Let them do it, so long as I am by his side. . . .' And let the king suffer, and Bülow, and herself, poor woman, through the pain she must inflict, so long as she was 'by his side.'

The king broke off all relations with her (had she not prevailed upon him publicly to pledge her innocence?), but not with Wagner. He could never forgive the beloved friend's treachery, but he could not cease to serve and revere the artist. . . . Bülow's situation was terrible. The interpretation of Wagner's music had been the mission of his life. He could not be the disciple of a master who betrayed him before the world. . . . He stayed on in Munich till June 1868, when he directed a wonderful production of *Tristan*; then, having filed a petition for divorce and sent their two daughters to Cosima, he went to Italy to recover his shattered nerves and begin life afresh. He never met Wagner again.

Wagner, too, was beginning life afresh. Their estrangement from the king, Bülow, Liszt (who had visited Wagner at Starnberg and at Triebschen), could mar Cosima's but not Wagner's profound happiness. His mate had joined him for ever in his secure, lovely home. . . . In June 1869 Cosima, who had already borne him two daughters, Isolde and Eva, crowned his happiness by bearing him a son—Siegfried.

The day before the birth of his son Wagner finished the musical sketches of the third act of *Siegfried*, in which, in the scene of Brynhilda's awakening by Siegfried, he gave exquisite expression to his happiness. It was a happiness deeper and more actual than that which he had expressed in *The Mastersingers*. Hans Sachs had passed away; Walther remained, no longer contemplated by a wiser, sadder second self, but embodying the soul of Wagner.

And then he turned to the final portion of the myth which he had abandoned two decades ago—*Siegfried's Death*, renamed *The Dusk of the Gods*. Now he would complete the tragedy of the world that destroyed Siegfried. In *The Rhinegold, The Valkyrie* and the first two acts of *Siegfried* he had depicted the tragic workings of the curse of desire and a vision of the liberating, splendid innocence of nature, for which mankind, represented by Wotan, yearned. Siegfried was the child of that yearning. But Siegfried became Tristan. The child of nature became tainted with a passion so fierce that he craved his doom, craved the release of death.

The Siegfried of the third act was eleven years older than that child of nature. He had expressed his fiercest passion. Now he craved life, not death. Now Wagner could make him the hero of a culminating tragedy—one worked not by a curse afflicting guilty passion, but by an inexorable, impersonal destiny dooming both the guilty and the innocent—dooming not only those who, like Alberich, Wotan, Siegmund and Tristan, steal either power or love or both, but Siegfried too—Siegfried, the guileless, radiant liberator.

This tragedy, when he had completed it, Wagner would not perform in Munich under the patronage of Ludwig II, but at a festival in a theatre he would build at some quiet spot far from the madding crowd of petty egoisms and noisy vulgarities that jostle in a great city—a festival to which an audience would be invited free of charge to partake like ancient Greeks in a solemn communal artistic act.

He had long ceased to regard his art as the organ of expression of a regenerated community. Art, he now believed, was a refuge from unalterable reality, a 'play', a 'dream-image . . . comforting us and lifting us above the sordid actuality of distress'. He had expounded this view (which left an imprint on *The Mastersingers*) in the article 'State and Religion' that he wrote for the king in 1864 to explain the changes in his outlook since 1848.

But he still believed that his art was supra-personal. 'The ideal of my art stands and falls with the rebirth of Germany,' he had written in 1866—of Germany the nation of supreme artistic potentiality. At times this belief misled him: in the article *German Art and Policy*, written in 1867, he disparaged foreign influences upon the development of German culture; in 1869 he reissued *Judaism in Music*. At other times it was the ideal standard by which he judged clearly the defects in the practice of music in Germany and diagnosed their remedy. In the *Report upon a German Music-School to be founded in Munich* (1865) and in *On Conducting* (1869) he criticized the current interpretation of classic operas and concert pieces and advocated the centralization of musical education in one great conservatory — on the scale of the Paris, Milan and

Naples conservatories—to build up a tradition of style inspired by the will to express the emotions implicit in the music of the great German masters from Bach to Wagner.

He had become a more practical idealist. His experiences since he had left Lucerne for Paris in 1859, dreadful and bitter though they had been, had given him cause to believe that such a style could be built up. He had met conductors, instrumentalists, singers, many of whom were teachable, some devoted, some gifted. One had been supremely gifted. He put his trust no longer in princes, no longer in revolution, but in the talent of the performer.

He revised his theory of music drama accordingly. In 1871 and 1872, while engaged upon *The Dusk of the Gods*, he wrote *The Destiny of Opera* and *Actors and Singers*, in which he emphasized the function of the actor. The art of the dramatist, he held, issued from the art of the mime. Shakespeare's dramas were 'fixed mimetic improvisations of the highest poetic worth.' Music was a supremely efficacious means of fixing and idealizing this improvisation. The music dramatist would write dramatic poetry like Shakespeare's—poetry which enabled the actor to embody characters in 'life's own image, mirrored with resistless truth to nature' —and set it to music like Beethoven's (who was Shakespeare's blood-brother)—to music, which, unfettered by conventional form, would catch the emotion of the moment and take 'the mind by storm.' Such music would have the 'sublime irregularity,' the 'ineffably vital shape of a Shakespearian drama.'

Events in the years 1869 and 1870 precipitated Wagner's resolve not to have *The Ring* produced in Munich under Ludwig II. After the production of *Tristan* in June 1869 the king had impatiently demanded that of *The Rhinegold* and *The Valkyrie*. Wagner could not prevent performances of the former[1] in September 1869 and of the latter in June 1870. He was furious that the operas should be thus given singly, inadequately prepared, without his indispensable co-operation.

The political events of 1870 and 1871—the defeat of France and the founding of the German Empire—on the other hand, filled him with hope. He wrote a celebration poem and the triumphal *Kaisermarsch.* He was not gratified by military victory, but by Germany's new solidarity, her pride. He hoped that the countless admirers which his early operas and now *The Mastersingers*—welcomed and applauded all over Germany—had won him, would be prevailed upon to finance his festival and create a new German culture.

The years which Wagner spent with Cosima in Triebschen, from November 1868 to April 1871, when he re-entered Germany to find a site for his festival theatre, were wonderfully creative. He composed and scored the third act of *Siegfried*, and composed the first two acts of *The Dusk of the Gods*; he wrote, besides several small polemical articles, his moving *Recollections of Ludwig Schnorr, On Conducting* and the weighty essay, *Beethoven*, in which he interpreted Beethoven's character and creative processes in the light of his own experience and reconstructed his theory of music drama with the material of Schopenhauerian metaphysics. He also completed his autobiography, begun in 1865 at the wish of the king, spending many happy evenings dictating its vivid eight hundred and seventy pages to Cosima.

He made a new friend, a youth of twenty-four, who came over from Basle, where he was professor of philology at the university, to spend week-end after week-end at Triebschen—Nietzsche. The two geniuses fascinated each other. Nietzsche,

[1] Wagner could not prevent the performances because the ownership of *The Ring* had been made over to Ludwig. Wesendonck had graciously ceded his rights.

like Wagner, was a Schopenhauerian; like Wagner he abhorred modern industrial civilization and idealized Hellenic art. It was his intercourse with Wagner that moved him in 1871 to write his book *The Birth of Tragedy from the Spirit of Music*, in which he expounded a Wagnerian conception of Greek drama.

The French authoress Judith Gautier, the daughter of the poet, also visited Triebschen during this period. In her book, *Wagner at Home*, she describes her visit. She leads us into the restful, luxurious drawing-room; we regard the portraits of Beethoven, Goethe and Schiller upon the walls, 'covered with yellow leather traced with arabesques of gold'; we move into the 'gallery'—'a long narrow room hung in violet velvet,' lined with small statues of Wagner's heroes and draped with tapestries portraying scenes from *The Ring* (the gift of Ludwig), and in one corner a butterfly collection and in another 'a gilded Buddha, Chinese incense-burners, chiselled cups—all sorts of rare and precious things.' Later we stroll through the glorious garden, the children and the Newfoundland dog, Russ, gambolling around us; we are guided by Wagner up a slope to a summer-house from which we behold the view: the house amid a mass of foliage, the sheep browsing on the hills, the limpid lake reflecting the white sails of the yachts drifting upon it and the immense violet-tinted summits behind; we glance at Wagner standing beside us,

> . . . upright, leaning both hands on the rough country fence, silent and with the earnest expression of concentration peculiar to him at times of internal emotion. His eyes, blue as the lake and almost motionless, seemed to be sucking in the picture, from which a world of ideas came streaming towards him. This place of refuge . . . made secure for him by the tenderness of the woman he loved at a time when he was most cruelly pursued by the bitter things of life; this lovely shrine, enlivened by children's laughter . . . it was of this that he was thinking with such thankfulness.

Judith Gautier visited Wagner in the summer of 1869. A year later Bülow's divorce proceedings were completed and Wagner was able to marry Cosima. On the morning of her first birthday after their wedding he assembled a small orchestra upon the staircase of their home and serenaded her with that piece in which he utters the thoughts Judith Gautier read in his eyes as he gazed upon the lake that day—the *Siegfried Idyll.*

In April 1871 Wagner sallied forth from Triebschen, like Siegfried from his enchanted mountain, 'to new deeds,' to found the Wagnerian theatre in Germany. Before departing he wrote a pamphlet to make public his intention: his theatre 'at first . . . should offer no more than the localized point of periodic meeting of Germany's best theatrical forces for practice and presentation of a higher German original style in their art, an exercise impossible in ordinary course of their labours. . . .' If successful, he hoped that his private institution would become 'an earnest object of some imperial authority nobly anxious for the nation's moral weal'—become nationalized, that is to say, by the formation of a 'union of all existing theatres, or at least the well-endowed among them.'

He had already in mind the ideal spot for his theatre, a town in Bavaria, his protector Ludwig's kingdom, situated in the centre of Germany; off the beaten track of the fashionable sightseer; small, unspoilt, pleasant, homely, *echt deutsch* Bayreuth. He went straight there, sounded the municipal authorities and found them sympathetic. Then he proceeded to the capital of the new empire, read his essay, *The Destiny of Opera*, to the academy, conducted a brilliant concert and rallied influential well-wishers to his cause. He even interviewed Bismarck. But Bismarck had never been very susceptible to music drama. After the interview he declared that he himself was by no means without self-conceit, but such a high grade of it in another as Wagner possessed he had not yet come across.

Important steps were taken in Berlin. Karl Tausig, the pianist, now a dominating figure there, and Frau von Schleinitz, the wife of a prominent member of the government, flung themselves heart and soul into the Wagner movement. They decided to form a society called *Wagneriana*, to support an orchestra, which would, under Tausig, perform Wagner's music in Berlin and later play at the festival; and to raise the three hundred thousand thaler needed for the building of the theatre by issuing a thousand shares, each worth three hundred thaler, to be taken up by patrons, whom they would find.

Wagner forthwith announced the opening of the first festival in 1873. He returned to Triebschen in May. He was then approached by one Emil Heckel, a music-dealer in Mannheim, who suggested the formation of provincial Wagner societies to collect funds from those who could not afford the expensive 'patronage shares,' yet desired to support the enterprise. Wagner, who intended to spend the summer composing the second act of *The Dusk of the Gods*, and writing an introduction to a collected edition of his literary works, referred him to Tausig, who favoured the idea.

Then in July Tausig died, even as Schnorr had done—struck down in the prime of his youth by a sudden senseless illness. Wagner found a successor to him — in so far as that was possible—in Baron Löen, the intendant of the Weimar theatre.

Meanwhile Wagner societies were being enthusiastically formed not only by Heckel in Mannheim, but in Berlin, Vienna, Munich and Leipzig. In November Wagner addressed to them a *Report*, narrating the history of *The Ring's* composition and gratefully welcoming their spontaneous aid.

In December he visited Bayreuth again, came to terms with the municipal authorities, who had sense enough to realize the prestige and money a Wagnerian festival would bring their little town, met the architects, with whom he had already made contact during his former visit to Germany that year, and chose a site. It was decided to lay the foundation stone the following spring. Then Wagner journeyed to Mannheim, to give a concert for the benefit of the local Wagner society.

Early in 1872 various difficulties arose: another site had to be chosen; the architectural plans were too costly; funds were flowing in too slowly. Wagner had to wrench himself from the composition of *The Dusk of the Gods* and make another trip to Germany. He viewed and approved a new site, and arranged to have the financial administration centralized in Bayreuth.

Another difficulty arose: Wagner intended to settle permanently in Bayreuth that spring and to have erected for himself a specially constructed house (he had already chosen a villa in which to live pending the building). But now the king, in a fit of angry disappointment at this final frustration of his hope that Wagner would one day return to Munich, threatened to cut off his income. The whole enterprise seemed jeopardized. However, the king relented and gave Wagner twenty-five thousand gulden with which to build his new home.

And so, in April 1872, Wagner left his beautiful Triebschen. Before he could settle into Bayreuth he had to rush off to Vienna to conduct a concert to raise funds for the Wagner society there. On 22nd May, his fifty-ninth birthday, the foundation stone of the Bayreuth theatre was laid with pomp and circumstance. The quiet town was filled with Wagnerians gathered from all parts of Europe to attend the ceremony. In pouring rain they trooped out of the town to the hill near by, where the theatre was to be built, and watched Wagner lay the stone with a hammer. 'Sei gesegnet mein Stein, stehe lang und halte fest,'[1] he said dramatically. Then they adjourned to the old-fashioned local opera house, listened to speeches, and later to a superlative performance of Beethoven's ninth Symphony by a host of specially invited distinguished musicians, conducted by Wagner.

When it was all over Wagner, very tired, withdrew into private life and devoted the rest of the summer to *The Dusk of the Gods*. While he composed, workmen reared his new home and his theatre.

[1] 'Be blessed, my stone, stand long and hold firm.'

CHAPTER VII

BAYREUTH

'I NEVER thought you would bring it off,' said the Emperor Wilhelm to Wagner, as he arrived in Bayreuth to hear the first performance of *The Ring,* in the summer of 1876, four years after the laying of the foundation stone. During those four years Wagner had had good cause to share that opinion. But for Ludwig II he would never have been able to 'bring it off.' Ludwig, his old friend and stand-by, whom he had so deeply injured, did not desert him.

By the end of 1872 it was clear that 'the achievements of the Wagner societies had disappointed even the most modest expectations.' And although Frau von Schleinitz had worked indefatigably, less than a third of the 'patronage shares' had been taken up. It was so much easier to attend meetings and applaud speeches than to write out cheques. Early in 1873 Wagner, who had just spent several exhausting weeks scouring western Germany for suitable singers, set out to raise funds by giving concerts in Dresden, Hamburg, Berlin and Cologne. At the end of the summer, which Wagner devoted again to *The Dusk of the Gods,* it seemed that the building operations would have to stop. In October a meeting of delegates of the Wagner societies issued an appeal to the public. But the public was either indifferent or distrustful. The post-war period was one of 'wild speculation, of frothy schemes and hysterical ideals.'[1] The press had dubbed Wagner a perverter of music, a crank; a psychiatrist had written an article to prove

[1] Ainslie Hight, *Life of Wagner,* vol. ii.

that he was insane. The only hope was Ludwig. If Ludwig would guarantee the costs, then perhaps more patrons would come forward. But Ludwig would not. All seemed lost. Wagner talked of boarding up the open side of the unfinished building, 'so that at least the owls won't nest there,' and awaiting better days. Then he learnt the reason for the king's refusal: he was offended by Wagner's neglect to fulfil a request he had caused to be made to him that he should set to music a certain poem. But Wagner had had no idea the request was the king's. He wrote at once, explaining the misunderstanding, begging desperately for help. 'No, no and again no!' the king replied. 'It must not end so! . . . Help must be given!' He guaranteed a credit of a hundred thousand thaler; the property bought with it was to belong to the king and the receipts from the patrons and societies were to be paid to him until they covered the credit.

The work could go on then: the festival could be held in 1876. If Germany could not be roused to support her new art by proclamation of 'the idea,' then she must be roused by the *fait accompli*—albeit carried out with borrowed money. Contracts were fixed up with Karl Brandt of Darmstadt, the stage engineer—a loyal, brilliant friend—and with Joseph Hoffmann, the Viennese painter and scenic designer. In the summer of 1874 singers were invited to Wagner's magnificent new home, Wahnfried, into which he had moved that spring, to be tested and coached by the master himself.

Wagner finished *The Dusk of the Gods* on 21st November of that year. Since he had settled in Bayreuth he had had with him a group of young musicians, the so-called *Nibelung-bureau,* who fair-copied the score, wrote out the orchestral parts, and were trained to the interpretation, notably Anton Seidl and Hermann Zumpe, who became famous Wagnerian conductors, and Joseph Rubinstein, a neurotic, gifted young

Jew, who adored Wagner and was befriended by him. All these people and many others were drawn into a *crescendo* of preparation that mounted through the years 1874 and 1875 to the grand climax of 1876.

Financial difficulties persisted all the time. To earn money Wagner gave concerts in Vienna, Budapest and Berlin in the spring of 1875, supervised a production of the Paris version of *Tannhäuser* and of *Lohengrin* in Vienna in the winter, and brought out *Tristan* in Berlin in March 1876 (but this was also a labour of love). Early in 1876 he confessed to Heckel that the undertaking was 'madly bold': only 450 of the 1,300 shares, which on a later reckoning they found were needed, had been taken up; he must have cash to pay the expenses of the musicians and singers, who were dispensing with salaries; he would appeal to the emperor for thirty thousand thaler (the appeal failed); '. . . as for the rest, we are keeping up our spirits. Everything will be got ready (on credit!).' . . . It was fortunate that just then he should be asked to compose a march for the celebration in Philadelphia of the American Declaration of Independence. For this he received twenty thousand marks. And the same sum was paid him, by special order of the emperor, from the profits of the *Tristan* production in Berlin.

Wagner was, of course, the life and soul of the rehearsals, of which there were two great series, in the summers of 1875 and 1876. He conducted the orchestra, ordered the stage hands about, instructed the singers. They must enunciate clearly, synchronize their gestures with the music, live their parts. Some were amenable. Unger, the Siegfried, for instance, had revised his vocal technique under a teacher, Julius Hey, and been coached at the piano by Wagner in every shade of expression. According to Hey, Wagner even tried to 'influence his temperament.' 'Your whole outlook on life,' he had said to him, 'seems to be too heavy and black, it must become gay and sunny.' Betz, the Wotan, on the other hand, resented instruction and Niemann, the Siegmund (who had sung Tannhäuser in Paris), was put off by it. Wagner gave way, cajoled, commanded, lost his temper, apologized, cracked jokes. He was the born leader, sympathetic yet determined, himself giving what he demanded of others; inspired himself and so inspiring others.

Although the press spread the report that an epidemic ot typhoid had broken out in Bayreuth; although for various reasons a new Sieglinde, a new Hagen and a new Hunding had to be found at the last moment; although, through lack of funds and lack of confidence that the festival would take place, many of the gas installers and scenery manufacturers were behind with their work—despite all this, the festival did take place! Well might the emperor say to Wagner: 'I never thought you would bring it off.'

Of course the performances were imperfect. Some of the singers failed, some of the scenery was inadequate. The scene-shifters made dreadful mistakes; the curtain more than once was raised too soon and one could see them darting about in shirt-sleeves. The neck of the dragon had not arrived; the head had to be jammed grotesquely on to the body. (It transpired afterwards that the neck, which had been manufactured by an English firm, had been dispatched by mistake to Beyrout in Syria!)

Nevertheless the festival could not but make a deep impression. The theatre was unique: the lovely rural surroundings; the simplicity of the auditorium; the orchestra concealed beneath the stage, that the dramatic illusion might be unimpaired, that the music might issue invisibly from 'mystic depths.' The magnitude, the multiformity of the work were astounding; the achievements of Niemann, Betz, Unger, Hill, Materna,

Richter, the conductor, prodigious. At the end of the first cycle Wagner came before the curtain to acknowledge the frantic applause. 'You have just seen what we can do,' he said solemnly. 'Now it rests with you. If you wish it, we shall have an art!'

Afterwards a banquet, speeches, ovations, receptions. Emperors, princes, dukes, archdukes, celebrities, flocked to congratulate him. And friends old and new—Frau von Schleinitz, Judith Gautier, Mathilde Maier, the Wesendoncks, the Willes, Jacob Sulzer, Pusinelli . . . and Liszt. Since 1872 Liszt had been his intimate friend again. He had reconciled himself to Wagner's marriage. And since she had settled in Rome and devoted herself to the study of theology he had seen less of the Princess Wittgenstein. . . . Ludwig II also came. But not to the reception. In the eight years since Wagner had last met him he had grown more and more peculiar. He shunned human contacts and craved the seclusion of fantastic castles, which he had built in the mountains near Munich. Thus he came by private train, and Wagner had to greet him in the middle of the night at a remote spot on the line. He stayed at a castle near by, went to the theatre by a secluded route and departed directly after the cycle was over.[1]

Nietzsche, too, was there. But he was acutely unhappy. His conception of Hellenic art had altered since he had written *The Birth of Tragedy*. In Bayreuth Wagner's music drama, which he had acclaimed as the renaissance of the Greek spirit, seemed to be the very antithesis of it. The Greeks, he had come to believe, affirmed life; Wagner, he now felt, denied it. Greek art was inspired by a will to live

[1] In 1886 Ludwig was dethroned and confined as a lunatic. Six days after, his body and that of his keeper were found drowned in a lake.

instinctively, powerfully, realistically; Wagnerian art was a refuge from reality, a hashish, intoxicating, enervating and baneful.

Gloomily he watched Wagner bask in his glory. Only a few weeks ago his own tribute to that glory had appeared: his book, *Richard Wagner in Bayreuth.* He winced when he was complimented upon it. That book was his last tribute to a friendship which had been the most precious experience of his life—the last triumph of affection over reason. For years he had stifled his doubts and worked heart and soul for Wagner's cause. Now he must utter the truth as he saw it, develop his own philosophy. And that meant severing his friendship with Wagner.[1]

Wagner had basked in his glory, but he was not dazzled by it. 'Never had an artist been so honoured,' he wrote afterwards. But, he added, it was the artist that had been honoured, not the art; the achievement, not the thing achieved. The emperor's remark: 'I never thought you would bring it off,' expressed a general feeling. None of the potentates who had honoured him thought of paying off the huge deficit of 120,000 marks which blocked the future of the festival.

[1] In 1878 Nietzsche wrote *Human, All Too Human,* in which he first expressed his changed attitude towards Wagner's art. Wagner, deeply offended by his apostasy, attacked him soon after in the article *Public and Popularity.* In 1888 Nietzsche wrote his sensational *The Case of Wagner,* a scathing indictment of Wagner's music drama as a source of degeneracy. But this book is probably the concern of the Nietzsche rather than of the Wagner biographer. This might be said of the entire relationship. In the words of Frau Förster-Nietzsche: 'For Wagner . . . the Nietzsche affair was but an episode of his latter days.' But for Nietzsche Wagner was an important stepping-stone in his development as man and thinker.

From Sorrento, whither he had travelled to rest after his tremendous exertions, Wagner appealed for help to his patrons and outlined to the King of Bavaria an elaborate plan for nationalizing the Bayreuth theatre. But in vain. In May 1877 he tried to save the situation by giving concerts in London. Again in vain. As conductor he was less than himself, for he was tired. And he had been induced to organize on too grand a scale. He had taken the Albert Hall, held nineteen rehearsals, each of which cost £200, and engaged several of the Bayreuth singers at lavish salaries.

But Wagner was determined to keep the flag flying at Bayreuth. He returned there to agitate on behalf of two long-cherished projects—the founding of a paper and of a school of musical interpretation. He realized the former. In February 1878 there appeared the first number of *Bayreuther Blätter,* under the editorship of Hans von Wolzogen, a young philologian resident in Bayreuth. Wagner contributed to it regularly for the rest of his life.

Early in 1878 the financial problem was at length solved. Ludwig II wished to have *The Ring* produced in Munich. He gave Wagner a royalty of ten per cent on the receipts from performances of his operas in that city; the royalties were to be paid into the royal treasury until the deficit on the festival was wiped out.

At the same time another valuable source of income was opened to Wagner by Angelo Neumann, the director of the Leipzig opera. Neumann was a Jew; he was enterprising and combined business acumen with artistic insight. Since the festival many managers had tried and failed to persuade Wagner to let them produce separate portions of *The Ring;* Neumann alone dared to propose a performance of the whole cycle. Wagner consented. The work was given in Leipzig in 1878 with conspicuous success. Other theatres followed suit. In 1881 Neumann produced it in Berlin and in 1882 in London. Wagner let him form a 'Richard Wagner Touring Company'; he took *The Ring*, lock, stock and barrel, all over Germany and later to Holland, Belgium, Italy, Austria and Russia.

That Wagner should have thus abandoned a principle to which he had clung for over half a century—the principle that *The Ring* should be performed only at a festival under his supervision—was no doubt partly due to the influence over him of Cosima. She had to consider her future and that of the children. In his old age Wagner's mode of life was more luxurious than ever; he was head over ears in debt.

But it was due also to the fact that, after the festival, the performance of *The Ring* ceased to be Wagner's supreme interest. He had, as he said, attained his goal *once* and shown the world the true meaning of his work. Once was enough. Five months after the festival he set himself to attain another goal, to execute another great artistic conception—*Parsifal.* He had written the poem before the concert season in London. For the sake of *Parsifal* rather than of *The Ring* he struggled to keep the flag flying in Bayreuth. In order to be able to live in security and execute *Parsifal* he bartered away *The Ring* to Neumann.

The legend of Parsifal, which Wagner had read in the early Paris and Dresden days, had gripped his imagination ever since the genesis of the idea of *Tristan.* We remember how in the interval between the composition of *The Valkyrie* and the first act of *Siegfried* Wagner had brooded over *Tristan* and a subject culled from a history of Buddhism. This subject expressed the idea of *Parsifal*—redemption through the abnegation of passion. On the Good Friday before his entry into the Asyl Wagner had recalled the Parsifal legend and jotted down a sketch for a Parsifal drama. While working at

Tristan he had planned to introduce Parsifal into the third act: 'Parsifal, in his quest for the Grail, is to come as a pilgrim to Kareol where Tristan lies dying in his desperate love-agony.'

The connection between the two ideas is evident: Tristan renounces life for the sake of passion—Parsifal renounces passion for the sake of eternal life. Parsifal embodies the yearning of Tristan's guilty conscience for salvation.

Wagner had not yet exorcized the Tristan in himself. Among the visitors who had flocked to Bayreuth in 1876 was Judith Gautier, and she had inspired a flame—faint, but a flame—of passion, in which the ageing man could not but rejoice.[1] He was near death; more than ever he yearned for salvation. He had expressed many things in music since he had composed *Tristan,* but not that yearning. In his last, greatest work, *The Dusk of the Gods,* he had expressed the tragedy of a humanity for which there was no salvation.

Wagner now turned in his old age from tragedy to religion. The change is reflected in his writings. In Munich he had held art to be a 'play . . . lifting us above the sordid actuality of distress.' Since the inception of *The Dusk of the Gods* he had been concerned mainly to define and analyse this 'play' and further its production; he had written *The Destiny of Opera, Actors and Singers*[2] and articles for his patrons and the Wagner societies. But now, it seems, in longing for redemption from his own distress, he longed to succour the distress around him. In his last years he inveighed against the eating of meat ('the thirst for blood') and racial impurity. Jehovah, the god of war, property and power, had corrupted Christianity, the religion of compassion and renunciation. It was the function of music, the language *par excellence* of the soul, 'to rescue the soul of

[1] The odd, touching story of Wagner's relation with Judith Gautier is told in the author's *Wagner and Judith Gautier* (*Music and Letters,* Vol. XVIII. No. 2). [2] See p. 102.

religion, to take those mystical symbols religion would have us believe actually true, and, by the ideal presentation of their symbolic values, to reveal the profound truths which they conceal'—to reveal, that is to say, man's tragic knowledge of his downfall; the sublimation of his sinful lusts into selfless pity for his fellows; his yearning for redemption and the sense of redemption which that yearning brings—to reveal, in fact, what Wagner was expressing so wonderfully in the music of *Parsifal*.

Wagner composed *Parsifal* in Bayreuth. He began it in August 1877 and by April 1879 had it ready for instrumentation. He worked comparatively slowly. His health was deteriorating. He suffered from heart-attacks and from an old gastric trouble and erysipelas. At the end of 1879 he fled from the cold, dreary German winter and settled with his family in a villa in Naples. He remained in Italy for ten months, reading, entertaining guests — notably Paul Zhukovsky, the Russian painter, and Heinrich von Stein, a young student of philosophy—making excursions, writing the essay *Religion and Art* and preparing the orchestral score of *Parsifal*. On the way home he visited Munich, conducted a private performance of the prelude for Ludwig (who irritated him by greedily demanding its repetition and then the *Lohengrin* prelude), and made arrangements for the production in Bayreuth. Ludwig waived a condition, which he had attached to the cancellation of the deficit on the festival, that *Parsifal* should be performed in Munich—a condition very offensive to Wagner, who held that the performance in an ordinary opera house of his '*Sacred* Dramatic Festival,' *Parsifal*, would be an act of violation. Ludwig now guaranteed three hundred thousand marks for a Bayreuth production and placed the choir and orchestra of the Munich Opera at Wagner's disposal free of charge.

Friedrich Bruckmann, Munich

RICHARD WAGNER

Drawing by Kietz

MATHILDE WESENDONCK

After a Drawing by Ernst von Kietz, 1856. From a Photograph in the possession of the Stadtgeschichtliches Museum, Leipzig

Unter dem Eindrucke der widerwärtigen Erfahrungen, welche im Betreff des durch die neu eingeführte Besteuerung der Hunde veranlassten Verfahrens gegen diese bisher so bevorzugten Hausthiere ~~bekannt~~ am hiesigen Orte bekannt geworden sind, hat sich ~~soeben~~ ein Verein von Thierfreunden gebildet, der es sich zur Aufgabe macht, nach Kräften dem hierauf bezüglichen, durchaus empörenden Unwesen entgegen zu treten. Diesem zur Folge sind die bisherigen Besitzer von Hunden, welche ihre Thiere, um der Steuerlast zu entgehen, zur Tödtung abzuführen entschlossen sind, aufgefordert, dieselben zuvor dem Beauftragten des Vereines (August Wilhelmj) — —, vorzuführen, um dieselben, nach Vermögen, zur Erhaltung nach den neugesetzlichen Vorschriften zu übergeben.

Der Verein
zur ~~Vermeidung~~ Verhütung der durch die neue Hundesteuer veranlassten Scheusslichkeiten.

Bayreuth — —

REPRODUCTION OF LETTER IN WAGNER'S HANDWRITING

Formerly in the possession of Professor Wilhelmj

RICHARD WAGNER IN 1861

From H. S. Chamberlain, 'Richard Wagner,' published by Friedrich Bruckmann, Munich

RICHARD AND COSIMA WAGNER

Museum der Gesellschaft der Musikfreunde, Vienna

FROM 'TRISTAN AND ISOLDE'

The score is in Wagner's handwriting

A CARTOON IN 'SCHALK VON LEIPZIG,' 5TH JANUARY 1879

Siegfried-Wagner hebt den Schatz der 'Niebelungen'

Da lieg auch du—dunkler Wurm!—	*There lie thou too—grim dragon!—*
Den gleissenden Hort heb' ich hurtig.	*The glittering hoard I carry off swiftly.*

The words are adapted from *The Ring.*

Below Wagner, on the right, crouches Paul Lindau, a prominent anti-Wagnerian critic; above him, on the left, is perched Frau von Schleinitz (or possibly Materna, the singer). On the doorway of Villa Wahnfried is posted, 'Jews forbidden to enter'; on its right-hand side stands Cosima, on the left Liszt.

Breitkopf and Härtel

THE THEATRE, BAYREUTH

The stage is set for the Grail Scene in 'Parsifal'

So far the patrons had subscribed only seventy thousand marks. Although Bülow raised an additional forty thousand by piano recitals—this, alas, was now the only contribution he could make to the cause!—Wagner was eventually compelled to open the festival to the general public, 'whose contributions are no longer given for the realization of an idea, but paid for a place in the theatre.' Later, however, he founded a special fund for the benefit of deserving Wagnerians who could not afford to pay the high price demanded.

The performances were fixed for the summer of 1882. The summer of 1881 was devoted to preparations. Singers were tested; stage appliances, scenery, costumes settled upon; the score continued and fair-copied (by the composer Humperdinck, among others). At the end of the year Wagner's failing health again forced him to flee southwards, this time to Palermo. He finished the instrumentation there on 13th January 1882. Zhukovsky describes how after supper that evening Wagner withdrew for a while and then returned with the score, announcing dramatically that he had that day completed *Parsifal*. In replying to a toast Wagner said that he had feared he would die before completing it.

The brilliant Mediterranean seascape, the prodigal, luscious vegetation made him feel young and vital again. He stayed in Sicily until the spring, then travelled to Venice, where he rented the Vendramini Palace on the Grand Canal for next winter, and thence to Bayreuth, to fling himself into the business of producing *Parsifal*.

There were difficulties, of course: defects in the scenery and the costumes had to be dealt with, quarrels between singers who played the same part on different nights had to be adjusted. Wagner still carried all before him—although he was subject to dangerous heart attacks. (During the fifth performance he collapsed; when he recovered he gasped: 'Another narrow escape!')

He could make the production more perfectly successful than that of *The Ring* in 1876. The undertaking was less enormous; the financial basis more solid; several of the leading singers had already been initiated into his style.

Zhukovsky designed the settings, Heinrich Porges trained the Flower-maidens, Hermann Levi, the Jewish conductor of the Munich Opera, was in charge of the orchestra. There were sixteen performances, the first two for the patrons, the rest open to the public. During the last performance Levi fell ill and Wagner took the baton from him. At the end the excited audience urged Wagner to mount the stage and make a speech. But Wagner remained at the conductor's desk and addressed not the audience but the orchestra and the singers lined on the stage before him. To them, he felt, not to this entertainment-seeking, mundane throng behind him, he owed his festival. He thanked them, congratulated them; he finished by inviting them to come again next year—would they come? Enthusiastically they shouted 'Yes!'

And yet it was precisely this despised throng that had ensured the festival. 'If you wish it, we shall have an art,' Wagner had said to his patrons at the close of the first cycle of *The Ring* in 1876. They had not wished hard enough. They had merged with the public who were prepared to pay thirty marks not to 'have an art,' not to share in the 'realization of an idea,' but simply to enjoy the Wagnerian music drama.

The creation of this public was the achievement of Bayreuth. Only by extraordinary effort could 'the true meaning' of Wagner's unique, elaborate art be revealed. Wagner made this effort, created a demand for this revelation, and set a standard of artistic endeavour by which all other attempts to interpret his music drama could be judged. Nowadays, when the imperfections of Wagnerian performance are so frequent that they tend actually to prejudice one's estimate of his work, we do well to recall that standard.

It was as if art, in generating for itself a Wagner, not only bestowed on him the power to conceive, but infused him with the devotion needed to realize his conceptions. Such devotion is denied other, lesser mortals, who do not create but only imbibe. . . . Perhaps Wagner was unjust in disdaining their applause; but who can blame him? He longed not for admiration, however sincere, but for the understanding of a community who valued art as he valued it. That understanding had always been and would always be denied him —save from friends and lovers and from fellow-artists who sang and played with him. And so on that final occasion he addressed those artists, not the public.

Wagner's life was over. He had worn himself out for the last time. In September 1882 he retired with his family to Venice, the lovely city in which years ago he had sung the praises of death. He lived quietly, wrote one or two articles for the *Bayreuther Blätter,* performed his early Symphony as a birthday surprise for Cosima. His great old friend Liszt arrived in November and remained with him until 13th January. Exactly a month later Wagner succumbed to a heart attack.

He was buried in Bayreuth with regal pomp and circumstance. Friend and foe alike mourned the death of this 'king among men,' as Bülow had once called him. As the coffin was laid beneath the catafalque, in which it was to be borne to its last resting-place in the garden of Wahnfried, the band played the funeral march for Siegfried from *The Dusk of the Gods*—solemn, glorious strains, which expressed, surely as nothing else could, the emotion men felt when Richard Wagner died.

CHAPTER VIII

WAGNER'S PERSONALITY

To comprehend another's personality we exert our powers of empathy, endeavour to enter his subjective world. Conditions are favourable so long as the personality attracts us; if it doesn't, if we keep running into unsympathetic traits inviting censure, empathy snaps. Instead of an exercise in understanding our study becomes a sort of accountant's exercise, a totting up of unsympathetic and sympathetic items in debit and credit columns. We reckon for instance that Wagner, who borrowed money from, lived in a house provided by, made love to the wife of, Otto Wesendonck, and afterwards in his Autobiography wrote disparagingly about him, was selfish, unscrupulous, ungrateful; on the other hand that he was a great artist, the gratification of whose abnormally urgent desires was necessary to his art. The reckoning will be just only if we resist the impulse to raise the voice at the mention of the attributes selfishness, unscrupulousness, ingratitude; only if we admit Wagner's values as well as our own and regard his gratifications, as he did, as serving tremendous purposes beyond themselves. He felt—he never ceased to feel—like D. H. Lawrence when he cried:

> I think . . .
> I could convulse the heavens with my horror.
> I think I could alter the frame of things in my agony.
> I think I could break the System with my heart.
> I think in my convulsion the skies would break.

Overweening egoism, in other words, was the concomitant of Wagner's greatness. If, for instance, Weissheimer was playing on the piano to Bülow an opera of his own, and Wagner in the room above wanted to sleep, word must be sent down to Weissheimer to stop playing. If Liszt could not visit him at a time when he craved his company, then the engagement which prevented him was 'trivial.' If he wished to indulge his luxurious tastes, then borrowed money must be spent. How fastidious, how exorbitant his tastes were can be gauged by the following order to his tailor for a dressing-gown:

Pink satin, stuffed with eiderdown and quilted in squares, like the grey and red coverlet I had of you; exactly that substance, light, not heavy; of course with the upper and under material quilted together. Lined with light satin, six widths at the bottom, therefore very wide. Then put on extra—not sewn on to the quilted material—a padded ruching all round of the same material; from the waist the ruching must extend downwards into a raised facing (a garniture) cutting off the front part. Study the drawing carefully [Wagner had enclosed a drawing]: at the bottom the facing, or *Schopp,* which must be worked in a particularly beautiful manner, is to spread out on both sides to have an all-in width and then, rising to the waist, lose itself in the ordinary width of the padded ruching which runs all round.[1]

If he wished to indulge his mania for reading his poems aloud, his friends must patiently listen for evenings on end. Frau Wille describes how on one occasion she was reproved when her child's illness called her out of the room: 'Wagner said that the boy was not dangerously ill; that it was a disagreeable criticism of an author to leave in that way; and he called me "Fricka." That settled it; I did not protest against the name.'[2]

[1] Quoted by H. T. Finck: *Wagner and his Works.* [2] Ibid.

This startling complaisance of Frau Wille's exemplifies the extraordinary fascination of Wagner. He was as expressive as his music; he compelled those about him to feel for him as he felt for himself. His presence was fascinating. His head was large in proportion to his body and so commanding that he seemed taller than he actually was. Every feature was extraordinary: the high, noble forehead; the translucent, greyish-blue eye, now flashing, now remote and dreamy; the big, boldly curving nose; the thick, jutting chin.[1] 'You lose your identity when in his presence . . .' said one, 'you . . . forget that there is something else in the world besides Wagner and his music. You are under an influence that sets every nerve at its highest key.'[2] Another said:

When he showed himself he broke out as a whole, like a torrent bursting its dikes. One stood dazzled before that exuberant and protean nature, ardent, personal, excessive in everything, yet marvellously equilibrated by the predominance of a devouring intellect. The frankness and extreme audacity with which he showed his nature, the qualities and defects of which were exhibited without concealment, acted on some people like a charm, while others were repelled by it. His gaiety flowed over in a joyous foam of facetious fancies and extravagant pleasanteries; but the least contradiction provoked him to incredible anger. Then he would leap like a stag, roar like a tiger. He paced the room like a caged lion, his voice became hoarse and the words came out like screams: his speech slashed about at random. He seemed at these times like some elemental force

---

[1] Wagner was thus described in the warrant for his arrest issued by the Dresden police in 1849: '. . . of medium stature, has brown hair, an open forehead; eyebrows, brown; eyes, greyish blue: nose and mouth, proportioned; chin, round, and wears spectacles. Special characteristics: rapid in movements and speech . . .'

[2] Hubert Herkomer, who painted Wagner. Quoted by H. T. Finck.

unchained, like a volcano in eruption. Everything in him was gigantic, excessive.[1]

His voice had 'something of the cry of a young eagle,' Liszt wrote. 'When he saw me again,' he continues—he is writing of one of his visits to Wagner in Zürich—'he wept, laughed and raved for joy for at least a quarter of an hour. . . .' He ordered other musicians about like a 'general,' but Liszt himself

he loves with all his heart and says continually: 'See what you have made out of me!' when the conversation turns upon his fame and popularity—twenty times a day he falls upon my neck—then rolls around on the floor, caressing his dog Peps and talking perpetual nonsense to him—while all the time he curses the Jews. . . . In a word: a great and overwhelming nature, rather like a Vesuvius, which when it erupts scatters forth sheaves of flame and at the same time sprays of rose and lilac.

Evidently Wagner's fascination lay not only in his expressiveness, but often in what he expressed. True, he 'loved his friends for his own sake, not for theirs'; [2] true, he could not interest himself in their operas or consider their engagements or their sick children. Yet few men ever loved so intensely as Wagner did 'after his fashion.' There is a naïve, childlike beauty in the very intensity of his egoistic loving. One feels this in the letters, of which he wrote an enormous number. (Nearly twenty volumes of them have been published, and they are not exhaustive. Sometimes he poured out as many as six a day.) His instinctive assumption that others must perforce be interested in his affairs, the gusto with which he unburdened himself, the spontaneity, the candour, the changes of mood — all this is childlike. He had, too, a child's fascinating sense of fun. He never, for instance, outgrew a

[1] Edouard Schuré, quoted by E. Newman, *Wagner as Man and Artist.*

[2] E. Newman, *Wagner as Man and Artist.*

passion for acrobatic stunts. This anecdote of Praeger's, one of his London friends, is delightful:

> I remember full well one day, when we were sitting together in the drawing-room at Triebschen (1871), on a sort of ottoman, talking over the events of the years gone by, when he suddenly rose and stood on his head on the ottoman. At the very moment he was in that inverted position the door opened, and Madame Wagner entered. Her surprise and alarm were great, and she hastened forward, exclaiming: 'Ach! lieber Richard! Richard!' Quickly recovering himself, he reassured her of his sanity, explaining that he was only showing Ferdinand he could stand on his head at sixty, which was more than the said Ferdinand could do.[1]

And he could climb up to the roof, slither up a tree or a statue, hang by his feet from a balcony railing. The onlookers' terror stimulated him. ('Above all things do not notice him: do not look surprised, or you can never tell where he will end,' said Cosima to Judith Gautier.) He would play about like a child, too, in his letters; would address a friend, 'much-tortured chamber-musician,' or 'O you most excellent fellow, man, brother, friend, chorus-director and music-copyist,' or 'dear old *play*-fellow.' [2] Like Beethoven, he was addicted to punning. Thus he describes an attack of erysipelas: 'The "roses"' ('Rosen' is the German name for the complaint) 'upon the thorns of my existence began to bloom, fading often, but budding again as often, and I had, like a good gardener, to give them almost three months of uninterrupted attention. And,' he runs on, 'I have still not managed to put my big child *The Valkyrie* to sleep.'

An interesting example of Wagner's playfulness was recently brought to light in the memoirs of Norman Douglas[3]—no less

[1] Quoted by H. T. Finck.

[2] Ibid.

[3] *Looking Back*, pp. 332–4.

than a new composition, a song! Mr. Douglas heard it sung in a restaurant in Naples by Peppino, Wagner's friend Zhukovsky's servant, who had been with Wagner in Naples and Bayreuth. It was a Neapolitan fisherman's song, written for and taught him by Wagner himself—so Peppino had explained to Douglas, who, struck with the Nordic flavour of the song, had questioned him about it. He had sung it in a garbled, incomprehensible German; he had forgotten the original, since there had been no demand for the song. And no wonder, for, as Mr. Douglas reproduces it, it is a trivial, banal little thing, with a jaunty, waltz-like rhythm. Its chief characteristic is the *Flying Dutchman*-like and non-Italian 'Ho-ja-ho' of the fisherman's call. It is easy to imagine Wagner gaily perpetrating it for Peppino, whose lovely voice and natural technique were a constant delight to him. He would spring it on the family as his latest composition, and what applause and laughter there would be!

A characteristic of Wagner which at first sight seems inconsistent with the picture drawn of him above as an overweening egoist is his passion for animals. For it was not a mere egoistic basking in the affection of one dog after another (his whole life long he was never without a dog), but a genuine solicitude for their welfare. When he gave away his pets' puppies he took great care that they should have 'a happy home in a large residence.' He 'wrote a long letter to a man in Vienna remonstrating against the cruelty of keeping his dog chained all the time.'[1] At Biebrich he adopted a vagrant bulldog and got bitten in the hand for his pains, with the serious result that work on *The Mastersingers* was held up for several weeks. All this seems to show how kind-hearted Wagner was, his egoism notwithstanding. . . . Or are the two qualities after all not incompatible? An egoist is not

[1] H. T. Finck.

necessarily a man who takes pleasure in unkindness, but who when his own feelings and interests are at stake cannot but sacrifice everything else to them. When he is in the mood he can be kind enough, and Wagner, with his childlike craving for affection, loved to be kind, loved to charm. His inferiors—his pets and his servants (many examples of Wagner's kindness to his servants could be cited)—were ideal objects, for they adapted themselves unquestioningly to his mood and did not expect him to adapt it to theirs. Not so his equals. Wagner could brook no equals therefore. His attitude towards others was, as Mr. Newman says, that of a 'benevolent despot.' He preferred the company of women to that of men because they were more sympathetic, more docile. His one big, permanently satisfactory relationship was with Cosima, whose object in life it was to minister to him.

As he grew older he became more relentlessly inconsiderate and self-obsessed. His misfortunes warped him. Because he had suffered so bitterly through Minna during and after their sojourn at the Asyl—through her understandable, intolerable (intolerable to one who believed with all his soul in the divine right of the genius to demand self-sacrifice of others) refusal to recognize the necessity of his relationship with Mathilde Wesendonck; through the expense of having to support her; through the inability to marry again—because of this he could write so coldly in *My Life* of her 'coarse misunderstanding,' and ruthlessly expose her limitations and frailties as if she were a character in a novel. At the time he had both felt, and as far as he could, behaved compassionately towards his 'alte Mutz,'[1] as he affectionately nicknamed her; had written her the cosy, chatty letters he knew she liked, had made plans for her, had tried to live with her again.[2] 'It is dreadful to think

[1] 'Old stump.'

[2] See above, p. 77.

that any one is suffering through me,' he had cried to Cornelius. And (after the Jessie Laussot episode) to Frau Ritter: 'Poor woman! She was so rich, so endowed, whom could she not have made completely happy! Alas that she lacked just one thing, the one thing without which all love is an illusion, all the cares of love a martyrdom, all union torment—the understanding of the one we believe we love. . . .'

And it was because he had suffered so bitterly through his failure to produce or even complete his great works, through the apparent hopelessness of ever being able to convince the world of the justice of his claims upon it, that he raised those claims and paid to himself the homage he knew the world owed him. His letters from Zürich show that his claims to a right to others' sacrifices did not preclude a sense of their sacrifice: they express genuine gratitude. But because Wesendonck had refused to harbour him after his flight from his Vienna creditors in 1864, he could write thus unfeelingly in *My Life* of his visits to him from the Asyl:

. . . it became really intolerable to me to give up whole evenings to conversations and entertainments in which my good friend Otto Wesendonck thought himself bound to take part at least as much as myself and others. His anxiety lest, as he imagined, everything in his house would soon go my way rather than his gave him, moreover, that peculiar burdensomeness with which a man who thinks himself slighted throws himself into every conversation in his presence, something like an extinguisher on a candle.

And in December 1861, in Paris, after he had abandoned the production of *Tristan and Isolde* and taken up *The Mastersingers,* he wrote this astounding letter to a young musician, Hornstein, with whom he had had a passing friendship in Switzerland:

Dear Hornstein,—I hear that you have become rich. In what a wretched state I myself am you can easily guess from my failures. I am trying to retrieve myself by seclusion and a new work. In order to make possible this way to my preservation—that is to say, to lift me above the most distressing obligations, cares, and needs that rob me of all freedom of mind, I require an immediate loan of a thousand francs. With this I can again put my life in order, and again do productive work.

It will be rather hard for you to provide me with this sum; but it will be possible if you *wish* it, and do not shrink from a sacrifice. This, however, I desire, and I ask it of you against my promise to endeavour to repay you in three years out of my receipts.

Now let me see whether you are the right sort of man!

If you prove to be such for me—and why should not this be expected of someone some day?—the assistance you give me will bring you into very close touch with me, and next summer you must be pleased to let me come to you for three months at one of your estates, preferably in the Rhine district. . . .[1]

Hornstein's curt refusal pained and surprised him. 'It would be wrong of me to pass over without censure an answer such as you have given me,' he writes. 'Though it will probably not happen again that a man like me will apply to you, yet a perception of the impropriety of your letter ought of itself to be a good thing for you. . . .'

If they had been written by any one save Wagner one would have said that these were the words of a crazy egomaniac.

Or had Wagner perhaps become slightly mad? Had he always been? Was that overweening egoism of his, which we have called the concomitant of his greatness, because it was natural to him with his temperament and genius to rate his interest higher than other people's, the cause of his misfortunes? Had he a madman's blindness to external realities? If he had been differently constituted could he have achieved his goal more easily? Certainly it does seem that if he had

[1] Quoted by E. Newman, *Wagner as Man and Artist.*

not spent other people's money on costly, elaborate dressing-gowns (not to mention stray pieces of silk and satin to strew round his room, silk underclothes, perfumes, slippers, bath-salts and much else besides), his career might have been easier. And if he had been less chronically pugnacious, less ready to alienate those whom he might have conciliated. 'The grudge,' he told Liszt, who disapproved of *Judaism in Music,* 'is as necessary to my nature as gall is to blood . . . and so I let fly.' He took a positive pleasure in riling critics (one recalls how he made an enemy of Hanslick by reading *The Mastersingers* to him). He had a biting pen. It is little wonder that the world paid him back in his own coin, derided and maligned him, accused him (him, of all people!) of perverting melody and violating the classics. He summed it all up once to Otto Wesendonck: 'We two, the world and I, are two stubborn fellows at loggerheads, and naturally whichever has the thinner skull will get it broken.' That was his attitude.

And if he had not imagined that he was the centre of the cosmos, that his art-work was the goal of all social, artistic progress, and poured out treatise after treatise to prove this, in which he waged war on facts as he did on his enemies and helped himself to one friendly theory after another—Feuerbach's, Schopenhauer's, Gobineau's—as unscrupulously as he did to his successive friends' pockets—if he had not thought and written thus, perhaps his path might have been less complicated.

His reading was wide, his memory retentive, his intellect powerful, yet the ten bulky volumes of his collected prose and poems contain much that is not only not worth reading but barely readable. Yet one must add that Wagner's ability as a prose-writer has been grossly under-estimated. In the English-speaking world this is partly due to the clumsiness of his indefatigable translator, W. Ashton Ellis. It is also because the longest, best-known, most biographically and aesthetically significant, *Opera and Drama,* is by far the worst written. Wagner lacked the poise and the discipline demanded by the task he was setting himself of imposing a revolutionary theory of art upon a recalcitrant world. But when writing unpretentiously of his feelings, perceptions and experiences he is readable and often fascinating.

Wagner's ability as a poet is another matter. He could throw off fine phrases and write passages of sustained eloquence (Sachs' *Wahn* monologue; Tristan's monologue in the third act of *Tristan*; Brynhilda's oration in the Immolation scene), but the poems are for the most part the work of a facile, idiosyncratic versifier—and none the worse for being so, since here the criterion is not literary quality but the demand, which they triumphantly meet, of music-dramatic effectiveness. Apart from this the poems (and for that matter certain passages in the theoretical writings, e.g. the discussion of the Oedipus myth in *Opera and Drama*) are remarkable for their depth-psychological insight. Wagner re-fashioned the myths which expressed the myth-makers' emotions and attitudes in order to give symbolic utterance to his deepest desires and fears—his passion and his shrinking from passion, his longing for power and his longing for death.[1]

[1] Robert Donington in his Jungian *Wagner's 'Ring' and its Symbols* maintains that, even though Wagner re-fashioned the myths, in *The Ring* they retain their traditional collective symbolism, as interpreted by Jung, and that it is this which constitutes the work's depth-psychological meaning. Others have employed the more prosaic Freudian assumption that its depth-psychological meaning is to be sought in Wagner's experience. As yet only one full-dress Freudian study has appeared: Louise Brink's *Women Characters in Wagner.* Freudian suggestions are to be found in the works by Thomas Mann, Bryan Magee and Robert W. Gutman listed in the Bibliography. The reader is also referred to the author's *A Freudian View of the 'Ring'* (*Music Review,* Vol. xxvi, No. 3).

And his vision of the musical world with which he had to traffic was penetrating. It *was* as he saw it—slipshod, commercialized, philistine, unprincipled; his music drama did need a special theatre, special organization, special funds, special efforts. The conclusion is irresistible that only a man of Wagner's peculiar qualities could have achieved what he achieved—a man whose egoism amounted to egomania; who acknowledged only his own values; who studied only himself; whom no scruple could deter from gratifying his wants, no matter how trivial or how grandiose; who waged relentless war on everything that did not suit him; who was incapable of compromise. For had he compromised—had he thwarted his needs by cutting down his expenses for his friends' sake; had he wasted his precious energy on another money-making *Rienzi*; had he let his huge works be shortened or simplified; had he let *The Ring* be produced piecemeal—had he done any of these things, he would have been lost. Yet it seemed that not to do them was to be lost. It never occurred to him to see himself as others saw him; he was secure in his magnificent egoism. He staked everything on the power of the truth which he apprehended. And in the end he won.

CHAPTER IX

WAGNER'S MUSIC

A STUDY of Wagner's music must start by cutting a path through the words he built around it. It must be established at the outset what truth there is in the contention that he was the successor of Beethoven, the child of the classical eighteenth and father of the romantic nineteenth century, in whose music drama was latent and of which Wagner's explicitly dramatic music was therefore the fulfilment of a potentiality.

Constant Lambert, in his brilliant *Music Ho!*, illuminatingly compared the difference of musical structure conveyed by the opposing terms 'classical' and 'romantic' to the difference between a formal Italian and an English landscape garden. In the Italian garden, in which the parts are assembled for the sake of the whole, 'it is not only excusable but desirable that one grove of trees should balance another, that the beds should be placed symmetrically.' But in the English landscape garden 'the sinister effect of an overshadowed ruin is completely spoiled if it recurs every hundred yards.' In Wagner's terminology the classical effect of the Italian garden is symphonic, the romantic effect of the English one dramatic. Wagner maintained that the emotions of the mature Beethoven called for musico-dramatic expression, and that it was Beethoven's 'all-puissant error'—an error akin to that of Columbus, who in discovering the New World believed he had re-discovered the Old—to attempt to utter emotions demanding a new medium of expression in an old one—the symphony.

To separate the gold from the dross in Wagner's theory one must pursue this distinction between the classical and the romantic a trifle further. Evidently the difference of structure is the outcome of a difference of sensibility. In the eighteenth century, it seems, a composer reconciled himself to his experience. In comparison to Beethoven—but the comparison must not be pushed too far, for they had many nineteenth-century moments—Haydn and Mozart were naïve, simple people to whom the symmetrical arrangement of the symphony seemed the ideal symbol of the universe as they apprehended it. But in Beethoven a new type of sensibility sought expression, one which felt more acutely the conflict between man and his environment, which struggled and raged and wept and loved and lost, and craved outlet. For this temperament life had not the facile, cheerful, dance-derived periodicity of the symphony: it was a drama with a beginning, a development, a climax and an outcome.

Beethoven, of course, never ceased to compose dance-derived movements capable of bearing the load of this new type of sensibility. But the Beethoven Wagner was invoking was the Beethoven of the dramatic development sections with their thrillingly modulating sequences, their dynamic range, their thematic cut-and-thrust. And it was the Beethoven of the late quartets with their increased number of movements, each seeming to lead inevitably to the next, converting the conventionally demarcated classical pattern of Allegro-Adagio-Scherzo-Finale into the continuum of a higher subjective unity. Wagner held that in the late quartets Beethoven was bringing music to the fulfilment of its deepest purpose, beyond the power of the dance-derived classical symphony: the expression of the continuum of the inner emotional life (in his essay on Beethoven of 1870 he went to the length—though he admitted he was only indulging a fancy—of interpreting the C sharp minor Quartet as the autobiography of the emotions of a day in Beethoven's life: the opening Adagio expressed the melancholy, tinged with prayerfulness, of one waking to yet another day of wishes unfulfilled; the recitative-like Allegro Moderato portrayed 'the Master, conscious of his art, preparing to exercise his magical power'; the ensuing Variations, the intoxicating exercise of this power; and so on). Wagner was overlooking that the drama of Beethoven's development sections was a drama firmly set within the framework of classical sonata form. And he was overlooking that this form provided the framework for most of the great movements of the late quartets (e.g. of the sublime finale of the C sharp minor, of which Wagner wrote that Beethoven was depicting 'the dance of the world itself: joy, grief, transports of love . . . and above all the mighty minstrel, compelling and controlling, proud and sure. . . .'). Berlioz and Mendelssohn, and in their way Chopin and Schumann, had proved, and Brahms, Tchaikovsky and Dvořák were to prove, that there was life in the old dog yet, that classical symphony could be adapted to the expression of romantic sensibility. Wagner himself for that matter in his early *Eine Faust Ouvertüre* had proved it, though the work is marred by unbalanced thematic working-out and excessive reliance on the diminished seventh (in places it sounds like a combined effort by Berlioz and Schumann at their worst). Yet he was not wrong in holding that the precedent of Beethoven pointed to a new kind of opera in which symphony would play a hitherto undreamt-of role.

The word 'symphony' here needs careful handling. Wagner's operas are weighted, as are no others, with 'symphonies,' that is to say, large-scale orchestral pieces, making their effect in purely musical terms. But it is not this which constitutes the essence of these operas' symphonic character. What constitutes it Wagner himself defined in words which provide the essential clue to the understanding of his genius. The structure of his music, he wrote, would have 'the unity of the symphonic movement, by *spreading itself over the whole drama* [italics mine], in the most intimate cohesion therewith—not merely over single, smaller, arbitrary parts' (i.e. not merely in single 'symphonic' purple passages, capable of transference to the concert hall). The 'spreading over the whole drama' would be effected by root-themes, 'pervading . . . the drama, themes which contrast, complete, reshape, divorce and intertwine as in the symphonic movement: only that here the needs of the dramatic action dictate the laws of parting and combining, which were there originally borrowed from the motions of the dance.'

These words, which claim the 'unity of the symphonic movement' but in the same breath make clear that the unity is *not* that of the classical symphonic movement derived 'from the motions of dance,' but a unity dictated by the 'needs of the dramatic action,' should be framed and hung over the beds of those who flatter themselves they are doing justice to Wagner by merely 'going to hear the music.' It is essential to give the 'needs of the dramatic action' the priority Wagner gave them, to read the dramas carefully and, in view of the weight of musical expression he loaded them with, savour them for *more* than they are worth. In fact the artist, like the man, must be swallowed whole; to bite and carp is to suffer indigestion. Swallow the artist whole and the essence of his greatness will be found to lie not in his music *as such*, not in its symphonic organization, which, save in the purple passages, neither has nor presumes to have any existence *as such*, but in his music's unique capacity to absorb drama: on the one hand bind and underpin the structure of the dramatic edifice; on the other, infiltrate its every nook and cranny.

In the early works we see at once how Wagner's art was rooted in Beethoven's and how his progress as original musician was bound up with his progress as music-dramatist. Of the instrumental works of his boyhood the chief quality is the expert 'vigour and confidence,' to use Mr. Newman's epithets, with which the traditional forms of Mozart and Beethoven were handled. The most noteworthy was the Symphony in C major, which was successfully performed in Leipzig in 1832. In his old age Wagner took an affectionate interest in this Symphony. In an article which he wrote after its performance during those last months in Venice he too praises its 'boundless confidence.' His standpoint, he says, was that of Beethoven in his second Symphony; his confidence he humorously attributes to an advantage that he enjoyed over Beethoven, namely that he already knew the *Eroica,* the C minor and A major Symphonies, which were still unknown to the master at the time he wrote the second, or 'at most could only have been floating before him in dimmest outline.'

In our short study, this Symphony, the sundry overtures, songs and occasional pieces which Wagner wrote in Magdeburg, Königsberg, Riga and Paris, and the first two imitative operas, *Die Feen* and *Das Liebesverbot,* can be mentioned only summarily. Here and there in the operas one can glimpse the child, the father of the man—in the dynamic verve with which he works up a situation, boldly reiterating a small quaver figure in the style of *Tristan,* in a melodic stroke characteristic of *Tannhäuser* and *Lohengrin,*[1] in the resourceful ensemble writing, in the promising sense of climax and so on. But opinions agree that this imitative music lacked the fancy and sparkle of the models imitated. *Die Feen* is held to be insipid, *Das Liebesverbot* garish.

Rienzi cannot be dismissed quite so easily. The proof of the pudding is in the eating; whereas *Das Liebesverbot* and *Die Feen* failed in their day and have been revived only as objects of curiosity, *Rienzi* triumphed and is still in the repertory of

[1] See E. Newman's *Wagner as Man and Artist,* p. 251.

continental opera. Military bands have made the overture familiar, indeed hackneyed. On the whole authorities agree that *Rienzi* is an uneven work. If Wagner transcended his models, the operas of Meyerbeer and Spontini, it was not because his artistry was superior—his choruses are often trivial and rhythmically monotonous, his orchestration is noisy and crude, his verse careless and mishandled—but because his muse already had a characteristic way of responding to the whip of a dramatic effect. He seems to take pleasure, for instance, in working up, with the gay tune which sports so lustily in the overture,

a vigorous choral paean to Rienzi at the close of the second act, in order to open the third act in a contrasting atmosphere of alarums and excursions, created by swift *staccato* chords, *tremolandi* and pattering quavers:

The work contains several such telling strokes. One might compare it to a massive stylized statue, of which essential features have been given individuality. Thus in the third act Roman burghers armed for war against the patricians tramp round to many bars of vapid military music; but Rienzi, the hero, enters to a stirring theme delivered by the orchestra in unison; soon he himself sings its first phrase to the words of the Romans' historic battle-cry, 'Santo Spirito Cavalieri,' and military trumpets on the stage complete it (one can imagine how wonderfully they must have set off Tichatschek's silvery, clarion tenor!). . . . Later on he returns triumphant from battle to be denounced by a patrician, Adriano, in the well-known aria, 'Gerechter Gott.' The part was written for Schröder-Devrient; the broad, flexible, declamatory periods seem to reflect Wagner's impression of the great singer's Romeo and Fidelio. Then the chorus takes up a joyful, flowing melody (reminiscent of the famous E flat subject of the *Freischütz* overture); Adriano's tearful, descending phrases intervene; when the joyous opening recurs it is whipped up to a dramatic conclusion on a loud diminished seventh as Adriano rushes off in a fury. The orchestra quickly closes the music upon the tonic. At once Rienzi reassures the agitated assembly in a short, conventional recitative, after which the joyous strains are repeated and this time ended happily. The recitative and the repetition are musically a complete anti-climax. They show how immature, how imitative Wagner's style still was. But the climax which they spoil is proof of the maturity he was beginning to attain.

After *Rienzi* came *The Flying Dutchman,* Wagner's first great original achievement. Hitherto he had conceived an opera as a series of separate vocal and instrumental numbers, whose relation to each other in the drama influenced, perhaps, but did not determine their form. But the subject of *The*

Flying Dutchman called forth themes and figures which, though they first took shape in his mind as the components of a number, Senta's ballad, could be—in Wagner's own phrase—'spread out' over the whole opera; could be isolated, remodelled, expanded, set in a different order, related to other themes. The accompanying figure to which Senta sings of the storm:

becomes an articulate motive as the Dutchman, the creature of the storm, enters:

The Dutchman's famous theme, with which the tubas prelude the stanzas of the ballad:

(its stark, sharp-rhythmed fourths and fifths bear a striking resemblance to the first subject of Beethoven's ninth Symphony), becomes quietly menacing, delivered *pp ma marcato* by the bassoons and cellos beneath the violas' *tremolando,* as Erik, Senta's lover, narrates to her the dream, so fearful to him, in which he beheld the Dutchman. It is reiterated every few bars in a rising sequence of minor keys, just as if it were the subject of a Beethoven development section. (No doubt Wagner profited not only from the example of Beethoven, which impressed him so deeply in Paris, but also from that of Berlioz, whose music he also heard there—from his elaborate, colourful orchestration and his poetic *idée fixe.*)

Wagner related the ideas of the ballad to the cheerful, rollicking themes of the Norwegian sailors, one of which he actually heard on his journey from Riga. Either he contrasted them: the Dutchman's gloomy scene is preceded by a jolly sailor's ditty. Or he combined them: contrapuntally in the third act when the Norwegian and the Dutchman's crew sing in double chorus, and symphonically in the overture when a phrase from the Norwegian chorus:

is repeated over and under the rushing chromatic scales of the strings to form a bridge passage leading out of the storm music to a new subject, the main theme of the Norwegian chorus. This phrase, it may be noted, he found further use for as the theme of the famous spinning chorus of Senta's maidens:

All this thematic development was, of course, linked in Wagner's mind with the dramatization of his subject. ('I am only attracted to matter the poetic and musical significance of which strike me simultaneously,' he wrote not long afterwards.) His desire to portray the Dutchman not only as Senta beheld him in her ballad, but as a concrete figure in a concrete background, stimulated him to 'spread out' the ideas of the ballad in the overture, in the Dutchman's scena, in Erik's dream, in the sailors' chorus. But these, for all their splendid expressiveness, were still only separate numbers. Wagner could not yet write continuous dramatic symphonic music. The subject as he conceived it, moreover, was undramatic.

Senta was not a flesh and blood woman whom the Dutchman found, won, lost, and with whom he died; she was an angel predestined to deliver him from a curse. The essential action began and ended in the number in which she dedicated herself to his salvation, in the ballad. Perhaps that was partly why the plot—the Dutchman's meeting with Senta's father, his introduction to Senta, their love-making, Erik's jealous intervention—occasioned numbers for the most part conventional and insipid.

The subject of *Tannhäuser,* on the other hand, attracted Wagner not only as a spiritual drama, but as a drama of situation. He created the situation by uniting two legends, both familiar to him: that of the Venusberg and that of the Singer's Tournament on the Wartburg. Their union was suggested by the version of the former which he came across in Paris and therefore, he tells us, had 'so much weight' with him.

No doubt the idea of the Singers' Tournament attracted Wagner because it afforded such an excellent dramatic pretext for writing fat operatic numbers. By combining it with the Venusberg legend he killed two birds with one stone—made an effect in the style of which he was a master and gave the effect the dramatic force of a 'reminiscence motive.' In the second act the force of Tannhäuser's involuntary repetition before the high-minded company on the Wartburg of the Hymn of Praise he has sung to Venus in the first act is electrifying. Wagner himself and others before him had already used the 'reminiscence motive,' but here and in the still finer scene in the third act, in which Tannhäuser, returning in despair from his fruitless pilgrimage to Rome, frantically invokes Venus again, it is made the dramatic high-light of an opera.

In the second act Wagner's style was still somewhat at

cross-purposes. Years later he told Mathilde Wesendonck that it was here he first realized 'the beautiful, convincing necessity of transition.' After Tannhäuser's song he discarded the operatic number. He modulated freely from episode to episode; preserved continuity by reiterating orchestral figures; made the assembly, pacified by Elisabeth's appeal for Tannhäuser's life, develop the famous melody of her Prayer in a moving chorus. But with the Landgrave's recitative, dispatching the sinner to Rome, the continuity snaps. The old operatic Adam was too strong in Wagner: he could not forbear working up a conventional grand choral finale, effective in itself, but detached from the rest of the music and holding up the action.

In the scene of the return from the pilgrimage Wagner forestalled more thoroughly his theory in *Opera and Drama* that, since the demarcated melody of the number spoils the continuity of a dramatic situation, the singer should sing an 'endless' declamatory melody, while orchestral motives, conveying the underlying emotion, should bear the brunt of musical expression. The very themes have a post-*Opera and Drama* feeling. The open augmented fourth motive of Tannhäuser's damnation:

recalls that of the dragon motive in *Siegfried*:

The pilgrimage motive:

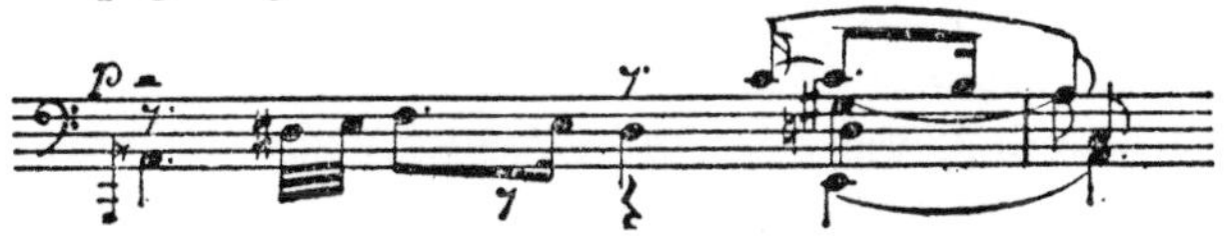

almost has the 'turn' and the line of that of Wotan's despair:

In *Tannhäuser,* then, Wagner travelled further afield than in *The Flying Dutchman.* He had 'spread out' Senta's ballad to represent an image in Senta's mind; he spread out the Venusberg music as a dramatic element, dashing Tannhäuser towards a disgraceful doom. Like that of the ballad, this music was the opera's initial inspiration. It was a wonderful discharge of elemental themes, a first fine, careless rapture of sexual discovery—so fine that whether in applying to it the technique, marvellous though it was, of *Tristan and Isolde* in the Paris version of 1861, Wagner was not doing violence to his own inspiration is a moot question.

If other scenes in the opera were on an inferior, conventional plane, perhaps it was because Wagner's desire to save Tannhäuser from his disgrace was not quite genuine. Passion is not in *Tannhäuser,* as it is in *Parsifal,* a torture, but a delight; religious aspiration is not tired old age's yearning for the ineffable serenity of another world; it is a neurotic attitude. Thus Tannhäuser's desertion of Venus in the first act is unconvincing. The Paris version here is infinitely superior. In the original, where Tannhäuser declares he must leave her, Venus starts up, instantly furious, and for most of the scene addresses him like a shrew, in a monotonously high-pitched, inflexible recitative, sparsely accompanied. In the Paris version she remains lying on her couch 'in quiet wonder' while the orchestra plays the languorous, syncopated sevenths so characteristic of *Tristan*. Gradually her emotion intensifies, gradually surprise gives way to the luxuriant despair of thwarted passion.

And because his desire to save him was insincere, Wagner failed to depict Elisabeth as his hero's saviour. In the well-known Greeting he depicted admirably the awakening of her passion for him; the sinuous, upward-curving phrases of the accompaniment resemble the Venusberg music. Her prayer for his life, too, is heartfelt; but that for his soul artificial. She departs to die for his sake to the yearning melody of Wolfram's Hymn to Chaste Love, which conveys no sense of salvation. And when at the end Tannhäuser, about to re-enter the Venusberg, is redeemed by the sight of her corpse, the funeral procession sings a banal hymn and then the yearning melody of the Pilgrims' Chorus, upon every crotchet of whose accompaniment the strings make a fascinatingly irreligious slur.

Evidently Wagner failed not because he lacked inspiration, but because his inspiration was inappropriate. In the Pilgrims' Chorus, in the Hymn to Chaste Love, in 'O Star of Eve,' in Elisabeth's Prayer, he seems to be drawing not away from, but towards the Venusberg. This music exhales a delicious melancholy, a sense of denial, a longing.

In *Lohengrin* Wagner consciously formulated this emotion —in the story of the holy knight who descends from Monsalvat to seek earthly delights, from which eventually his divinity debars him, and in the music of the prelude. . . . A high A major chord, held alternately by a chorus of eight violins and by flute and oboe, depicts ethereal, shimmering Monsalvat. Soon the upper violins play a long, hovering melody· then flute, oboe and clarinet take it up, and later the horn, while the violins in counterpoint soar above, like doves, creatures of the element from which Lohengrin is descending. As the orchestration thickens the melody seems to draw nearer; at last the brass delivers the first phrase and draws it to a powerful cadence, upon which the second phrase is dashed by the full force of the wind orchestra. But the force soon spends itself. Yearning is exhausted. As the end only the violins' counter-point theme remains, still soaring above. Slowly, gently it floats down, then mounts back to the high chord of the opening. It is as if Lohengrin has been gathered and wafted to the shimmering reaches of his home.

The story of *Lohengrin,* however, attracted Wagner not only as the programme of a tone poem, but for its own sake. Like *Tannhäuser,* it contained a powerful dramatic situation. It attracted him so keenly that he began the composition with the scene that contained it. Lohengrin and Elsa have just been married; she has promised that she will never ask him who he is and where he comes from; her fear and curiosity, which have been worked upon by Ortrud, Lohengrin's enemy, drive her to break her promise. The situation lent itself ideally to the 'reminiscence motive.' When Elsa recalls the mystery of her husband's origin Wagner sounds the motive to which in the first act Lohengrin forbade her to question him:

When she is obsessed by fear and curiosity, the coiling, sinister motive to which Ortrud in the second act corrupted her:

When she wails that one day he will leave her suddenly,

magically as he came, the little motive to which he took leave of the swan that bore him to her:

And when, Elsa having put the fatal question, Lohengrin sighs: 'Ah, now for ever our joy has fled!' Wagner depicts his fading vision of that joy; the clarinet and then the melancholy oboe play the sweet tune which at the beginning of the act Elsa sang to him:

In working backwards and forwards over the rest of the opera Wagner seldom lost sight of this situation and the emotions proper to it. The first act and the conclusion of the third one are dominated by the music of the prelude, the second by Ortrud's motives and by Elsa's bridal music, similar in feeling to the tune which Lohengrin recalls so pathetically. As a good music-dramatist Wagner only permitted himself two solitarily effective pieces—the introduction to the third act and the Wedding Chorus. He had not yet found, however, how to sustain musical interest through a long opera without them. In the mature works he continuously developed his 'reminiscence motives.' In *Lohengrin* he was only groping towards this discovery. When Elsa recounts her vision of Lohengrin a phrase from the prelude is lifted into a new context; when he leaves her a motive which expressed her joyful welcome is repeated in a minor key. But for the most part the motives are only baldly reiterated.

For Wagner still thought mainly in terms of vocal melody, not of orchestral motive. *Lohengrin* is a series of recitatives, ariosos, lyrics and choruses leading uninterruptedly into each other as the drama demands, but not thereby creating a cumulative effect. The king's, the herald's and Ortrud's recitatives only serve to make clear the plot; the choruses serve the music in that they vary and fill out the vocal line, but do so at the expense of the drama. The chorus here is not a protagonist as in the second act of *Tannhäuser,* but only a spectator; its constant interjections have no dramatic justification.

In *Opera and Drama,* the fruit of the years of cogitation which followed the composing of *Lohengrin,* Wagner repudiated choruses and all vocal ensembles as destructive of dramatic effect under any circumstances; and for the sake of dramatic effect formulated the cardinal principle of his music drama: the symphonic development of the orchestral motive.

In *The Flying Dutchman, Tannhäuser* and *Lohengrin* we have seen the dramatist in Wagner constantly stimulating him to develop his musical inspirations. But in all three he shot his chief musical bolt before the opera began. The overture to *The Flying Dutchman* was a symphonic expansion of Senta's ballad; the overture to *Tannhäuser* contained the one full exposition of the Venusberg music and the clinching of its relationship to the Pilgrims' Chorus; the prelude to *Lohengrin* was a tone-poem in which the emotion of the story was once and for all crystallized. In *The Nibelung's Ring,* however, the actual drama itself, its course and outcome, inspired musical developments. For musical ideas were now capable of 'spreading over the whole drama,' root themes which could 'contrast, complete, reshape, divorce and intertwine as in the symphonic movement.' Wagner was entering the New World which he had mapped in *Opera and Drama.*

Not that at all times he rigorously put into practice the theories he had outlined. He took full advantage, of course, of the freedom afforded to the vocal line by the orchestra's taking over the burden of musical thought; he made it match every nuance of the text—Alberich's dissonant, *staccato* tones, the Rhinemaidens' mocking laughter, Erda's level, solemn periods. But at times the singer took complete possession of the music, and not merely to announce or repeat the orchestra's motives, but, forgetting he was the protagonist of a drama, to sing a melody of his own—an absolute, self-contained melody like an aria, and unlike it only in that it formed part of a greater whole. When the music-dramatic occasion warranted Wagner even harked back to the choruses and vocal ensembles which he had repudiated. In the closing passage of *The Rhinegold,* for instance, the trio of Rhinemaidens plays a decisive part as well as the orchestra.

This passage also brilliantly exemplifies the unique symphonic structure of Wagnerian music drama. In the first scene the Rhinemaidens acclaim the Rhinegold by singing the happy motive of the opening bars of this example:

And in the second scene this solemn motive typifies Valhalla, the home of the gods:

Alberich steals the gold from the Rhinemaidens; Wotan wrests it from him and pays it to the giants for building Valhalla. At the close the gods triumphantly enter their new home, while the maidens in the Rhine below wail for their stolen gold. This is the culminating situation; now, not till now, Wagner combines the two motives. The gods advance to the Valhalla music, but they are interrupted by the Rhinemaidens' motive transformed into a yearning cry:

After a few bars the Valhalla music is resumed as the gods move forward ignoring the interruption. But again the maidens cry out their melody, this time distended, passionate, and to the inexorable rhythm of the gods' march:

'Tender and true 'tis but in the waters:
False and base are those who revel above,'

they sing; upon the last syllable the Valhalla theme breaks through again and swells to a grand coda as the gods reach their home.

'Let us tell the musician,' Wagner had written in *Opera and Drama,* 'that every, even the tiniest, moment of his expression *in which the poetic aim is not contained* and which is not conditioned necessarily by that aim and its realization—that every such moment is superfluous, disturbing, bad.' Other examples of the inspiration of this 'poetic aim' leap to the pen. To depict the elemental, unchanging Rhine, he wrote the prelude, one of his most daringly original compositions, in which he remained for 136 bars on the tonic chord of E flat major, reiterating and elaborating a simple arpeggio. To depict Fasolt's consternation when Wotan refuses to give up Freya, whom the Supreme Lawgiver had pledged to him as his reward for building Valhalla, he drew Wotan's, the giants' and Freya's theme into a moving arioso passage. To depict the piling-up of Alberich's hoard, which was to ransom Freya, whom the giants had dragged off, he put a variant of the Wotan motive into canon and combined it with the Nibelung motive and the rhythm of the giants:

With wonderful skill, too, Wagner made the orchestra lead

the episodes into each other, not merely uninterruptedly, but inevitably. Either he blended into the closing phase of an episode the motive of the succeeding one;[1] or he transformed the concluding motive of an episode to resemble the motive of the succeeding one;[2] or, having boldly begun a new episode, blended into it material from a preceding one.[3] Episodes thus related preserved a musical continuity matching the dramatic one.

The 'needs of the dramatic action' of *The Rhinegold* did not, as did those of the subsequent operas, *often* demand that the music rise above the task of preserving continuity to climaxes of purely musical inspiration (twice only did such heights have to be scaled: in the theft of the gold of the first scene and in the entry into Valhalla of the last). Frequently, perhaps too frequently—in Wotan's wrangling's with Fricka and haggling with the giants, in Loge's double-crossing of Alberich—no more is demanded than a vocal line declamatory rather than melodious, punctuated by the bare statement of motives bearing on the matter in hand. If, notwithstanding, the work triumphs, it is because the motives are such that their bare statement, no matter how loose the musical context, rejoices one. In Wagner, who was so consciously susceptible to the symbolism of music (one recalls how the open fifths of the violins' tuning conjured ghosts to his childish fancy), the common chord, the arpeggio, the diatonic scale, the chromatic scale, altered chords, dotted, syncopated rhythm—all this and much more roused thoughts 'too deep for tears.' It is as if in the clear mountain air of Switzerland, free from the old cramping life in Dresden, he rediscovered the elements of his art. The common chord, for

[1] See *The Rhinegold* piano score, pp.30–1 (Schott edition).

[2] Ibid, pp. 54–5.

[3] Ibid, pp. 77–80.

instance, symbolized for him the majesty of natural forces and so he struck from it the rainbow, the thunder, the sword and the gold motive:

The pure arpeggio symbolized the passionless flow of water; the adulterated one the outpouring of love:

The slur of a resolving dominant ninth conveyed the Rhine-maidens' playful cry; [1] that of a diminished seventh Alberich's cry of hatred:

---

[1] See p. 150.

Syncopation conveyed the baffled, insistent throb of his despair:

Small wonder that at times Wagner was content simply to formulate these wonderful discoveries. *The Rhinegold,* moreover, was written as a prelude; its function was to expound, not to draw conclusions. Thus a third of the ninety motives of *The Ring* already appear in it. And each of the other music dramas, though each longer than its predecessor, contained a smaller proportion of new motives. As Wagner's art matured he revelled more and more in drawing conclusions, in fulfilling the potentialities for symphonic development of these simple plastic themes.

Already in the next composition, the first act of *The Valkyrie,* he worked on a far grander scale. The remorseless six-crotchet rhythm of the prelude not only depicts the terrible pattering of the storm which throws Siegmund, the Volsung, into Hunding's hut; it counterpoises the tentative love themes to which Siegmund and Sieglinde, Hunding's wife, first address each other. As their feelings become more defined the themes unravel themselves, until in a little, deliberate orchestral passage their meaning is fully revealed. Then, suddenly, Hunding enters, and the passage breaks before a theme whose sudden entry is so swiftly, surpassingly beautiful that it is as if all before had been but a preparation for it—as if Wagner had been unfolding his other themes in order to show how he could split them with one clean cut (as a dexterous swordsman displays his skill by cleaving through a cushion). Then he relaxes for a while. Siegmund's narrative is an interlude, during which the interest shifts from the orchestral motivation to the stanza-like periods of the vocal recitative. But Wagner does not let it impair the unity of the act: throughout the orchestra recalls the storm, the love and the Hunding motives (perhaps he felt that with them he had created a situation so strong that he did well merely to hold it for a while); and the periods are rounded off by themes which play an important part later on, the Valhalla and the Volsung motives.

When Hunding, having recognized in Siegmund a member of an enemy clan, declares he will kill him next day, defenceless though he is, and departs, driving Sieglinde off, the orchestra draws their motives together again, expressing their every gesture—Hunding's as he angrily bears down upon Siegmund, Sieglinde's as she intervenes, Siegmund's and Sieglinde's as they exchange glances. At the last moment Wagner characteristically anticipates the first theme of the next episode, the sword motive. Here he actually dramatizes the anticipation: Sieglinde regards the hilt of the sword which Wotan had planted in the tree in the centre of the hut; Siegmund, she feels, is the hero for whom it is destined; he will pluck it out and save himself.

Left alone Siegmund broods in despair, the fearful rhythm of the Hunding motive hammering through his brain. He, too, thinks of a sword—the sword which it had been prophesied he would find in his hour of direst need. The two motives are united:

Soon he bursts into an impassioned melody, at the end of each phrase of which the sword motive flashes through the orchestra as the sword's hilt flashes in the flicker of the dying fire. Sieglinde returns to tell him of Wotan's planting of the sword in the tree: the Valhalla motive is extended and run into the sword motive. Declaring her love for and belief in him, she too breaks into an impassioned melody, goaded on by an agitated violin figure. The Volsung motive announces Siegmund's reply, yet another fiery melody, matching it, similarly figurated. Through a glorious augmented sixth modulation it leads into the famous song, 'Winter storms have waned in the moon of May,' of which the second stanza passes into the love music which pervaded the early part of the act:

But now, like a theme in a Beethoven development section, it acquires a new meaning, a new character. It becomes loud and grand; it seems to be raised aloft, to swell out and transcend itself. Every few bars it returns, sweeping every melody and motive and figure into its greater orbit. Some of them are its offshoots—this melody of Sieglinde's, for instance, is derived from the last phrase:

—and this little motive, which foreshadows the chromaticism of *Tristan and Isolde,* from the opening notes of the first phrase:

When Sieglinde ponders their relationship the tension gradually drops; the Valhalla motive, which has reappeared, bounded by the ever-recurring love theme, now leads alone quietly beyond it. She questions Siegmund in a recitative of which the phrases recall his narrative earlier in the act, while the first chords of the Valhalla motive, sounded every few bars, indicate the coming situation. 'Beside herself,' she proclaims him her brother, goaded by the same agitated violin figure to which she had declared her love. Again the Volsung motive, but this time in a sequence leading to the sword motive, announces Siegmund's reply, which is a repetition of his cry for the sword at the beginning of the scene. Then, grasping the hilt, he sings that same eloquent phrase which Alberich sang as he grasped the gold in the first scene of *The Rhinegold.* As he strains and heaves the cry for the sword breaks from him louder and louder, in three terrific periods, rising through a succession of semitones to a long diminished seventh, which resolves upon C major, the chord of the subdominant, as at last he draws forth the sword. Triumphantly the full orchestra brandishes the sword motive. This is the culminating climax; now the themes tumble pell-mell over each other to the close proclaimed by that mighty subdominant. At the very end the love theme drives forward ever faster and faster as the lovers rush out into the forest. First so:

Then pushed on by the sword motive:

And falling away over itself:

In this act Wagner reveals his full stature. He reconciles symphonic with dramatic logic; each episode in the music and in the drama conditions the other and leads to a climax in which every issue is clinched and resolved.

The subject-matter of the second act of *The Valkyrie* is not a single developing situation, but a chain-reaction of disastrous encounters involving issues presented in *The Rhinegold.* At times therefore Wagner lowers his musical sights and employs his motives not expressively but referentially as *Leitmotive* 'guide-motives', symbolical of those issues.

It is only in such passages that this widely used term, *Leitmotiv*, can be employed without creating a false impression. Wagner did not employ it, but Wolzogen, the editor of *Bayreuther Blätter*; it was Wolzogen too who gave the motives their well-known labels, thereby facilitating their discussion, but heightening the false impression that they were intended by Wagner purely as sign-posts to the drama—as dramatic 'visiting cards,' to use Debussy's ironical phrase.[1] At his finest, as we have seen, Wagner uses them not merely referentially, but expressively. Indeed sometimes in the heat of music-dramatic expression he forgets the referential function: when Siegmund as he grasps the sword sings the theme to which Alberich grasped the gold or when Brynhilda bids farewell to her horse, Grane, to the theme of Siegmund and Sieglinde's love, Wagner is not asking us to think back to a previous scene but expressing a quality of emotion common to both.

Wotan's Narration in the second act of *The Valkyrie* where, in order to explain why he must reverse his command to Brynhilda to protect Siegmund, the god expounds the story of *The Rhinegold,* is the *locus classicus* of referentially employed *Leitmotive.* But, galvanized as it is by outbursts of eloquent

[1] This false impression was fostered by anti-Wagnerians. Dame Ethel Smyth relates how Joachim used to raise his hat to Clara Schumann and murmur 'Guten Tag' at every appearance of a *Leitmotiv.*

anguish as the narrator bares his heart, the long recitative provides the Wotan with a grand histrionic opportunity. It is rather when the dramatically loaded poem is being set to a not in itself memorable 'endless melody' and articulated above a not in itself memorable, richly scored, elaborately illustrative orchestra that Wagner becomes a trial. Unless one has so soaked oneself in a work as to be aware of the gist of every sentence (not that this condition cannot be fairly easily met in this age of tapes and records) one is liable to feel that his is a dangerously self-indulgent, over-loaded form of artistic communication, and to sympathize with critics who allege that by sacrificing the clarity of lightly accompanied recitative for 'endless melody' coupled with an 'endless' symphonic fantasia based on repetitive symbolic motives Wagner was making the worst of both worlds, producing unintelligible drama and unimpressive music. One should rather regard comparatively uninspired passages that occur in even the finest acts as the product of a mind that projected on to the stage musical and literary ideas loaded with obsessional significance. ('Your music—dear me, it is a sort of luggage van to the kingdom of heaven', said the painter Lenbach.) Perhaps the wonder is they do not occur more frequently.

In the first act of *Siegfried* Wotan has another less straightforward, more ingenious narration. Wotan the Wanderer appears in order, in the form of a question-and-answer game with Mime, to remind the audience of the past history enacted in the previous operas of the cycle. The reminder was dramatically redundant, but it gave the music-dramatist the opportunity to depict Wotan's change of heart in terms of thematic transformation. In the long duologue he does more with *Leitmotive* than employ them referentially or merely repetitively; he combines and develops them with fresh ones so that they take shape as the majestic periods of a formal strophic pattern.

Space forbids description of the act as a whole (as it has forbidden that of the great symphonic-dramatic episodes within the second and third acts of *The Valkyrie*; 'Brynhilda's Annunciation,' 'The Ride of the Valkyries,' 'Wotan's Farewell'). As a *tour-de-force* of cumulative symphonic-dramatic planning it matches the first act of *The Valkyrie*. But it does not have the same impact, we do not feel with Siegfried as we do with Siegmund and Sieglinde. The music has a rhythmic drive unlike anything else in Wagner and the poem is rich in subtle characterization, but on the stage they do not completely fuse; the rhythmic drive tends to ride roughshod over the subtleties. Siegfried, supposed to embody the ultimate of youthful *joie de vivre,* seems merely a lively young bully. And of course there remains the fact—which Wagner, absorbed in the poem and writing without concern for immediate performance, for the time being put out of mind—that this imperfect world does not contain the *Heldentenor* capable of portraying a lively *young* bully, let alone the ultimate of youthful *joie de vivre* (the memory of Lauritz Melchior, who had abundant *joie de vivre,* flinging himself on his ample stomach and kicking his heels is still with me).

In the second act of *Siegfried* Wagner was dealing with a situation, dramaturgically different from that of the lovers in Hunding's hut and the hero in Mime's cave: not a situation implicit from the beginning and worked upon by external factors to develop and reveal itself, but one created by the continual interpenetrating of two conflicting elements—the dark, treacherous Nibelung element and the bright element of love depicted in the Forest Bird's song. The song does not grow out of the scenes between Alberich, Wotan and Fafner and between Siegfried and Mime which precede it, but contrasts with them, and the effect of this contrast is the abiding inspiration of the act. Again and again the song pours in, like a lovely, great rondo theme bounding every episode—the conflict with Fafner, the dwarfs' quarrel, the undoing of Mime.

At the close the bird sings of the sleeping Brynhilda, interrupted by the agitated Siegfried to a variant of the sleeping Brynhilda motive. The difference between the original:

and the variant:

typifies most admirably that between the world of *The Ring* and that of *Tristan and Isolde* into which the bird actually led Wagner. The feeling of the one is diatonic, of the other chromatic; the former phrase glides down easily to its goal, the D sharp of the dominant seventh, the latter strains against the bass of a flattened supertonic; the one seems to depict effortless attainment, the other anguished effort to attain. So Wagner made music of his yearning for Mathilde Wesendonck. The adulterated chords formed by unprepared suspensions, passing notes, altered notes, appoggiaturas symbolized for him longing fixated and unfulfilled. With such chords he wrought a new, unique idiom.

Not that chromatic harmony was in any sense a perquisite of Wagner. He admitted to Bülow that 'since I got to know

Liszt's compositions' (during the cure at Mornex, after the completion of *The Valkyrie,* he had studied the symphonic poems) 'I have become a very different sort of harmonist from what I was formerly.' The uniqueness of Wagner's idiom lay less in the harmony as such than in the melody which conditioned it and which it conditioned. The famous theme of the *Tristan* prelude:

is made so haunting and harrowing by the altered diminished seventh under G sharp; but only in this context could this so-called *'Tristan'* chord have this potent effect.

With the subtle, multiform apparatus of chromatic harmony Wagner could make a little melody go a very long way. Precisely this long way, this long-drawn-out agony of craving was the subject of his expression. In the supreme climax of the opera, the celebrated *Liebestod,* he repeated the little group of semitones, which closed the theme of the prelude, in a chain of twenty-six sequences, in which he used astounding, excruciating discords (each frantically endeavouring to resolve upon the other):

But he used them not for their own sake—like so many of his imitators—but to make possible that protracted, terrific sequence.

Wagner, in other words, mixed new colours not for their own sake, but for that of a new picture. He could depict a theme in enchantingly various guises. The motive which opens the second act:

could be transformed thus in the course of the act (to cite only a few examples):

He could often and easily mingle his themes in counterpoint: [1]

[1] Here the shepherd's motive of the third act (in the upper part); the 'wounded Tristan' motive of the first act, quoted below (in the middle part); and the opening motive of the second act (in the bass) are combined.

And since the slightest phrase could have melodic significance—even, as we have seen, a mere cluster of semitones—he could draw several themes from one theme, spin a network of ideas from one idea as a spider spins a complex web of gossamer from his tiny body. Thus (and again one can cite only a few examples) this phrase, which introduces the third act, is drawn from the last four notes of the theme of the prelude:

Inverted they form the motive to which Isolde sings of the wounded Tristan:

Inverted, the first three notes of the theme of the prelude form the motive to which she plots his death:

And with the enharmonic modulation possible to chromatic harmony Wagner could vary his picture with the ravishing lights and shades of remotely related keys.

Since, in his own words, he was actuated above all by a 'longing beyond bounds to revel in music,' *Tristan* contains little action and exposition. The characters are called upon to feel rather than to do; to pour out their emotions in long duologues. What little exposition there is is contained in a grand symphonic ballad, the famous narrative of Isolde, through which the motive of the wounded Tristan recurs, sweeping on in stanzas which mount upon each other to a wonderful climax.

Wagner regarded his subject less as a drama, less as a series of actions and consequences of actions, than as the incarnation of a feeling underlying action, unchanged by it, transcending it. Thus, the lovers' drinking of the magic potion is not a dramatic event, for the music has already revealed their suppressed craving for each other (but in *The Dusk of the Gods,* when Siegfried drinks Gutrune's cup, the music depicts the liquid stealing through his veins, intoxicating him). Thus, when Marke surprises the lovers the music does not reflect the rhythm of the situation (as it does when Hunding surprises the lovers in *The Valkyrie*); Marke chooses this moment to deliver a long address into which he pours all the cumulated yearning and grief of his life.

Whereas the music of *The Ring* is no less rich in contrast than the drama, that of *Tristan* tends to be dominated by a single pervasive idea. For all that Brangäne and Kurwenal are characterized, Brangaene responds to Isolde's narration in the language of her mistress and Tristan apostrophizes Kurwenal's loyalty to the 'Tristan' chord of the Prelude. The sea-wind blows only that we may feel it driving Isolde to her destiny with fresh, fearful power. The horns of the hunt echo the throbbing in her heart as she awaits Tristan. The solitary shepherd pipes Tristan's solitary cry of woe.

If the criterion by which one judges music is its power to overwhelm one with emotion, then *Tristan and Isolde* is probably Wagner's most wonderful achievement. Perhaps no other artist ever let forth such a flood of expression, tearing down the secret places of the heart. Many recoil from such revelation. They turn to *The Mastersingers,* not as Wagner did, as a reaction from *Tristan,* but as to something greater because more cheerful, more balanced, more philosophical.

The Mastersingers may or may not therefore be the greater. Certainly therefore its structure differs fundamentally from that of *Tristan* and *The Ring.* Since the poem of *Tristan* had been primarily the voicing of a musical process, Wagner had in it already discarded the alliterative verse which he had used in *The Ring,* because it was the 'purely human' form of the 'folk' who fashioned the myth; he had used end-rhyme, *vers libre,* anything that suited his musical purpose. The poem of *The Mastersingers* was rhymed throughout, for it was the stylized libretto of a comic opera—a libretto full of ingenious situation, delicate characterization, parody, polemic, philosophy.

The original draft, sketched in 1845 in a mood of reaction from the passion of *Tannhäuser,* Wagner had intended simply 'as a satire on the Wartburg contest.' Now, when he came to set it to music, the idea of the singing contest served him, as it had done in the second act of *Tannhäuser,* as a brilliant dramatic expedient for composing set operatic numbers—songs, marches and choruses. For these were the forms in which the music inspired by his reaction from *Tristan* took shape in his mind. He could use them without forfeiting his individuality. He saw the diatonic melodies and harmonies of broad daylight with the eyes of an Orpheus, mellowed by suffering in the chromatic nether world.

He applied the chromatic technique of *Tristan* to traditional diatonic polyphony. In *Tristan* and in *The Ring* he had used polyphony primarily as a means of symphonic development. He had elaborated in order to intensify. In *The Mastersingers* he no longer worked mainly with Beethovenian orchestral motives, but with vocal melodies which he seems to have elaborated in the spirit of Bach, out of a joyous superabundance of creative power. Towards the close of the overture, for instance, he plays now two, now three such melodies against each other in free counterpoint for thirty bars:

Strings, horn and clarinet play the melody of the Prize Song; strings and wind the March of the Mastersingers in diminution; double bass, bass tuba and bassoon the opening theme of the Mastersingers. The ingenuity of it makes one leap for joy. (It made the conservative anti-Wagnerians who called the creator of *Tristan* a musical anarchist grind their teeth, for it proved that Wagner could beat them at their own game.)

The form of this overture points the fundamental difference of structure between *The Mastersingers* and the other mature works. The preludes in *The Ring* and in *Tristan* are intended only to depict the mood in which the act opens. They flow into their context. This is true even of self-contained pieces like the prelude to the third act of *The Valkyrie* and to the first act of *Tristan*. The chorus of Valkyries at once takes up the music of their ride; throughout the length and breadth of

Tristan the themes of the prelude are developed. But in *The Mastersingers* overture, as in that to *The Flying Dutchman* and to *Tannhäuser,* and in the *Lohengrin* prelude, Wagner capped all that followed.

Not that the form of *The Mastersingers* was simply a reversion to the type of his early operas. It was hybrid. Wagner's inspiration was not exhausted by the overture, Walther's songs, Sachs's monologues, the quintet and the grand contrapuntal choral finales. He delighted in disseminating this music through the opera; in fashioning a string of delicately linked episodes to match the comedy. Its involutions stimulated his fancy. Thus in the second act Walther and Eva under the lime tree outside her home have planned to elope; Eva has retired to disguise herself; Walther waits for her behind the tree. The Watchman, whose ox-horn blown in the distance has already interrupted their love-making, enters, delivers his call, blows his ox-horn again and retires. Sachs, who in his house over the way has overheard all, decides to block their flight. Eva returns; Sachs lights his lamp, draws up his shutter and exposes them to his view. Beckmesser enters to serenade Eva. Sachs puts his cobbler's bench in his doorway and sits there working and singing to keep the lovers at bay and to spoil Beckmesser's serenade. Wagner keeps order in this complicated scene by reiterating through it the pungent little motive (very like Siegfried's forging motive) which typifies Sachs the cobbler:

Its distinctive note, the F sharp of the augmented triad, is forestalled by that of the Watchman's ox-horn; when blown again, the horn leads into the motive itself, not in its final shape, however, but forming the dominant of B major:

the key in which Walther and Eva have been making love. When Eva returns, disguised, the Prize Song melody, which had been hinted at a little while ago when she agreed to elope, possesses the music, modulating it into its characteristic key, C major. The lovers are about to rush off when Eva notices Sachs. 'Alas! the cobbler!' she cries. Then we hear Sachs's theme in its true form, while at the same moment the Watchman blows his ox-horn again in the distance (as if Wagner wished to underline their relationship). While Beckmesser tunes his lute, while the lovers discourse in agitated undertones, while Sachs prepares to work in the doorway, the cobbling theme is sounded again and again; finally, as Sachs bursts into song, it dominates the music completely—as completely as Sachs dominates the situation.

But the music cannot always thus match the comedy. When David is expounding the Mastersingers' rules and Sachs teaching Walther how to write the Prize Song its wings are clipped and the composer forced to over-repeat himself. What mattered here was not Wagner's emotional reaction from *Tristan* but his desire to parody his critics and give the world a music-lesson.

The great theme of Sachs's grief is the solitary expression of that from which Wagner had reacted. It is orchestral, not vocal. It transcends words. Like Marke's theme it bends down; it is a gesture of renunciation. Sachs himself noticed the resemblance.

'My child, of Tristan and Isolde the grievous tale I know;
Hans Sachs was wise and would not through King Marke's
torments go,'

he tells Eva, whom he loves but is too old to marry. But in Sachs's theme there is no chromatic harshness; it is calm and impersonal. It could, in the prelude to the third act, dissolve before the nobly cheerful strains of the *Wach' auf* chorus—the chorus in which the populace in the concluding scene of the act acclaims him. Sachs could forget his grief in his love for Nuremberg and in its love for him.

And then Wagner returned to *The Ring* tetralogy which he had abandoned thirteen years before. He composed the third act of *Siegfried* and *The Dusk of the Gods*.

Inevitably after that long interruption there was a change in his style, yet it did not mar but on the contrary furthered the organic unity of the whole. With the marvellous harmonic, contrapuntal apparatus he had fashioned in *Tristan and Isolde* and in *The Mastersingers* he could delineate the great shadow cast by Siegfried's tragedy upon the world that bore him. Themes which had symbolized disparate elements, scenes and figures he could draw together beneath this shadow, revealing their latent affinities, transforming them; or he could mingle them with the themes to which the tragedy was played. He was able not merely to complete, but to synthesize the *Ring* cycle. It is almost as if he had composed *Tristan and Isolde* and *The Mastersingers* in order to be able to accomplish this.

It is in *The Dusk of the Gods* that this synthesis is fully achieved. In the early scenes of the third act of *Siegfried*—Wotan's invocation of Erda, Siegfried's conquest of Wotan, journey through the fire and soliloquy before the sleeping Brynhilda—new motives and relevant old ones are magnificently swept into fresh, dramatically compelling co-ordination. But when the awakened Valkyrie joyously greets the youth who owes his life to her ('before thou wert born, my shield was thy guard'), recoils before his passion, implores him to preserve his innocence and finally abandons herself, a sense of strain, even of incongruity, is created by the sumptuous expression of the intimately subjective—one might say, Freudian—poem—above all by the final grand-operatic duet when the lovers become a soprano and tenor bringing the scene to a close in a blaze of vocal glory.

As we have seen, it was while he was engaged upon *The Dusk of the Gods* that Wagner wrote the two essays, *The Destiny of Opera* and *Actors and Singers,* in which he revised his theory of music drama in order to emphasize the mimetic function of the actor-singer. Since the actor-singer is capable of exercising this function not only in declamatory recitative and arioso, but within the purely musical pattern of the formal aria and *ensemble,* Wagner was in effect relinquishing the ideal of a music drama having the ebb and flow of reality. He was bowing to the obvious, acknowledging that music drama was different in kind from spoken drama, that it was stylized musical representation of drama, that it was in fact opera—opera immensely expanded and refined upon, but nevertheless an art whose principal medium of stylization was the singer. In the solitude of Switzerland building up vast scores, inspired by subjects of intimate personal significance and conceived regardless of the possibility of performance, he had put out of mind the truth that their realization was bound up with the appearance, inflections and gestures of the singer. His subsequent struggles in Germany, above all the superb Tristan of Ludwig Schnorr, had brought the truth home. And so in *The Dusk of the Gods* that compromise between the method of *Opera and Drama* and the method of conventional opera the signs of which we have already noted in the *Ring,* not to mention *The Mastersingers,* was carried further. Here Wagner made the best of both worlds, gathered the lessons of his experience into a supreme synthesis.

The poem, written before the theories of *Opera and Drama* had been evolved, was fundamentally grand-operatic. Wagner came to it from *Lohengrin* and its plot is in many respects similar: in both the action is laid by a river; in both a hero embarks and plays the rôle of champion; in both the hero's wife becomes the tool of a conspiracy hatched by enemies; in both the climax is a scene of marital misunderstanding. But not only this: like *Lohengrin,* and unlike the other, epically conceived, *Ring* poems, the plot had the conventional virtues of a well-knit drama, governed by the Aristotelian unities of time and place. Furthermore the poem, which Wagner had of course revised to bring into harmony with the other poems,[1] gave the orchestra the opportunity to enact the role of chorus in a Greek tragedy (the analogy was Wagner's). It could direct its mighty cargo of themes into symphonic-dramatic episodes outside the swift complex action—forebode in the scene of the Norns; depict in 'Siegfried's Journey to the Rhine'; mourn in the 'Funeral March'; sum up in 'Brynhilda's Immolation.' The poem, it is true, contained two long passages of narrative, but both had a dramatic significance which Wagner magnificently exploited. In 'Valtraute's Narrative,' as he had done in the Wanderer's duologue with Mime, he depicted—in terms of the theme he had used there, further transformed—a further stage in Wotan's spiritual development. In 'Siegfried's Narrative,' delivered in the hour of his death, he created an

[1] Originally not Waltraute but a band of Valkyries had visited Brynhilda and narrated events bearing on the subsequent *Valkyrie.* Likewise the Norns had narrated events bearing on the subsequent *Rhinegold.* Hagen's and Alberich's scene was revised, and the Immolation scene in the light of the decision to end the work tragically. These were the chief revisions.

overwhelming effect of tragic irony by recapitulating relevant passages from *Siegfried*.

Within the swift complex action the orchestra's function, for all the weight of thematic reference it carries, is throughout propulsive. When Hagen has the stage to himself after Sieg-fried's and Gunther's departure, the descending interval of his massively dynamic motive:

and that of Gutrune's fleeting, pathetic one:

re-appears as a downward stab piercing Siegfried's joyous hunting-call:

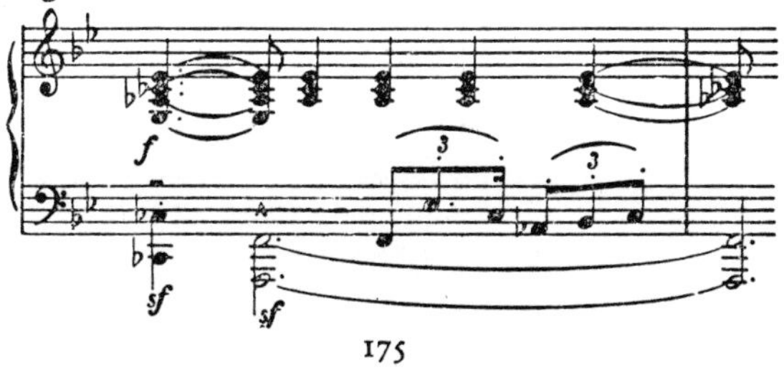

In manifold ways this downward stab—combining with the motives of Siegfried's sword and Wotan's spear:

combining with another Hagen theme:

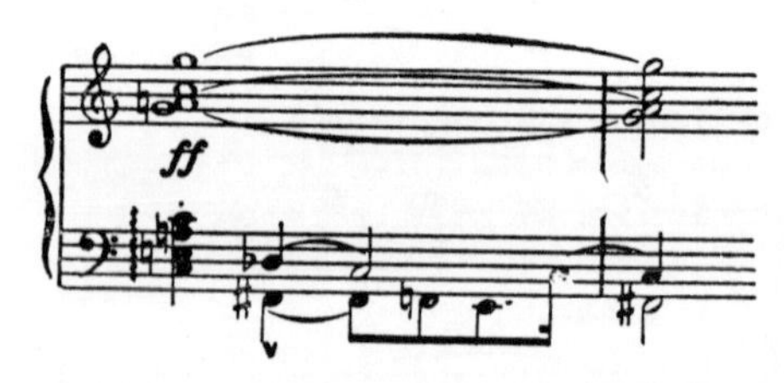

—penetrates the music of later scenes, in which the music is expanded and enriched as Hagen's plan matures. When the plan has matured Wagner turns to grand opera in order that Hagen may give formal expression to his triumph. In a choral episode of stirring sinister power Hagen summons the vassals to greet the captured Brynhilda who, seeing Siegfried affianced to Gutrune, will denounce him:

'Love well your lady,
faithfully help:
if she be wronged,
swift be your vengeance!'

As Brynhilda steps on shore the vassals deliver a formal paean of welcome. Grand opera comes into its own too at the end of the act when Brynhilda, Hagen and Gunther pool their individualities in a conventional trio of vengeance.

The full force of the synthesis of *The Dusk of the Gods* is revealed in the supreme opportunities the opera gives the Brynhilda. It is as though all that had been enacted and sung and played throughout the cycle converges on her, as though every gesture, every inflection, the very quality of her voice had become charged with a cosmic significance. If she has, as Frieda Leider had, the gift of dramatic empathy; if she can endure that formal paean of welcome with the air of one writhing inwardly and yet with a sullen dignity acknowledging the inevitable, the moment is unforgettable. If she has the voice of a Flagstad or Nilsson ringing above the orchestra with a joy of self-abandonment tuned to the highest pitch, the climax of her ride to join Siegfried in death—that climax forestalled long ago in *The Valkyrie* by Sieglinde ecstatically greeting the annunciation of Siegfried's birth—remains in the memory as a unique revelation of the wonder of human personality. It is in virtue of such moments, crowned by the singer-actor, that a fine performance of *The Ring* can become the cherished experience of a lifetime.

In his old age Wagner could not endure Siegfried's tragedy. He renounced the joys of earthly fulfilment, longed for redemption from the burden of the flesh. He composed *Parsifal*.

In *The Dusk of the Gods* he had achieved a synthesis between grand opera and music drama. In *Parsifal* he stood the two in apposition: on the one hand the grandiose processional and choral music of the Temple of the Grail, couched in the diatonic idiom of the solemn scenes of *Tannhäuser* and *Lohengrin*; on the other hand the chromatic idiom of *Tristan* wrought to a pitch of pathological intensity, with discords no longer piled upon each other to heighten the ecstasy of the moment of ultimate resolution, but failing to achieve this resolution, surrendering themselves masochistically to their dissonance:

They can only finally resolve when, having spent their anguish, a diatonic melody rescues—one can say redeems—them.

This redemption, which can be thought of as a musical event, is the theme of *Parsifal*; but Wagner did not make of it a truly dramatic theme. A drama, as he said, is a 'becoming.' It is a sequence of events manifestly leading to a climax. In his previous works it was precisely this climax which had inspired motives to transcend themselves; therein lay their strength. But at the dramatic climax of *Parsifal*—the 'pure fool's' rejection of the seduction of Kundry in the second act—motives do not transcend themselves. Necessarily not. Parsifal rejects her because, through the desire she evokes, he comprehends the suffering, which in the first act he had witnessed uncomprehendingly, of Amfortas, the Guardian of the Grail, who had succumbed to Kundry. At the climax, therefore, Wagner recalls the motives of Amfortas's suffering not that they should transcend themselves—the situation does not demand it—but in their original form in order to express Parsifal's identification with Amfortas. In the course of the long scene the motives are varied and intensified, it is true, but in that Wagner's aim is to express the agony of unfulfilled guilt-laden desire the music necessarily lacks the cumulative power of his great scenes. It is as though the longed-for redemption were a phantom; as though, in the guise of a 'pure fool' bewailing his lost purity, Wagner were expressing the yearning of his old age for release from the burden of carnal desire.

The moment of redemption, when it comes, is brought by the orchestra: Parsifal returning to Monsalvat on the morning of a radiant Good Friday, overcome by the beauty of the early spring, experiences the change of heart expressed by the Good Friday music, the most eloquent passage in the opera. Is it significant that the uplifting theme occurred to Wagner not in his old age, but on the Good Friday after he had moved into the *Asyl,* a time of hope and joy? Does it suggest that for all the pomp and ceremony of the Grail scenes the only redemption Wagner could really find was in the heart-easing recollection of younger, happier days?

'*Parsifal,* majestic in its sclerotic languor,' wrote Thomas Mann. The words aptly describe the slow heavy dotted rhythms of the solemn processional music of the two Grail scenes. Yet Wagner's limbs could still move with their old suppleness when he sat down to sup with the devil, depict the insidious charm of the Flower Maidens and Kundry. In the scenes leading to the climax of Kundry's rejection —Parsifal surrounded by the maidens caressing and teasing in twelve-part operatic *ensemble* (two trios for solo voices combining with two three-part choruses); Kundry's tale of the death of Herzeleide, Parsifal's mother, fluid, declamatory, yet crystallizing in pure melody; Parsifal's shock and grief—in these scenes Wagner again achieves the synthesis of *The Dusk of the Gods,* draws grand opera into a sequence of music-dramatic episodes leading into and surmounting each other in the old wonderful way.

In the last year of his life Wagner contemplated composing a symphony. Whether one wishes he had contemplated this sooner and found a way of casting into symphonic form the musical inspirations of his 'Sacred Festival Play'—above all the Good Friday music, conveying a poetry of feeling beyond the traffic of the stage—partly depends upon how susceptible one is to the impressive ritual and tonal effects of the Grail scenes: the bells, the boys' voices floating out from the dome, the modally inflected cadences. Partly also it depends upon whether one views the musically inspired purple passages in the operas as the works of a symphonist in the royal line of Beethoven. I have tried to show how misleading it is to regard the operas themselves in this light; it remains to emphasize that this is no less true of their purple passages. Wagner, we saw, regarded the Beethoven symphony as out of date because it did not express the nineteenth-century sensibility. He meant of course that it did not express his sensibility. Even the overtures to *The Flying Dutchman* and *The Mastersingers,* which approach the classical model of sonata form, reveal a difference in kind. The contrasts between the fury of the Dutchman's subject and the yearning of Senta's and between the stiff, bustling Mastersingers' subjects and the lyrical, rhapsodical Prize Song motive at the beginning of the development section (Wagner marked the passage 'sehr zart und ausdrucksvoll' [1]) break the rhythmic continuity which is the *sine qua non* of the dance-derived classical model. It is in virtue of his command of thematic development —above all, of thematic polyphony—that Wagner is symphonic, and this symphonic command he exercised in forms which enabled the development of a single theme (as in the *Lohengrin* prelude) or cluster of combining themes (as in the *Tristan* prelude) to proceed continuously with growing volume and thickening orchestration to a mighty climax. Delivered by the battery of Wagner's augmented brass (augmented for this very purpose), the climax has a force of assault, a power to swamp

[1] Bar 56.

and shatter, beyond anything Beethoven could have dreamt of. But (and I say this in order to differentiate, not derogate) in the nature of the case an argument propounded to drive home a single overwhelming proposition lacks the enduring appeal of the great classical movement based on variety underpinned by rhythm. The shock of the assault, because it *is* a shock, wears off.

In those exceptional cases where the propulsive force is the sheer rhythmic impetus of a theme, the assault is delivered by a thrilling modulation—by the sweep from B major to C major of Donner's outburst; from B minor to B major of 'The Ride of the Valkyries'; from F major to A major when Siegfried, journeying down the Rhine, is greeted by the Rhine motive. In the symphonic ballad of 'Isolde's Narrative'—symphonic because its texture is thematic, a ballad because its scheme is strophic—the assault is delivered outside the strophic scheme by the ringing peroration of Isolde's Curse. In 'Brynhilda's Annunciation,' where again the form is strophic, again the assault is delivered outside the scheme by Brynhilda at the last moment dropping her role of messenger of death and rallying to Siegmund. And in 'Wotan's Farewell,' the greatest of these symphonic-strophic passages, the assault is delivered outside a strophic scheme. The first strophe is the melody of the 'Farewell' sung by Wotan above the murmuring of the Sleep motive, wreathed around a C major triad:

In the second strophe, during which Wotan lays Brynhilda to rest, the orchestra takes over the melody, bringing the Sleep motive into the foreground, and omitting its middle section in order to repeat the haunting final bars:

There follows the interlude—from the point of view of the strophic scheme—of the summoning of Loge and welling up of the Fire motive:

Then the Sleep motive re-enters in E major, the key of the second strophe, and it seems that the strophic pattern is about to re-establish itself. But Wotan has another thought now than to bid farewell:

> He who my spearpoint's sharpness feareth
> Shall cross not the flaming fire!

The strophic pattern is shattered by the magnificent assault of the Siegfried theme sung through the Sleep motive and a sheen of fiery arpeggio, and then, as Wotan stretches forth his spear, proclaimed by three trumpets, four trombones and bass tuba:

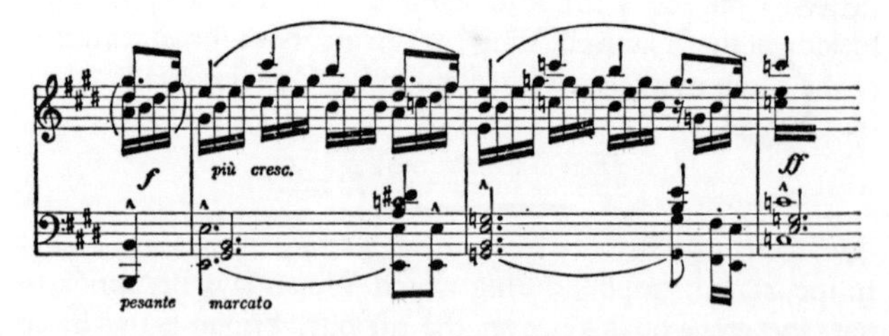

Yet just before the end—and herein lies the surpassing beauty of the passage—the strophic design re-forms. As the departing

Wotan looks back on Brynhilda the Siegfried theme gives way to those haunting final bars of the Farewell.

Anything less Beethovenianly symphonic than that last-minute appearance of the Siegfried motive can hardly be imagined. Heard merely in the concert-hall, at every performance the shock of the revelation, alas, wears off. Heard in the opera-house it is another matter—and heard by one who has already heard the whole of the *Ring,* and steeped himself in its symbolism, still another matter. The theme points back to the moment of its first delivery by Sieglinde, when she learns she is to bear a hero, and forward to the hero's tragic future. The soaring arch of the Sleep motive points to the instrument of his tragedy, the Brynhilda he will awaken. The sheen of fiery arpeggio playing round the Sleep motive points to the fire which will in the end consume them both. No passage more tellingly reveals the fruits of that power to unite the thematic with the dramatic which was the essence of Wagner's genius.

Wagner composed one work, though, which could plausibly be held to point to a symphony-that-might-have-been: the purely instrumental *Siegfried Idyll.* Other occasional pieces written in his mature years (the American Centennial March, *Kaisermarsch* and *Huldigungsmarsch*) are pot-boilers of no consequence; but the *Siegfried Idyll,* which he composed in the December of 1870 to celebrate Cosima's first birthday after their marriage, and had performed at Triebschen by a chamber orchestra, is a masterpiece of pure music occupying a unique place in his output. It is, though, a very Wagnerian kind of purely musical masterpiece. Characteristically it lacks rhythmic continuity: the thread snaps in the transition passage from first to second subject, where Wagner, marking the score 'Immer langsamer werdend,' moves more and more slowly, tapering the texture down to nothing but violins contemplatively trilling through four whole bars:

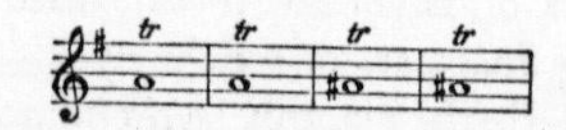

Characteristically its two subjects are combined in a display of thematic counterpoint building cumulatively through sequences and thickening texture and orchestration to a thrilling polyphonic climax. And characteristically it is an autobiographical document. The first subject, and almost certainly the second,[1] had been conceived during that fateful week when Cosima joined Wagner at Starnberg: he had planned to work them as a string quartet dedicated to her, celebrating the bliss of their acknowledged love. In 1869 their long-desired son Siegfried was born: so that thrilling polyphonic climax is built up and its last bars crowned by jubilant Siegfried motives from *Siegfried,* of which the third act Wagner composed in 1869. Thus the *Idyll* is unique in Wagner's output not only in being his only purely musical masterpiece, but in that it is the record of a unique experience in his life. As such, it is hardly a pointer to a symphony-that-might-have-been.[2]

Since the *Idyll* had been conceived originally as a quartet it was arranged some years ago for that medium and broadcast

[1] See Ernest Newman, *Life of Wagner,* vol iii, p. 263.

[2] The relation to *Siegfried* appears to have been two-way: besides drawing Siegfried motives into the *Idyll,* Wagner worked portions of the contemplated Starnberg Quartet into the love duet of the third act. They occur when Brynhilda, after having shrunk from Siegfried's embrace, invokes the ideal of happy youth unclouded by passion. In the eyes of some authorities the calmly flowing formal periods of the quartet make an incongruous effect. But it could be argued that they restore the musical balance of the scene, threatened by the episode of Brynhilda's resistance, and pave the way to the ecstatic final section.

as a feature on the 'Third.' The effect of the arrangement was what one would have expected it: it emphasized the music's dependence on the orchestra. Not that Wagner's dependence on the orchestra, the subject which in these penultimate paragraphs we have to consider, was so absolute that one could say of him, as one could of Berlioz, that the very blood and bone of his thinking is orchestral, that his ideas have no life save in that form. His scores were built up, as Berlioz's were not, at the keyboard; at Wahnfried he used a piano with a specially fitted desk. A pianist with a command of tone-colour and a feeling for the idiom can bring the purple passages to life (I once heard Josef Hoffman bring the Liszt transcription of the *Liebestod* to such orgiastic life that a member of the audience seated on the platform had an epileptic fit). But since these pianistically realizable scores were destined for the stage, and such a stage, they demanded an undreamt-of wealth of orchestral vesture, upholstery and underpinning. Just as Wagner spared no pains and no expense to flatter his other senses—obtain silk underclothes and satin dressing-gowns—so he stopped at nothing to gratify his exquisite sense of dramatically appropriate tone-colour. The structure of *The Ring* is underpinned by augmented, subtilized brass. It rises out of brass: the prelude to *The Rhinegold* is begotten of the interplay of arpeggiating horns—not of the usual two or four, which would not have sufficed to create the atmosphere Wagner wanted of infinite watery depth, but of eight horns; the rich reposeful grandeur of the Valhalla theme is begotten of the four 'Wagner' tubas, hybrids combining the structure of tuba and horn, which he had specially built. This theme and others associated with Wotan, as they stride through the drama, meeting and mingling with other themes and undergoing transformation, are invested by Wagner's brass with a stature larger than life, their sheer sound vibrating through his audience's subconscious memory, underpinning the thematic-dramatic pillars upon which the structure of the cycle rests.

Not that the brass section especially attracted Wagner or that he normally went to the length of having a special instrument designed. As a rule it sufficed to expand and subtilize all that was up to date in the orchestration of his day. His employment of the brass in chromatically modulating four-part harmony—as in the Valhalla music—he owed to the invention of the new valved brass which came into general use in the latter half of the century. His fastidious handling of the English horn, bass clarinet and viola, regarded in Beethoven's day as merely accessory; his exquisite blending of wood-wind and string tone; his way of launching brass unison themes into swirling seas of violin figuration had been anticipated by Berlioz, Meyerbeer and Mendelssohn. But since Wagner's scoring was coupled with the workings of a music-dramatic imagination of transcendent range and subtlety, it had a greater scope and accordingly a greater influence than theirs.

To realize this one has but to open at random the score of any one of his great works—at that heart-rending passage in the third act of *Tristan,* for example, in which Tristan, having been told that Isolde's ship cannot be seen, listens sadly to the melancholy tune of the shepherd's pipe, which the English horn had delivered unaccompanied before the curtain rose. As he listens his sadness mounts to despair. The English horn, which had been playing the tune again, gives way to the oboe, clarinet and horn each taking up a phrase in turn, as though pleading to each other in different accents of grief, while violas and cellos draw out a long, shuddering *tremolando.* Soon Wagner directs the strings to remove their mutes. Now combined wood-wind have the tune; brass add the anguished theme of the second act; violins and cellos make swift stabbing figurations. As though unable to bear the emotion thus let loose the violins sweep the tune into their upper register and discharge its agony with a force which sends it hurtling back across the stave in a searing descending arpeggio. All passion spent for the time being, the English horn then resumes the tune, its melancholy deeper and more hopeless than ever. . . .

Having touched upon Wagner's influence in the sphere of orchestration, it remains finally to touch upon his influence in a general sense.

In the sphere of opera Wagner's influence was in the short run dangerous, since the method which in his hands was a line of most resistance, demanding unique powers of dramatic, thematic and orchestral cross-fertilization, appeared to others to offer a line of least resistance. Write or get written a play and claim that it needs a through-composed score to reveal its significance; claim that your themes have dramatic significance and work them hard; employ a large orchestra, lay on its colours thick, and keep up an incessant flow of modulation, and it is open to any mediocrity to compose whole operas and cycles of operas. The only post-Wagnerian operas firmly established in the international repertory are the *Rosenkavalier, Elektra, Ariadne auf Naxos,* and *Salome* of Richard Strauss and the *Hänsel und Gretel* of Humperdinck. . . . Regarded in the perspective of the hundred years which have passed since the composition of *Tristan,* Wagner's influence takes on another aspect, becomes one among other forces in the operatic *Zeitgeist* of the latter half of the nineteenth century seeking to assimilate the realities of life outside the opera-house. In the year that Wagner composed *Lohengrin* Verdi composed the first *verismo* opera, based on a contemporary novel: *La Traviata.* As *Lohengrin* stands to *The Dusk of the Gods,* Wagner's supreme masterpiece, so *La Traviata* stands to Verdi's *Otello.* What appears significant now is not just how far Wagner influenced Verdi and how far he influenced Bizet, Moussorgsky, Puccini, Charpentier,

Massenet and their contemporaries, but the trend which he together with them represents. For us who, in Berg's *Wozzeck,* Menotti's *The Consul,* Dallapiccola's *The Prisoner,* have witnessed attempts to assimilate realities outside the opera-house undreamt-of by Wagner and Verdi, the burning question is: How far and on what terms can the process be carried?

As Wagner's influence as an orchestrator was less that of an innovator than of one who expanded and subtilized existing methods, so was his influence as a composer. 'As Beethoven is the morning and Wagner the high noon, so Delius is the sunset of that great period which is called Romantic,' wrote the late Philip Heseltine in his study of Delius. Beside Wagner stand Liszt, Chopin, Schumann, Brahms, Tchaikovsky; beside Delius, Strauss, Mahler, Elgar, Hugo Wolf, Cesar Franck and other post-Wagnerians, whose idiom was a refining upon the chromaticism of Wagner and his contemporaries. Wagner exerted the greatest influence mainly because his marriage of musical to dramatic logic gave him a formal freedom to undermine tonality by chromatic modulation, and mainly because he exploited as no one else the searing expressiveness of the chromatic sequence. Of *Tristan* Ernest Newman wrote that 'it reveals more of the dreadful capacity of our poor human nature for pain than all our natural experience of life has done.' The revelation is more dreadful still in *Parsifal,* where the agony of the chromatic discord's impotence to resolve is wrought to the pitch of masochistically surrendering the hope of resolution. Carried still further by the post-Wagnerians, Wagner's revelation came to be the explosive force producing in our century that chain-reaction of atonality, *Expressionismus* serialism, Webernism, post-serialism, post-Webernism, the consequences of which are unforeseeable.

Of that other chain-reaction produced by the explosive effect of Wagner's racialist theories on the mind of Hitler, who perverted the tragic epic of *The Ring* into a paranoidal gospel of violence (*Mein Kampf* is saturated with *Nibelungen* phraseology), this would not be the place to speak—were it not that it is partly responsible for a current attitude towards the operas of which the biographer of a 'Master Musician' must take cognizance. Although Wagner by now is forgiven his influence on Hitler, the fact has to be reckoned with that modernistic production of Wagner, making a clean sweep of many of the traditions he created, is in many quarters tolerated and even welcomed.

The standards set by the original Bayreuth performances were musical, histrionic, dramaturgic, but not of course scenic. Wagner, who had to make shift with gas-lighting and steam jets (for The Magic Fire), found it a torture to see the landscape of his imagination realized on that stage; he even said: 'Now that I have created an invisible orchestra, I would like to invent an invisible theatre.' This expression of his disillusion was seized upon by the directors of post-war Bayreuth, Wagner's grandsons Wieland and Wolfgang, as the warrant for an aesthetic of production making a *tabula rasa* of the past, an aesthetic dictated in *principle* not by Wagner's vision, but by the subjective vision of a modern producer applying the latest techniques of stage effect. Not only were demands of Wagner ignored which have long been regarded as miscalculated or outmoded—for fussily realistic scenery littered with mythological 'props'; for Valkyries in cumbersome armour; for a flesh-and-blood Grane. Practicable, dramatically essential demands were ignored. In Wolfgang Wagner's *Ring* in 1960 the first act of *The Valkyrie*, where it is dramatically essential that the setting be domestic, the action sighted in relation to a couch, a table, a hearth, was played in a bare circular hall; throughout the whole of *The Dusk of the Gods* there was no hint of the Rhine; after the tempestuous 'Ride of the Valkyries' the curtain rose on a group of Valkyries gracefully reclining. Travesties such as these, stamped with the prestige of Bayreuth and name of Wagner, have been imitated not only by producers in Germany —where audiences are pardonably glad to see the operas stripped of associations that meant so much to Hitler—but also in this country. One can only hope that in a not too distant future the disease will produce its remedy, that the vogue of the subjective producer, having had its fling, will give way to the novelty of endeavouring to re-create in the spirit of Wagner's dramatic vision.

Perhaps there is a grim poetic justice in the spectacle of Wagner to-day being subjectively interpreted in the name of Wagner. He himself was the first great subjective interpreter of his century. Conductors before him had usually been either ex-orchestral players, who were court hangers-on, as content merely to beat time like metronomes as to indulge the whims of virtuoso instrumentalists, or else conservatoire products devoted to the Mendelssohnian ideal of 'classical' restraint—the 'musical temperance society' Wagner dubbed them. He was the first to raise subjectivity to the status of an ideal. He did not make a virtue of indulging in a personal wayward rubato, riding roughshod over the composer's directions, but he put his trust in imaginative perception of the latent poetic and dramatic content of a composition and hence the power to re-create its indefinable nuances of tempo, accent and colour. 'Perpetual modification of tempo' was the principle which he laid down in his famous treatise *On Conducting* for the interpretation of romantic music and of Beethoven.

That inspired subjectivity was the hallmark of Beethoven's own playing, contemporary accounts agree. And one can point to a long line of great conductors in the Wagnerian tradition: Bülow, Richter, Mottl, Levi, Nikisch, Mahler, Strauss, Furtwängler, Seidl, Walter, Karajan. Inspired subjectivity is indeed the guarantee of fine performance—from which it does not follow, alas—as witness the Bayreuth of to-day—that subjectivity contains any guarantee of inspiration. To exalt it as Wagner did was dangerous doctrine.

Dangerous doctrine . . . everything about this volcanic genius, endowed with surpassing eloquence and with insight reaching to the exalted heights of the mind and to its subterranean depths, spells danger. It is no accident that the Wagner who, seeking to assimilate the realities of life outside the opera-house, paved the way to *Wozzeck* and who, revelling in the masochism of unresolved dissonance, paved the way to atonality, is the Wagner who would have wrecked his own life but for the allegiance of the psychopathic Ludwig of Bavaria and the Wagner who inflamed the lunatic mind of Adolf Hitler.

Let Liszt, who compared Wagner to a volcano, have the last word:

. . . twenty times a day he falls upon my neck—then rolls around on the floor, caressing his dog, Peps, and talking perpetual nonsense to him—while all the time he curses the Jews. . . . In a word: a great and overwhelming nature, rather like a Vesuvius, which when it erupts scatters forth sheaves of flame and at the same time sprays of rose and lilac.

APPENDICES

APPENDIX A

CALENDAR

(Figures in brackets denote the age reached by the person mentioned during the year in question.)

Year	*Age*	*Life*	*Contemporary Musicians*
1813		Wilhelm Richard Wagner born, May 22, in Leipzig, son of Karl Friedrich Wilhelm Wagner (43), clerk to the city police. Death of W.'s father from typhus, Nov. 22. His mother, *née* Johanna Pätz (34), is befriended by Ludwig Geyer (33), a painter and actor.	Dargomizhsky born, Feb. 2/14; Grétry (72) dies, Sept. 24; Macfarren born, March 2; Verdi born, Oct. 10. Auber aged 31; Balfe 5; Beethoven 43; Bellini 12; Berlioz 10; Bishop 27; Boieldieu 38; Cherubini 53; Chopin 4; Clementi 61; Donizetti 16; Dorn 9; Field 31; Glinka 10; Gossec 79; Halévy 14; Hérold 22; Hummel 35; Lesueur 53; Liszt 2; Loewe 17; Lortzing 10; Marschner 18; Méhul 50; Mendelssohn 4; Mercadante 18; Meyerbeer 22; Nicolai 3; Paer 42; Paisiello 72; Potter 21; Rossini 21; Salieri 63; Schubert 16; Schumann 3; Spohr 29; Spontini 39; Weber 27.
1814	1	Removal to Dresden	

Appendix A.—Calendar

Year	*Age*	*Life*	*Contemporary Musicians*
1815	2	Marriage of W.'s mother (36) to Geyer (35).	Franz born, June 28; Heller born, May 15.
1816	3		Paisiello (75) dies, June 5.
1817	4		Gade born, Feb. 22; Méhul (54) dies, Oct. 18.
1818	5		Gounod born, June 17.
1819	6		Offenbach born, June 21.
1820	7		Serov born, Jan. 11/23; Vieuxtemps born, Feb. 20.
1821	8	Death of Ludwig Geyer (41), Sept. 30. W. sent to Eisleben, where Geyer's younger brother takes his education in hand.	
1822	9	Returns to Dresden during the year. Sent to the Kreuzschule there, Dec.	Franck born, Dec. 10; Raff born, May 27.
1823	10	At school attracted by study of Greek tragedy.	Lalo born, Jan. 27; Reyer born, Dec. 1.
1824	11	Growing enthusiasm for Weber (38), with whom his mother (45) is acquainted. Learns piano from Humann, but plays fragments from operas instead of practising. His sisters Clara and Rosalie make their first appearance as opera singers, the former in Rossini's (32) *Cenerentola,* the latter in Weber's *Preciosa.*	Bruckner born, Sept. 4; Cornelius born, Dec. 24; Smetana born, March 2.
1825	12	Writes prize poem commemorating death of schoolfellow.	Salieri (75) dies, May 7; Strauss (J. ii) born, Oct. 25.

Year	*Age*	*Life*	*Contemporary Musicians*
1826	13	Family move to Prague. Left alone, W. neglects school studies and indulges his tastes. Begins long, gruesome Shakespearean tragedy.	Weber (40) dies, June 4–5.
1827	14	Abandons Kreuzschule and rejoins family at Leipzig, whither they have moved. Enters the St. Nicholas school there.	Beethoven (57) dies, March 26.
1828	15	Intercourse with Uncle Adolf stimulates him to complete Shakespearean tragedy, and hearing of Beethoven's symphonies at the Gewandhaus and acquaintance with the *Egmont* Overture stimulates him to set it to music. He secretly studies thoroughbass and writes a piano Sonata in D minor, a Quartet in D major, an aria and a pastoral play.	Schubert (31) dies, Nov. 19.
1829	16	Is now allowed to study the violin and theory, but shows no liking for the former, while he resents the restraint of the latter; but he studies Beethoven's scores with passionate interest. Hears Wilhelmine Schröder-Devrient (25) in *Fidelio* and is deeply im-	Gossec (95) dies, Feb. 16.

Year	*Age*	*Life*	*Contemporary Musicians*
		pressed. The new Leipzig theatre being opened, Aug. 2, Dorn (25), who is appointed conductor, shows interest in W.	
1830	17	Is passionately in sympathy with the July Revolution in Paris. He takes an active part in the Leipzig Revolution, Sept. Piano arrangement of Beethoven's ninth Symphony, autumn. Dorn (26) performs W.'s Overture, B flat major, at the theatre, where orchestra and public receive it with derision.	Goldmark born, May 18; Rubinstein born, Nov. 16/28.
1831	18	Enters Leipzig University, Feb., and studies harmony and counterpoint under Weinlig (51) at the Thomasschule. Concert Overture, D minor, finished, Sept. 26 and revised, Nov. 4. Sonata, B flat major, Polonaise and Fantasy, F sharp minor, for piano composed.	
1832	19	Weinlig (52) informs him that he can teach him nothing more. Overture to Raupach's (48) *König Enzio,* Feb. Concert Overture, C major, March. C major Symphony com-	Clementi (80) dies, March 10.

Year	Age	Life	Contemporary Musicians
		posed, spring. Visit to Vienna, summer, and to Prague, autumn. There the Symphony is performed by the Conservatoire students' orchestra. Libretto for the opera, *Die Hochzeit,* written in Prague. Return to Leipzig, end of Nov. Music for the first scene of *Die Hochzeit* finished, Dec. 5. His sister Rosalie declares the work unsuitable for the stage, and he abandons it. Libretto for the opera, *Die Feen,* on Gozzi's *La donna serpente* drafted.	
1833	20	Performance of C major Symphony at a Gewandhaus concert, Jan. 10, at which Clara Wieck (14) appears. W. becomes chorus master at Würzburg, Jan. Sketch of the opera, *Die Feen,* worked out.	Brahms born, May 7; Hérold (42) dies, Jan. 19.
1834	21	*Die Feen* finished, Jan. Returns to Leipzig for its production, which falls through. Friendship with Laube. Bad performance of Beethoven's ninth Symphony and wonderful one of Schröder-Devrient (30)	Boieldieu (59) dies, Oct. 8; Borodin born, Oct. 30 Nov. 12.

Year	*Age*	*Life*	*Contemporary Musicians*
		in a Bellini (33) opera stimulates enthusiasm for Italian and French opera at expense of German. Writes article, 'Die deutsche Oper,' in *Die elegante Welt.* Joins Bethmann company, of which Minna Planer (25) is a member, as conductor at Lauchstädt, July. Company removes to headquarters at Magdeburg, where he begins composition of *Das Liebesverbot,* autumn.	
1835	22	Overture to Apel's (24) drama, *Columbus,* performed at the Magdeburg theatre, spring. W.'s benefit concert, at which Wilhelmine Schröder-Devrient (31) appears, May 2. Tour made to find new singers for Magdeburg, summer, and return there, autumn. Minna Planer (26) goes to Berlin, he proposes to her, and she returns.	Bellini (34) dies, Sept. 24; Cui born, Jan. 6/18; Draeseke born, Oct. 7; Saint-Saëns born, Oct. 9.
1836	23	Production of *Das Liebesverbot* at the Magdeburg theatre, March 29. The second performance, March 30, given for W.'s benefit, badly attended and	Balakirev born, Dec. 31 (O.S.).

Year	Age	Life	Contemporary Musicians
		abandoned owing to a quarrel among the singers. Collapse of the Bethmann company. C major Symphony submitted to Mendelssohn (27) in Leipzig. Engagement at the Königsberg theatre hoped for, but not obtained. Minna Planer (27) is there. Marriage to her, Nov. 24. Opera, *Die hohe Braut,* begun and offered to Scribe (45) for translation into French.	
1837	24	Overture, *Rule, Britannia,* performed at Königsberg, March. Begins but abandons text of light opera, *Die glückliche Bärenfamilie.* W. appointed conductor at the theatre, spring. It goes into liquidation and Minna (28) suddenly leaves him, early summer. He takes refuge with sister, Ottilie Brockhaus, in Dresden, where he conceives *Rienzi.* Appointment to the theatre of Riga. W. petitions for divorce, summer. Return of Minna, Oct. W. pursued by Magdeburg and Königsberg creditors.	Field (55) dies, Jan. 11; Lesueur (77) dies, Oct. 6.

Year	*Age*	*Life*	*Contemporary Musicians*
1838	25	Absorbed in composition of *Rienzi.*	Bizet born, Oct. 25; Bruch born, Jan. 6.
1839	26	Riga conductorship transferred to Dorn (35), Jan. W. resolved to go to Paris. Departure, end of June. Stormy voyage takes them to coast of Norway, whence to England, early Aug. After a week in London, they stay at Boulogne, where W. meets Meyerbeer (48). Arrival in Paris, very poor, Sept. 16. Vain promises, but no real encouragement held out to him in Paris. French songs composed without success. After hearing Beethoven's ninth Symphony under Habeneck (58) at the Conservatoire, W. composes the Overture to Goethe's *Faust,* Nov.	Mussorgsky born, March 9/21; Paer (68) dies, May 3.
1840	27	A winter of misery and privation. *Das Liebesverbot* prepared as *La Novice de Palerme* at the Théâtre de la Renaissance, which goes into liquidation just as W. and Minna (31) have moved to better quarters, spring. Writes libretto of one-act opera on the subject of the Flying Dutchman	Götz born, Dec. 17; Svendsen born, Sept. 3; Tchaikovsky born, April 25/May 7.

Year	Age	Life	Contemporary Musicians
		for the Opéra. The director accepts the libretto, but for composition by a French musician. He writes articles and does hack work for publishers. Composition of *Rienzi* finished, Nov. 19.	
1841	28	Removal to Meudon. W. reluctantly accepts 500 francs for the libretto of the one-act *Le Vaisseau fantôme.* The money, however, gives him leisure to expand it into a full-length opera for Germany. Libretto written in May and composition finished, Sept.; overture, Nov. *Rienzi* accepted by Dresden for eventual production, July. W. and Minna (32) continue to live in privation.	Chabrier born, Jan. 18; Dvořák born, Sept. 8; Pedrell born, Feb. 19.
1842	29	*Der fliegende Holländer* provisionally accepted by Berlin, March. W. attracted by the legends of Tannhäuser and the Singers' Tourney on the Wartburg. Giving up all hopes of Paris, W. and Minna (33) leave for Dresden, April 7. W. is anxious to see *Der fliegende Holländer* produced	Boito born, Feb. 24; Cherubini (82) dies, March 15; Massenet born, May 12; Sullivan born, May 13.

Year	Age	Life	Contemporary Musicians
		in Berlin. (*Le Vaisseau fantôme* by Dietsch (34) being prepared for performance in Paris, but it is again deferred, June.) Summer holiday at Teplitz, where a draft of the *Tannhäuser* libretto and some sketches for the music are made. Production of *Rienzi* at Dresden, Oct. 20. W. appointed second conductor at the court opera.	
1843	30	Production of *Der fliegende Holländer* at Dresden, Jan. 2. *Das Liebesmahl der Apostel,* for male chorus and orchestra, composed, June.	Grieg born, June 15: Sgambati born, May 28.
1844	31	Composes paean of welcome to King of Saxony, Aug. and music for funeral of Weber, Dec. Composition of *Tannhäuser* finished, except for the instrumentation, Dec. 29.	Rimsky-Korsakov born, March 6/18.
1845	32	*Tannhäuser* completed, April 13. Summer holiday at Marienbad, where he sketches the libretto of *Die Meistersinger von Nürnberg,* which he abandons for that of *Lohengrin.* Production of *Tannhäuser* at Dresden, Oct. 19.	Fauré born, May 13.

Year	*Age*	*Life*	*Contemporary Musicians*
1846	33	A memorial suggesting improvements submitted to the court theatre, March. It is shelved. W. performs Beethoven's ninth Symphony, April 5. Music for *Lohengrin* begun during a holiday at Gross-Graupe, May. First meeting with Hans von Bülow (16).	Bungert born, March 14; Weigl (80) dies, Feb. 3.
1847	34	Having undertaken to publish his works on his own account, W. continues to be very poor. Composition of *Lohengrin* finished, Aug. 28, except the scoring. *Rienzi* performed in Berlin, with little success, Oct. 24.	Mackenzie born, Aug. 22; Mendelssohn (38) dies, Nov. 4.
1848	35	Shows great sympathy with the revolutionary movement that spreads through Europe after the February Revolution in France. He joins the radical 'Vaterlandsverein,' May. Beginning of friendship with Liszt (37). Libretto of *Siegfrieds Tod* finished, Nov. 28, and that of *Jesus von Nazareth* abandoned, Dec.	Donizetti (51) dies, April 8; Duparc born, Jan. 21; Parry born, Feb. 27.
1849	36	Many intrigues afoot against him at court, his democratic views being interpreted as revolutionary.	Chopin (39) dies, Oct. 17; Nicolai (39) dies, May 11.

Year	*Age*	*Life*	*Contemporary Musicians*
		On the outbreak of the Revolution, he sides with the people, May. The revolt failing, he flies to Liszt (38) at Weimar, where *Tannhäuser* was produced in Feb. W. hears from Minna (40) that a warrant for his arrest has been issued at Dresden. Flight to Switzerland, May 28, after a separation from Minna. After a fruitless visit to Paris, he settles at Zürich, end of June. Essay, *Die Kunst und die Revolution,* written, July. Minna joins him again, Sept. Writes *Das Kunstwerk der Zukunft.*	
1850	37	Poverty forces him to seek career in Paris again. He abandons the libretto of an opera, *Wieland der Schmied,* which he meant to submit to the Opéra, March. Situation saved by allowance from Julie Ritter and Jessie Laussot. Visits the latter in Bordeaux and plans to elope with her. He resolves to leave Minna (41) for ever, but suddenly Jessie decides to remain with her husband, May.	

Year	Age	Life	Contemporary Musicians
		He again settles down at Zürich with Minna, who agrees to forget the affair, July. Liszt (39) produces *Lohengrin* at Weimar, Aug. 28, in W.'s absence. W., who conducts some opera performance at the Zürich theatre, secures the appointment of Bülow (20) as conductor there, Oct. Bülow resigns in Dec. and W. too withdraws.	
1851	38	Book, *Oper und Drama*, finished, Feb. 16. Friendship with Herwegh (34). The Weimar court theatre commission W. to complete *Siegfrieds Tod*, and he writes the book for a preliminary music drama, *Der junge Siegfried*, June. During a cure for an abdominal complaint at Albisbrunn, W. expands his two Siegfried dramas into a cycle based on the Nibelungen Saga, Sept. Julie Ritter grants him an annuity, Nov.	d'Indy born, March 27; Lortzing (48) dies, Jan. 21; Spontini (77) dies, Jan. 14.
1852	39	Book of *Das Rheingold* sketched, March. Book of *Die Walküre* finished, July 1. Book of the former completed, Nov. The two earlier dramas converted	Stanford born, Sept. 30.

Year	Age	Life	Contemporary Musicians
		into *Siegfried* and *Götterdämmerung,* end of year.	
1853	40	After a cure at St. Moritz, W. goes to Italy, but soon returns to Zürich, Aug. Piano Sonata composed and dedicated to Mathilde Wesendonck (25). Visit to Paris with Liszt and meeting with his daughter Cosima (16) for the first time, Oct.	
1854	41	Music of *Das Rheingold* completed, May 28. Composition of *Die Walküre* begun, June 28. While Minna (45) spends some time in Germany, W. becomes more and more attracted to Mathilde Wesendonck (26), and under this powerful new impression conceives the idea of a music drama on the subject of Tristram and Iseult.	Humperdinck born, Sept. 1; Janáček born, July 4.
1855	42	Visit to London at the invitation of the Philharmonic Society, March. He conducts eight concerts; the public is appreciative, but the press hostile. Friendly meetings with Berlioz (52), who conducts the opposing New Philharmonic concerts. Return	Bishop (69) dies, April 30; Chausson born, Jan. 21; Liadov born, April 29/May 11.

Year	Age	Life	Contemporary Musicians
		to Switzerland, June. Friendship with Gottfried Keller (36).	
1856	43	Music of *Die Walküre* finished, end of March. Libretto for a Buddhist music drama, *Der Sieger,* sketched, May. W. undergoes a cure for erysipelas at Mornex, near Geneva, July, and returns to Zürich in good health. Composition of *Siegfried* begun, Sept. 11.	Martucci born, Jan. 6; Schumann (46) dies, July 29; Sinding born, Jan. 11; Taneiev born, Nov. 13/25.
1857	44	First sketch for *Parsifal* made, April. Removal to the Asyl in the grounds of Otto Wesendonck's (42) house, end of April. The poem of *Tristan und Isolde* begun, early Aug. Hans (27) and Cosima (20) von Bülow visit W. and Minna (48), Sept. Songs, *Der Engel, Träume* and *Schmerzen,* to words by Mathilde Wesendonck (29) composed, winter. Music of first act of *Tristan und Isolde* finished, Dec. 31.	Bruneau born, March 1; Elgar born, June 2; Glinka (54) dies, Feb. 15.
1858	45	Visit to Paris, Jan.–Feb. Two more songs to words by Mathilde Wesendonck (30) composed: *Stehe still* and *Im Treibhaus,* Feb. and	Leoncavallo born, March 8; Puccini born, June 22.

Year	*Age*	*Life*	*Contemporary Musicians*
		May. Music of first act of *Tristan und Isolde* finished, early April. Minna (49), whose jealousy of Mathilde comes to a head, leaves for Germany, while W. renounces Mathilde and goes to Venice with Karl Ritter, Aug. Composition of *Tristan* resumed there, Oct. W. is once more in serious financial straits.	
1859	46	Second act of *Tristan und Isolde* finished, March. He goes to live at Lucerne. Third act of *Tristan* completed there, early Aug. Serov (39) visits W. Farewell visit to friends at Zürich and departure for Paris, Sept. Negotiations for the production of *Tannhäuser* at various theatres. Minna (50) joins W. again, Nov., having tried in Dresden to secure him an amnesty.	Spohr (75) dies, Oct. 22.
1860	47	Conducts a successful concert of fragments from his works in Paris, Jan. 25. Friendship with Baudelaire (39) and rupture with Berlioz (57), Feb. Napoleon III (52) commands a production of *Tannhäuser*	Albeniz born, May 29; Charpentier born, June 25; Mahler born, July 7; Wolf born, March 13.

Year	*Age*	*Life*	*Contemporary Musicians*
		at the Opéra, March. W. refuses to write a ballet for it, which is deemed essential. W. at last receives permission to enter Germany, except the kingdom of Saxony, and goes to Baden-Baden to thank the Princess Augusta of Prussia for her intervention and to fetch back Minna (51), who has just undergone a cure at Soden, Aug. Rehearsals of *Tannhäuser* begin at the Opéra, Sept. Revised version of the Venusberg scene composed.	
1861	48	Venusberg scene finished, end of Jan. First Paris performance of *Tannhäuser*, at the Opéra, March 13, without serious opposition. At the second and third, March 18 and 24, the Jockey Club creates a great disturbance and the work is doomed. W. withdraws it. Visit to Karlsruhe, where *Tristan und Isolde* is to be produced in the autumn, April, and to Vienna, where he hears *Lohengrin* for the first time, May. An ideal production of *Tristan* planned there.	MacDowell born, Dec. 18; Marschner (66) dies, Dec. 14.

Year	*Age*	*Life*	*Contemporary Musicians*
		Return to Paris, only to leave it for good, July. He stays in Vienna, where difficulties begin to arise in the preparation of *Tristan,* which he has in the meantime withdrawn from Karlsruhe, Nov. Visits the Wesendoncks in Venice. Fired by Mathilde's (33) suggestion that he should take up *Die Meistersinger von Nürnberg,* he abandons *Tristan* in Vienna and, Dec., proceeds to Paris, where he sets about the libretto of *Die Meistersinger.*	
1862	49	Libretto finished, end of Jan. Visit to Mainz, where Schott accepts *Die Meistersinger* for publication, Feb. W. settles down at Biebrich, where he begins the composition, March. Friendship with Mathilde Maier and love affair with Friederike Meyer. An amnesty granted to W. which allows him to enter Saxony again. Concerts of extracts from his works at Leipzig, Nov., and Vienna, Dec., for which he has made an	Debussy born, Aug. 22; Delius born, Jan. 29; Halévy (63) dies, March 17.

Year	*Age*	*Life*	*Contemporary Musicians*
		orchestral arrangement of *The Ride of the Valkyries* from *Die Walküre.* Production of *Tristan* wilfully delayed in Vienna.	
1863	50	After two more concerts in Vienna, W. gives one in Prague, Feb. 8, then four at St. Petersburg and Moscow, March and April. W. gives up his Biebrich lodgings and settles at Penzing, near Vienna, where Brahms (30) visits him. Two concerts at Budapest, July. Although these and other concerts are profitable, he is more than ever in debt.	Mascagni born, Dec. 7.
1864	51	Threatened with imprisonment for debt, W. leaves Vienna secretly, March, and goes to Zürich, then to Stuttgart, end of April. There he is sought by the secretary of Ludwig II of Bavaria (19), to whose court he becomes attached, not as an official, but as an intimate friend and adviser. He is to produce his works under ideal conditions. He has Bülow (34) appointed conductor and Cosima von Bülow (27) takes it upon herself to become the	d'Albert born, April 10; Meyerbeer (73) dies, May 2; Strauss (R.) born, June 11.

Year	*Age*	*Life*	*Contemporary Musicians*
		chief worker in W.'s cause. She and W. soon fall deeply in love. W. soon discovers that he is regarded as an influential royal favourite, to be flattered and used for a variety of intrigues. *Huldingungsmarsch* composed for the king. The architect Semper (61) called to Munich to submit plans for a new theatre to be built specially for the production of *Der Ring des Nibelungen,* Dec. The courtiers and civil servants become alarmed at W.'s influence and a campaign is set secretly afoot against him.	
1865	52	Production of *Tristan und Isolde* in Munich, June 10, with Schnorr von Carolsfeld (29) and his wife, Malvina (40), in the title parts. There had been nearly a month's delay, which had been dexterously exploited by W.'s enemies in the government and the clerical party. They engineer a public agitation against W. and persuade Ludwig II (20) that it is national. Nov.	Dietsch (57) dies, Feb. 20; Dukas born, Oct. 1; Glazounov born, July 29/Aug. 10; Sibelius born, Dec. 8.

Year	*Age*	*Life*	*Contemporary Musicians*
		Ludwig asks W. to leave him, at least for a time. W. goes to Switzerland, Dec. 10, and his departure is at once interpreted by his antagonists as a final dismissal. He takes refuge on the Lake of Geneva, first at Vevey, then at the Campagne aux Artichauts, near Geneva.	
1866	53	First act of *Die Meistersinger von Nürnberg* finished, Feb. Cosima von Bülow (29) joins W., March. They discover a house at Triebschen on the Lake of Lucerne, where W. settles down while Cosima returns temporarily to Munich, April. She joins him with her children, followed by Bülow, (36), who has accidentally discovered the truth about her relation with Wagner. His marriage having been extremely unhappy, he is not averse from a separation; his chief concern is to silence gossip. Second act of *Die Meistersinger* finished, end of Sept. Richter (23) engaged as W.'s amanuensis. W.	Busoni born, April 1.

Year	*Age*	*Life*	*Contemporary Musicians*
		starts to dictate *Mein Leben* (begun in 1865) to Cosima.	
1867	54	Composition, but not orchestration, of *Die Meistersinger von Nürnberg* finished, early March. Three visits to Munich, where Ludwig II (22) vainly tries to persuade W. to remain again and where *Lohengrin* is prepared by Bülow (37), who is now court conductor and principal of the new School of Music. Cosima (30) once more joins her husband at Munich, for the sake of appearances, April.	Granados born, July 29.
1868	55	Time divided between Triebschen and Munich, where *Die Meistersinger von Nürnberg* is prepared for production by Bülow (38) and Richter (25). First performance, June 21. Cosima (31) definitely settles at Triebschen, autumn, where W. resumes the composition of the third act of *Siegfried.* Meeting with Nietzsche (24) during a visit to Leipzig.	Bantock born, Aug. 7; Rossini (76) dies, Nov. 13.
1869	56	Son, Siegfried, born to W. and Cosima (32), June 6. Triebschen visited by Serov	Berlioz (66) dies, March 8; Dargomizhsky (56) dies, Jan.; Loewe (73) dies,

Year	*Age*	*Life*	*Contemporary Musicians*
		(49), Catulle Mendès (28) and his wife, Judith (*née* Gautier) (19), July. Although against the separate performance of *Das Rheingold* in Munich, he goes there to patch up the production.	April 20; Pfitzner born, May 5; Roussel born, April 5.
1870	57	Composition of first act of *Götterdämmerung* begun, Jan. Cosima (33) divorced from Bülow (40), July 18 and married to W., Aug. 25. Scheme for a festival theatre at Bayreuth takes shape during the year. *Siegfried Idyll* composed for Cosima's birthday, and performed on the staircase at Triebschen, Dec. 25.	Balfe (62) dies, Oct. 20; Mercadante (75) dies, Dec. 17; Novák born, Dec. 5; Schmitt born, Sept. 28.
1871	58	Scoring of *Siegfried* completed at Triebschen, Feb. 5. *Kaisermarsch* for the celebrations of the Prussian victory, March. First visit to Bayreuth, which he finds to be the ideal place for his festival theatre, April. Successful visits to Leipzig and Berlin, April–May.	Auber (89) dies, May 12; Potter (79) dies, Sept. 28; Scriabin born, Dec. 25 (O.S.); Serov (51) dies, Jan. 20/Feb. 1.
1872	59	Composition of the third act of *Götterdämmerung* finished, Feb. Triebschen left for Bayreuth, April. Excavations for the festival	Vaughan Williams born, Oct. 12.

Year	*Age*	*Life*	*Contemporary Musicians*
		theatre begun. Visit to Vienna to give a concert in aid of the theatre, which proves a brilliant success, and return to Bayreuth with Richter (29), May. Foundation stone laid, May 22, W.'s birthday, with a great festivity. The German press attacks the Bayreuth scheme. W. and Cosima (35) go to Weimar to visit Liszt (61), who has been somewhat estranged from them since his daughter's desertion of Bülow (42). Copying of orchestral parts of *Der Ring des Nibelungen* begun by several disciples, autumn. Tour through Germany to discover artists for the *Ring*, to float Wagner Societies and collect funds.	
1873	60	Finding subscriptions too slow in coming in, W. is obliged to give concerts again in various centres, much against his will, Jan.–Feb. Concert for 60th birthday arranged by Cosima, including the old C major Symphony, May 22. Erection of the roof of the festival theatre	Rachmaninov born, March 20/April 1; Reger born, March 19.

Year	*Age*	*Life*	*Contemporary Musicians*
		celebrated, Aug. 2. The scheme threatening to collapse, propaganda on a grand scale is organized, Nov. First act of *Götterdämmerung* finished in full score, Dec. 24.	
1874	61	The Bayreuth scheme is as near collapse as possible, when Ludwig II (29), who is already verging on insanity and has for a time refused all help, suddenly advances 100,000 thaler, March. Removal to the Villa Wahnfried, April. Preliminary studies of *Der Ring des Nibelungen* begun there, Richter (31) and Seidl (24) assisting, summer. Second act of *Götterdämmerung* completed in full score, June 26. The whole work finished, Nov. 21.	Cornelius (50) dies, Oct. 26; Holst born, Sept. 21; Schoenberg born, Sept. 13; Suk born, Jan. 4.
1875	62	Concerts in Vienna and Budapest, March. Two concerts in Berlin, April. Preliminary rehearsals of *Der Ring des Nibelungen* with some of the principal artists begun, May. All the artists assembled, July, and stage rehearsals begun at the festival theatre, Aug.	Bizet (37) dies, June 3; Ravel born, March 7.

Year	*Age*	*Life*	*Contemporary Musicians*
		2. Performance of the Paris version of *Tannhäuser* in Vienna, Nov. 22. Hugo Wolf (15), who studies at the Vienna Conservatoire, approaches W., whom he worships.	
1876	63	The festival still in jeopardy. W. receives 5,000 dollars for a March commissioned by the U.S.A. for the centenary of the Declaration of Independence, Feb. First Berlin performance of *Tristan und Isolde,* March 20. Mottl (20) joins the Bayreuth staff, May. Rehearsals of *Der Ring des Nibelungen* begun, Richter (33) conducting under W.'s supervision, June 3. First cycle of performances, Aug. 13–17. The whole work is given three times, with an immense success, but a deficit of 120,000 marks. Utterly exhausted, W. takes the family for a holiday in Italy, Sept.	Falla born, Nov. 23; Götz (36) dies, Dec. 3.
1877	64	Earlier sketches of *Parsifal* shaped and elaborated, Jan. Eight concerts in aid of Bayreuth given in London, May. After a	Dohnányi born, July 27.

Year	*Age*	*Life*	*Contemporary Musicians*
		cure for his old abdominal complaint at Ems, June, W. and Cosima (40) return to Bayreuth, end of July. Composition of *Parsifal* begun, end of Aug. W.'s complaint begins to cause heart trouble, Oct.	
1878	65	First number of *Bayreuther Blätter* published. In spite of much suffering from his complaint and from rheumatism, the composition of *Parsifal* progresses. First complete performance of the *Ring* outside Bayreuth, at Leipzig, April. Prelude to *Parsifal* privately performed on Cosima's (41) birthday, Dec. 25.	
1879	66	Composition of *Parsifal* finished in short score, April 26. The *Ring* deficit is still not cleared and W. continues to send out appeals for funds. He begins to suffer from erysipelas again, Nov.	Bridge (Frank) born, Feb. 26; Ireland born, Aug. 13; Medtner born, Dec. 24; Respighi born, July 9; Scott (Cyril) born, Sept. 27.
1880	67	At Naples, Jan.–Aug. Humperdinck (26) becomes attached to W. there, spring. W. ill again, July. Removal first to Perugia, then to Siena, Aug. After a stay in	Bloch born, July 24; Offenbach (61) dies, Oct. 4; Pizzetti born, Sept. 20.

Year	*Age*	*Life*	*Contemporary Musicians*
		Venice, Oct., W. and Cosima (43) return to Bayreuth, with a visit to Munich, Nov. 17. Orchestration of *Parsifal* resumed, Nov. 23. Angelo Neumann proposes to produce the *Ring* in London, St. Petersburg and the U.S.A., Dec.	
1881	68	Orchestration of first act of *Parsifal* finished, April 25. Gobineau (65) visits W. at Bayreuth, May. Heart seizure during an ovation after the *Ring* performances in Berlin, May 29. Preliminary studies for *Parsifal* begun, Humperdinck (27) assisting. Scoring of second act finished, Oct. 19. Arrival at Palermo for the winter, Nov. 5.	Bartók born, March 25; Miaskovsky born, April 8/20; Mussorgsky (42) dies, March 16/28; Vieuxtemps (61) dies, June 6.
1882	69	Orchestration of *Parsifal* completed at Palermo, Jan. 13. After two stays at Acireale and Messina, the W.'s go to Venice, April. Return to Bayreuth, May 1. Rehearsals for *Parsifal* begin, July 2. First performance, reserved for patrons, July 26, and first public performance, July 30. Levi (43) is the	Kodály born, Dec. 16; Malipiero born, March 18; Raff (60) dies, June 24–5; Stravinsky born, June 5/17.

Year	*Age*	*Life*	*Contemporary Musicians*
		conductor. At the last (16th) performance, Aug. 29, W. notices that Levi is indisposed during the third act and conducts the work to the end. Departure for Venice, much exhausted, Sept 14. W. is in poor health and has frequent heart attacks.	
1883	70	W. wishes to write a Symphony, Jan. His health deteriorates more and more and he is subject to great depression. Wagner dies at Venice from heart failure, Feb. 13.	Bax born, Nov. 6; Casella born, July 25; Szymanowski born; Webern born, Dec. 3. Albeniz aged 23; Balakirev 47; Bantock 15; Bartók 2; Bloch 3; Boito 41; Borodin 49; Brahms 50; Bridge (Frank) 4; Bruch 45; Bruckner 59; Bruneau 26; Bungert 37; Busoni 17; Chabrier 42; Charpentier 23; Chausson 28; Cui 48; Debussy 21; Delius 21; Dohnányi 6; Dorn 79; Draeseke 48; Dukas 18; Duparc 35; Dvořák 42; Elgar 26; Falla 7; Fauré 38; Franck 61; Gade 66; Glazounov 18; Goldmark 53; Gounod 65; Granados 16; Grieg 40; Holst 9; Humperdinck 29; d'Indy 32; Ireland 4; Janáček 29; Kodály 1;

Appendix A.—Calendar

Year	*Age*	*Life*	*Contemporary Musicians*
			Lalo 60; Leoncavallo 25; Liadov 28; Liszt 72; MacDowell 22; Mackenzie 36; Mahler 23; Malipiero 1; Martucci 27; Mascagni 20; Massenet 41; Medtner 4; Miaskovsky 2; Novák 13; Parry 35; Pedrell 42; Pfitzner 14; Pizzetti 3; Puccini 25; Rachmaninov 10; Ravel 8; Reger 10; Respighi 4; Reyer 60; Rimsky-Korsakov 39; Roussel 14; Rubinstein 53; Saint-Saëns 48; Schmitt 13; Schoenberg 9; Scott (Cyril) 4; Scriabin 12; Sgambati 40; Sibelius 18; Sinding 27; Smetana 59; Stanford 31; Strauss (J. ii) 58; Strauss (R.) 19; Stravinsky 1; Suk 9; Sullivan [illegible]1; Svendsen 43; Taneiev 27; Tchaikovsky 43; Vaughan Williams 11; Verdi 70; Wolf 23.

APPENDIX B

CATALOGUE OF WORKS

THIS list is based upon the completed portion of Breitkopf & Härtel's collected edition and upon Ernest Newman's catalogue in his *Wagner as Man and Artist.* The dates given are those of composition, not of publication.

OPERAS

Die Hochzeit (unfinished) (1832).
Die Feen (1833–4).
Das Liebesverbot (1835–6).
Rienzi (1838–40).
Der fliegende Holländer (1841).
Tannhäuser (1843–4).
Lohengrin (1846–8).
Der Ring des Nibelungen (1853–74):
- *Das Rheingold* (1853–4).
- *Die Walküre* (1854–6).
- *Siegfried* (1856–69).
- *Götterdämmerung* (1869–74).

Tristan und Isolde (1857–9).
Die Meistersinger von Nürnberg (1862–7).
Parsifal (1877–82).

ORCHESTRAL WORKS

Marches

Huldigungsmarsch (1864).
Kaisermarsch (1871).
American Centennial March (1876).

Appendix B.—Catalogue of Works

Overtures

Overture in C major (1830) (unpublished).
Overture in B flat major (1830) (unpublished).
Concert Overture in D minor (1831).
Concert Overture in C major (1832).
Overture to *König Enzio* (Raupach) (1832).
Christoph Columbus Overture (1835).
Rule Britannia Overture (1836).
Polonia Overture (1836).
Eine Faust Ouvertüre (1840).

Symphony

Symphony in C major (1832).

Symphonic Poem

Siegfried Idyll (1870).

Choral Works

For Male Chorus

Weihegruss for the unveiling of the memorial to King Friedrich August I of Saxony (1843).
Gruss seiner Treuen an Friedrich August den Geliebten (1844).
An Webers Grabe (1844).

For Male Chorus and Orchestra

Das Liebesmahl der Apostel (1843).
Song for the unveiling of the memorial to King Friedrich August I of Saxony (1843).

For Mixed Chorus and Orchestra

Neujahrs-Kantate (1834).
Nicolai. National hymn for a solo voice and choir (1837).
Descente de la Courtille. Vaudeville chorus (1840).

Incidental Music

Incidental music to a play, J. Springer's *Die letzte Heidenverschwörung in Preussen, oder der Deutsche Ritterorden in Königsberg* (1837).

Songs

Seven Compositions to Goethe's *Faust* (1832):

1. *Lied der Soldaten.*
2. *Bauern unter der Linde.*
3. *Branders Lied.*
4. *Lied des Mephistopheles.*
5. *Lied des Mephistopheles*
6. *Meine Ruh ist hin.*
7. *Melodram.*

Vampyr-Aria (*allegro* to aria in Marschner's *Der Vampyr*) (1833).
Romance for bass (addition to K. Blum's *Singspiel* of *Marie, Max und Michel*) (1837).
Song for bass (addition to J. Weigl's *Die Schweizerfamilie*) (1837).
Aria, with male chorus, for bass (addition to Bellini's *Norma)* (probably 1837).
Der Tannenbaum (Scheuerlein) (1838).
Les Deux Grenadiers (Heine) (1839–40).
Dors, mon enfant (1840).
Mignonne (Ronsard) (1840).
Attente (V. Hugo) (1840).
Les Adieux de Marie Stuart (Béranger) (1840).
Tout n'est qu'images fugitives (Reboul) (1840).
Fünf Gedichte von Mathilde Wesendonck:

1. *Der Engel* (1857).
2. *Stehe still!* (1858).
3. *Im Treibhaus* (1858).
4. *Schmerzen* (1857).
5. *Träume* (1857).

Kraft-liedchen (unaccompanied humorous song of thanks to Herr Kraft, a hotel manager in Leipzig) (1871).
Fischerlied (unaccompanied humorous song for Peppino, a Neapolitan singer) (unpublished) (1880?).

Appendix B.—Catalogue of Works

Piano Music

Sonata in D minor (unpublished) (1829).
Sonata in B flat major (1831).
Polonaise in D major for four hands (1831).
Fantasia in F sharp minor (1831).
Ein Lied ohne Worte (1840).
Album Sonata in E flat major (for Mathilde Wesendonck) (1853).
Albumblatt in A flat major (1861).
Albumblatt: Ankunft bei den schwarzen Schwänen (for Countess Pourtalès) (1861).
Albumblatt in C major (for Princess Metternich) (1861).

Violin and Piano Music

Albumblatt in E flat major (1875).

Chamber Music

Quartet in D major (unpublished) (1829).

Arrangements

Ninth Symphony (Beethoven) for piano (unpublished) (1830).
Soirées Musicales—Les Mariniers (Rossini) for small orchestra (1838).
La Favorita (Donizetti) for piano, etc. (1840).
L'Elisir d'Amore (Donizetti) for piano (1840).
La Reine de Chypre (Halévy) for piano, etc. (1841).
Le Guitarrero (Halévy) for piano (1841).
Iphigénie en Aulide (Gluck) revised and added to (1846).
Stabat Mater (Palestrina) with expression marks (1848).
Don Giovanni (Mozart) revised and added to (1850).

APPENDIX C

PERSONALIA

d'Agoult, Marie Catherine Sophie de Flavigny, Countess (1805–67), French novelist and political and historical essayist (under the *nom de plume* 'Daniel Stern'). The mistress of Liszt and mother of Cosima Wagner.

Auber, Daniel François Esprit (1782–1871), French operatic composer. His chief work, *La Muette de Portici,* influenced the youthful Wagner.

Bakunin, Mikhail (1814–76), influential Russian anarchist, the father of Nihilism. Associated in the Dresden revolution with Wagner, who vividly describes him in *My Life.*

Baudelaire, Charles Pierre (1821–67), French poet, critic and essayist, author of *Les Fleurs du mal,* one of the foremost 'decadents.' Associated with Wagner in the Paris *Tannhäuser* period, and was fascinated by his music.

Betz, Franz (1835–1900), German baritone singer, who created Hans Sachs and Wotan. Also famous as Falstaff in Verdi's opera.

Breitkopf & Härtel, publishing firm at Leipzig, founded in 1719 by Bernhardt Christoph Breitkopf (1695–1777).

Bülow, Hans von (1830–94), German pianist and conductor, first husband of Cosima Wagner. Wholly devoted to the cause of Wagner and the New German School at first, later leaning towards Brahms.

Cornelius, Peter (1824–74), German composer, follower of Liszt and Wagner, author of the comic opera, *Der Barbier von Bagdad.*

Davison, James William (1813–85), music critic in London.

Devrient, Philipp Eduard (1801–77), German baritone singer, actor and author of a history of German acting. Director of the court theatre at Dresden, 1844–6, and at Karlsruhe, 1852–69.

Dietsch, Pierre Louis Philippe (1808–65), French composer and conductor. Composed unsuccessful opera to the original French version of *The Flying Dutchman* libretto. Conducted *Tannhäuser* in Paris, 1861.

Doré, Paul Gustave (1833–83), French painter and illustrator associated with Wagner in the Paris *Tannhäuser* period.

Dorn, Heinrich Ludwig Egmont (1804–92), composer, teacher and conductor, pupil of Zelter in Berlin, operatic conductor in Hamburg and Riga, where he succeeded Wagner in 1839. Finally conductor of the Royal Opera in Berlin, 1849–68, and professor.

Eckert, Karl Anton Florian (1820–79), German violinist, pianist, composer and conductor. In 1853 became director of the Vienna court opera; in 1860 of the opera in Stuttgart, whither in 1864 Wagner fled from his creditors.

Esser, Heinrich (1818–72), German composer and conductor. Long career in Vienna. Discovered Hans Richter for Wagner.

Feuerbach, Ludwig Andreas (1804–72), German philosopher who aimed to subjectivize religion. Author of *Philosophie und Christentum*, 1839, in which he attacked Christianity, and *Das Wesen des Christentums*, 1841. Greatly influenced Wagner.

Gautier, Louise-Judith (1850–1917), French authoress, daughter of Théophile Gautier, who visited and wrote of Wagner.

Gervinus, Georg Gottfried (1805–71), German historian, whose *History of German Literature*, 1835–42, was the first of its kind. In it Wagner found the material for *The Mastersingers*.

Gobineau, Joseph Arthur, Comte de (1816–82), French diplomat and author. Propagated theories of racial purity in his *Essai sur l'inégalité des races humaines*, 1853–5, which affected Wagner, whose friend he was.

Gutzkow, Karl Ferdinand (1811–78), advanced 'anti-romantic' German novelist and dramatist. Author of *Wally, die Zweiflerin* and *Die Ritter vom Geiste*. Quarrelled with Wagner in Dresden.

Habeneck, François Antoine (1781–1849), French violinist and conductor. Founder of the Société des Concerts du Conservatoire in Paris. Conductor at the Opéra, 1824–47.

Halévy, Jacques François Fromental Elie (1799–1862), French-Jewish operatic composer, whose opera, *La Reine de Chypre*, Wagner arranged for Schlesinger in Paris in 1841. Described by Wagner in *My Life*.

Hanslick, Eduard (1825–1904), music critic in Vienna, lecturer on musical history.

Hauser, Franz (1794–1870), baritone singer and singing teacher. Recipient of well-known letters from the theorist Moritz Hauptmann. One of Wagner's chief antagonists.

Hérold, Louis Joseph Ferdinand (1791–1833), French operatic composer. His *Zampa* famous in Germany in Wagner's youth.

Herwegh, Georg (1817–75), German revolutionary poet, author of *Gedichte eines Lebendigen.* In 1848 fled to Switzerland, where he became Wagner's friend.

Hoffmann, Ernst Theodor Amadeus (1776–1822), German musician and *littérateur,* one of the greatest influences upon the musical romantic movement in Germany and France in the early nineteenth century.

Humperdinck, Engelbert (1854–1921), German operatic composer. The scoring of his masterpiece, *Hänsel und Gretel,* obviously influenced by Wagner, with whom he was associated in the *Parsifal* period.

Klindworth, Karl (1830–1916), German pianist and conductor, pupil of Liszt and arranger of music for his instrument, including vocal scores of Wagner's works. Had a school of music of his own in Berlin.

Lachner, Franz (1803–90), Bavarian composer and conductor, in Vienna, Mannheim and Munich.

Laube, Heinrich (1806–84), German novelist, dramatist and theatre director, associated with Wagner in his youth in Leipzig and in Vienna in the sixties.

Levi, Hermann (1839–1900), German-Jewish conductor associated with Wagner. 1872–96 director of the Munich court theatre. Conducted the first performances of *Parsifal.*

Lipinsky, Karl Joseph (1790–1861), Polish violin virtuoso. Dedicatee of Schumann's *Carneval. Konzertmeister* at Dresden, 1839–61.

Logier, Johann Bernard (1777–1846), German musician who settled in Dublin. Inventor of a system of pianoforte technique and author of the text-book for composition which Wagner first studied.

Magnan, Bernard Pierre (1791–1865), French marshal, who played leading part in Napoleon III's *coup d'état* in 1851. Was attracted by Wagner's music and supported the 1861 production of *Tannhäuser.*

Materna, Amalie (1845–1918), Austrian dramatic soprano singer. Created the parts of Brynhilda and Kundry at Bayreuth.

Mottl, Felix (1856–1911), German conductor, associated with Wagner. Conducted *Tristan und Isolde* at Bayreuth in 1886, the *Ring* in London in 1898 and *Parsifal* in New York in 1903–4.

Neumann, Angelo (1838–1910), German-Jewish baritone singer, later theatre director, the first to introduce the *Ring* into the ordinary world of opera as a business proposition.

Niemann, Albert (1831–1917), German tenor singer. Sang Tannhäuser in Paris in 1861, and Siegmund at Bayreuth in 1876.

Nietzsche, Friedrich Wilhelm (1844–1900), eminent German philosopher.

Nikisch, Arthur (1855–1922), Hungarian conductor, violinist and pianist. Played under Wagner in the performance of Beethoven's ninth Symphony at the laying of the foundation stone of the Bayreuth theatre. Trained and accompanied Elena Gerhardt.

Paer, Ferdinando (1771–1839), Italian opera composer, popular in France and Germany.

Reissiger, Karl Gottlieb (1798–1859), German conductor and composer. From 1827 to his death conductor of the Dresden Opera.

Richter, Hans (1843–1916), Austro-Hungarian conductor, intimately associated with Wagner and later with Brahms, frequent visitor to London and conductor of the Hallé Orchestra in Manchester, 1897–1911.

Rubinstein, Joseph (1847–84), Russian-Jewish pianist and composer of drawing-room music and devotee of Wagner. Made a notorious attack upon Brahms and Schumann in *Bayreuther Blätter.*

Sainton, Prosper Philippe Catherine (1813–90), French violinist, who in 1845 settled in London as professor at the Royal Academy of Music and leader of orchestras.

Schlesinger, publishing firm in Berlin, founded in 1810 by Adolf Martin Schlesinger (died 1839), and in Paris, founded in 1834 by his eldest son, Moritz Adolf (died 1871).

Schnorr von Carolsfeld, Ludwig (1836–65), German tenor singer devoted to Wagner, the creator of Tristan, and a pianist, composer and arranger of songs. He also wrote poetry and painted.

Schott, publishing firm at Mainz, founded in 1773 by Bernhard Schott.

Schröder-Devrient, Wilhelmine (1804–60), German dramatic soprano admired by Wagner. Created Leonore in the revival of *Fidelio* in Vienna in 1822, and Adriano, Senta and Venus in Wagner's operas. Inherited great dramatic talent from her mother, Antoinette Sophie Bürger, a famous actress.

Scribe, Augustin Eugène (1791–1861), prolific French dramatist and librettist. Wrote librettos of successful operas for Meyerbeer, Auber and Verdi.

Seidl, Anton (1850–98), Hungarian conductor associated with Wagner. Conducted Angelo Neumann's 'Richard Wagner' touring company. From 1885 active in New York.

Semper, Gottfried (1803–79), German architect and art-theorist, associated with Wagner in Dresden, Zürich and Munich. Planned or shared in the planning of famous buildings in Dresden, Zürich, Vienna and London (the South Kensington Museum).

Smart, George Thomas (1776–1867), composer and conductor in London.

Stein, Heinrich Freiherr von (1857–87), German philosopher and poet, associated with Wagner, who influenced him. 1879–80 Siegfried's tutor. Chief works *Die Entstehung der neuen Aesthetik* and dramatic pieces, *Helden und Welt.*

Tausig, Karl (1841–71), Polish pianist, arranger and composer for his instrument. Played an active part in initiating the Bayreuth movement.

Tichatschek, Joseph Aloys (1807–86), German tenor singer. The creator of Rienzi.

Uhlig, Theodor (1822–53), German violinist, composer and author of theoretical works. Recipient of important letters from Wagner.

Unger, Georg (1837–87), German tenor singer. The creator of Siegfried. The first so-called 'Heldentenor.'

Viardot-Garcia, Michelle Ferdinande Pauline (1821–1910), Franco-Spanish mezzo-soprano singer. Sang Venus in Paris in 1861.

Weigl, Joseph (1766–1846), Viennese conductor and composer of popular German and Italian operas, notably *Die Schweizerfamilie.*

Weinlig, Christian Theodor (1780–1842), German composer and teacher of musical theory. From 1823 to his death was cantor of the Thomasschule in Leipzig (Bach's position). Taught Wagner, who described his methods in *My Life* in a well-known passage.

Wolzogen, Hans Paul Freiherr von (born 1848), editor of *Bayreuther Blätter* and author of many works on Wagner's music and theories.

Zumpe, Hermann (1850–1903), German conductor, associated with Wagner. In 1900–3 conducted famous Wagner performances in Munich.

APPENDIX D

BIBLIOGRAPHY

Preliminary Note on 'recommended reading'

THE standard biography is Ernest Newman's great *Life*: this is 'required' reading, though it must be borne in mind that its four volumes, intensely readable though they are, are directed to the specialist. A comprehensive, balanced large-scale study in the light of contemporary thought and knowledge is still outstanding. Hight's conspectus of the life and works appeared in 1925; Gutman's comparatively recent one is richly informed, insightful and trenchantly written, but unbalanced by his hostility towards everything about Wagner save his music.

Newman's *Study of Wagner* and *Wagner as Man and Artist* are also 'required' reading, though Newman's approach is to a certain extent splintered by the contrast between his admiration for the composer and rigorously critical attitude towards other aspects of Wagner. Equally 'required' therefore are Paul Bekker's profound study of Wagner's life in relation to his works, Thomas Mann's brilliant essay *The Sufferings and Greatness of Richard Wagner* and the illuminating chapters on Wagner in Joseph Kerman's *Opera as Drama.*

Of Wagner's own writings the most notable as literature are the moving and witty early Parisian pieces and the revealing account of his youth and childhood in *Mein Leben. On Conducting* is still interesting. *A Communication to my Friends,* though heavy going, gives an illuminating account of Wagner's artistic development up to *The Ring.* Many important letters will be found in the Altmann selected edition. Other recommendable collections are the exciting letters to Liszt, Uhlig and Röckel, written during the genesis of *The Ring*; the letters to Ludwig; the Burrell collection, which contains moving early love-letters to Minna; and the letters to Mathilde Wesendonck, which vividly convey the emotional and philosophical background of *Tristan.*

Appendix D.—Bibliography

The following bibliography is a selection of the vast literature. In compiling it use has been made of the bibliographies in Grove's *Dictionary*, Newman's *Life* and Hight's and Gutman's biographies. Marked with an asterisk are not only those works mentioned above, but others of especial value.

Wagner's Correspondence

General Collections

* 'Richard Wagners Briefe.' Selected and edited by Wilhelm Altmann. 2 vols. (Leipzig, 1933.)
* 'Letters of Richard Wagner.' Selected and edited by Wilhelm Altmann. Translated by M. M. Bozman. 2 vols. (London and Toronto, 1927.)
* 'Richard Wagners Briefe nach Zeitfolge und Inhalt.' W. Altmann. (Leipzig, 1905.)
* 'Richard Wagners Gesammelte Briefe.' Edited by Julius Kapp and Emmerich Kastner. (Leipzig, 1914.) (Not completed.)
* 'Letters of Richard Wagner: the Burrell Collection.' Edited with notes by John N. Burk. (London, 1951.) 'Richard Wagners Sämtliche Briefe,' Vols. I and II. Edited by Gertrud Strobel and Werner Wolf. (Leipzig, 1967.) Contains letters up to 1849.

Special Collections

* Richard Wagner an Theodor Apel.' Edited by Theodor Apel the Younger. (Leipzig, 1910.)
* 'Bayreuther Briefe von Richard Wagner' (1871–83). Edited by C. F. Glasenapp. (Berlin and Leipzig, 1907.)

'Richard Wagner's Briefe an Hans von Bülow.' (Jena, 1916.)

* Familienbriefe von Richard Wagner' (1832–74). Edited by C. F. Glasenapp. (Berlin, 1907.)
* 'Family Letters of Richard Wagner.' Translated by W. A. Ellis. (London, 1911.)

'Richard Wagner an Freunde und Zeitgenossen.' Edited by Erich Kloss. (Leipzig, 1912.)

'Die Briefe Richard Wagner an Judith Gautier.' Edited by Willi Schuh. (Zürich and Leipzig, 1936.)

'Richard Wagners Briefe an Emil Heckel.' Edited by K. Heckel. (Berlin, 1899.)

'Richard Wagner's Letters to Emil Heckel.' Translated by W. A. Ellis. (London, 1899.)

'Zwei unveröffentlichte Briefe Richard Wagners an Robert von Hornstein.' Edited by Dr. Ferdinand Freiherr von Hornstein. (Munich, 1911.)

'Richard Wagner an seine Künstler.' Edited by Erich Kloss. (Berlin, 1908.)

* 'Briefwechsel zwischen Wagner und Liszt.' Edited by Erich Kloss. 2 vols. (Leipzig, 1919.)

* 'Correspondence of Wagner and Liszt.' Translated by F. Hueffer. 2 vols. (London, 1897.)

'Ludwig II und Richard Wagner: Briefwechsel.' Edited by Otto Strobel. 4 vols. (Carlsruhe, 1936.)

'Richard Wagner an Mathilde Maier' (1862–78). Edited by Dr. Hans Scholz. (Leipzig, 1930.)

'The Nietzsche-Wagner Correspondence.' Edited by E. Förster-Nietzsche. Translated by C. V. Kerr. (London, 1922.)

'Briefe Richard Wagners an eine Putzmacherin.' Published by O. Spitzer. (Vienna, 1906.)

* 'Richard Wagners Briefe an Frau Julie Ritter.' Edited by S. von Haussegger. (Munich, 1920.)

* 'Richard Wagners Briefe an August Röckel.' (Leipzig, 1894.)

* 'Richard Wagner's Letters to August Röckel.' Translated by E. C. Sellar. (Bristol, 1897.)

* 'Richard Wagners Briefe an Theodor Uhlig, Wilhelm Fischer, Ferdinand Heine.' (Leipzig, 1888.)

* 'Richard Wagner's Letters to his Dresden Friends Theodor Uhlig, Wilhelm Fischer, Ferdinand Heine.' Translated by J. S. Shedlock. (London, 1890.)

'Richard Wagners Briefwechsel mit seinem Verlegern.' Edited by W. Altmann. (Leipzig, 1912.)

* 'Richard Wagner an Minna Wagner.' 2 vols. (Berlin and Leipzig, 1908.)
* 'Richard Wagner to Minna Wagner.' Translated by W. A. Ellis. 2 vols. (London, 1919.)
* 'Richard Wagner an Mathilde Wesendonck.' Edited by W. Golther. (Berlin, 1904.)
* 'Richard Wagner to Mathilde Wesendonck.' Translated by W. A. Ellis. (London, 1905.)
* 'Richard Wagners Briefe an Otto Wesendonck.' (Berlin, 1905.)
* 'Richard Wagner's Letters to Wesendonck and Others.' Translated by W. A. Ellis. (London, 1899.)
* 'Fünfzehn Briefe von Richard Wagner. Nebst Erinnerungen und Erläuterungen von E. Wille.' (Berlin, 1894.)

BIOGRAPHIES

* *Burrell, The Hon. Mary,* 'Richard Wagner's Life and Works, 1813–34.' (London, 1898.)

Chamberlain, Houston Stewart, 'Richard Wagner.' (Munich, 1896.) Translated by G. A. Hight. (London, 1897.)

Dannreuther, Edward. Article on Wagner in Grove's 'Dictionary of Music and Musicians.' (3rd edition, London, 1928.)

* *Ellis, W. A.,* 'Life of Richard Wagner.' 6 vols. Begun as translation of Glasenapp's biography, but last 2 vols. independent. (London, 1902–8.)

Engel, Erich W., 'Richard Wagners Leben und Werke im Bilde.' 2 vols. (Vienna and Leipzig, 1922.)

Finck, Henry T., 'Wagner and his Works.' 2 vols. (London, 1893.)

* *Glasenapp, C. F.,* 'Das Leben Richard Wagners.' 6 vols. (3rd and 4th editions, Leipzig, 1894–1911. The standard biography.)

Gutman, Robert W., 'Richard Wagner—The Man, His Mind and His Music.' (London, 1968.)

Hadow, Sir Henry, 'Richard Wagner.' (London, 1934.)

* *Hight, George Ainslie,* 'Richard Wagner: a Critical Biography.' 2 vols. (London, 1925.)
Kapp, Julius, 'Wagner.' (Berlin, 1922.)
Koch, Max, 'Richard Wagner.' 3 vols. (Berlin, 1907–19.)
* *Newman, Ernest,* 'The Life of Richard Wagner.' Four volumes. (London, 1933–47.)
* *Pourtalès, Guy de,* 'Richard Wagner.' Translated by Lewis May. (New York, 1932.)
Strobel, Otto, 'Neue Urkunden zur Lebensgeschichte Richard Wagners, 1864–1882.' (Carlsruhe, 1939.)
Tappert, Wilhelm, 'Richard Wagner, sein Leben und seine Werke.' (Elberfeld, 1883.)

STUDIES

Aderne, Theodor W., 'Versuch ueber Wagner.' (Berlin, 1952.)
* *Bekker, Paul,* 'Wagner. Das Leben im Werke.' (Stuttgart, 1924.) Translated by M. M. Bozman. (London and Toronto, 1931.)
* *Brink, Louise,* 'Women Characters in Richard Wagner.' (Washington, 1924.)
Buesst, Aylmer, 'The Nibelung's Ring.' (London, 1932.)
Dannreuther, E., 'Wagner and the Reform of the Opera.' (2nd edition, London, 1904.)
* *Donington, Robert,* 'Wagner's "Ring" and its Symbols.' (London, 1963.)
* *Drews, Arthur,* 'Der Ideengehalt von Richard Wagner.' (Leipzig, 1931.)
Gal, Hans, 'Richard Wagner—Versuch einer Würdigung.' (Frankfurt-on-Main, 1963.)
Gollancz, Victor, 'The Ring at Bayreuth.' (London, 1966.)
Gilman, Lawrence, 'Wagner's Operas.' (New York, 1937.)
* *Kapp, Julius,* 'Richard Wagner und die Frauen.' (Berlin, 1912.)
* —— 'The Women in Wagner's Life.' Translated by Hannah Waller. (London, 1932.)
* *Kerman, Joseph,* 'Wagner: Thoughts in Season.' *The Score,* No. 28, 1961.

Krehbiel, H. E., 'Studies in the Wagnerian Drama.' (London, 1891.)

Lavignac, Albert, 'The Music Dramas of Richard Wagner.' Translated by Esther Singleton. (London, 1898.)

Lichtenberger, Henri, 'Richard Wagner, Poète et Penseur.' (Paris, 1931.)

Lippert, Woldemar, 'Richard Wagners Verbannung und Rück-kehr, 1849–62.' (Dresden, 1927.)

Liszt, Franz, 'Lohengrin et Tannhäuser.' (Leipzig, 1851.) 'Der fliegende Hollander.' (1845.) 'Das Rheingold.' (1855.) In 'Gesammelte Schriften.' Vol. III. (1881.)

Loos, Paul Arthur, 'Richard Wagner: Vollendung und Tragik der deutschen Romantik.' (Munich, 1952.)

Lorenz, Alfred, 'Das Geheimnis der Form bei Richard Wagner.' 4 vols. (Berlin, 1924, etc.)

Magee, Bryan, 'Aspects of Wagner.' (London, 1968.)

* *Mann, Thomas,* 'Past Masters.' Translated by H. T. Lowe Porter. (London, 1933.)

Moser, Max, 'Richard Wagner in der englischen Literatur des 19. Jahrhunderts.' (Berne, 1938.)

* *Newman, Ernest,* 'A Study of Wagner.' (London, 1899.)

* —— 'Wagner as Man and Artist.' (2nd edition, 1923.)

—— 'Fact and Fiction about Wagner.' (1933.)

* —— 'Wagner Nights.' (London, 1949.)

Nietzsche, Friedrich, 'Die Geburt der Tragödie aus dem Geiste der Musik.' (Chemnitz, 1872; 2nd edition, 1878.)

—— Richard Wagner in Bayreuth.' (1876.)

—— 'Der Fall Wagner.' (1888.)

—— 'Nietzsche contra Wagner.' (1889.)

Pohl, Richard, 'Richard Wagner, ein Lebensbild.' (Leipzig, 1883.)

Porges, H., 'Die Aufführung von Beethovens neunter Symphoni unter Richard Wagner in Bayreuth.' (Leipzig, 1872.)

—— 'Die Bühnenproben zu den Festpielen im Jahre 1876.' (Chemnitz, 1883.)

* *Rayner, Robert M.*, 'Wagner and *Die Meistersinger*.' (Oxford, 1940.)

Runciman, J. F., 'Richard Wagner, Composer of Operas.' (London, 1913.)

Schneider, Marcel, 'Wagner.' (Paris, 1960.)

Shaw, G. B., 'The Perfect Wagnerite; a Commentary on the Nibelung's Ring.' (2nd edition, London, 1903.)

* *Skelton, Geoffrey*, 'Wagner at Bayreuth.' (London, 1965.)

Soubies, A., and *Malherbe, C. T.*, 'Mélanges sur Wagner.' (Paris, 1892.)

Stein, Herbert von, 'Dichtung und Musik im Werk Richard Wagners.' (Berlin, 1962.)

Stein, Jack M., 'Richard Wagner and the Synthesis of the Arts.' (Detroit, 1960.)

Von Westernhagen, C., 'Richard Wagner: sein Werk, sein Wesen, sein Welt.' (Zürich, 1956.)

Weingartner, Felix, 'Bayreuth.' (2nd edition, 1904.)

* *Weston, Jessie*, 'Legends of the Wagner Drama.' (London, 1896.)

Wolzogen, Hans Paul Freiherr von, 'Thematische Leitfaden . . . der Ring des Nibelungen.' (Leipzig, 1876.) Translated by E. von Wolzogen. (London; Leipzig, 1882.)

—— 'Thematische Leitfaden . . . Parsifal.' (Leipzig, 1882.) Translated by W. A. Ellis. (London, 1889.)

—— 'Tristan und Isolde. Ein Leitfaden durch Sage, Dichtung und Musik.' (Leipzig, 1880.) Translated by B. L. Mosely. (Leipzig, 1884.)

Zuckerman, Eliot, 'The First Hundred Years of Wagner's Tristan.' (London, 1964.)

Memoirs

Fricke, 'Bayreuth vor dreissig Jahren.' (Dresden, 1906.)

* *Gauthier, Judith*, 'Wagner at Home.' Translated by E. D. Massie. (London, 1910.)

Kietz, G. A., 'Richard Wagner in den Jahren 1842–9 und 1873–5.' (Dresden, 1905.)

Neumann, Angelo, 'Erinnerungen an Richard Wagner.' (Leipzig, 1907.) Translated by Edith Livermore. (London, 1909.)

Perl, Henry, 'Richard Wagner in Venedig.' (Augsburg, 1883.)

* *Praeger, Ferdinand,* 'Wagner as I knew him.' (London, 1892.)

Schuré, Edouard, 'Richard Wagner, son œuvre et son idée.' (Paris, 1930.)

Weissheimer, W., 'Erlebnisse mit Richard Wagner, Franz Liszt und vielen anderen Zeitgenossen nebst deren Briefen.' (Stuttgart and Leipzig, 1898.)

Wolzogen, Hans von, 'Erinnerungen an Richard Wagner.' (Vienna, 1883.) Translated by A. and C. Simpson. (Bayreuth, 1894.)

General Works

* *Bulthaupt, Heinrich,* 'Dramaturgie der Oper.' Vol. II. (Leipzig, 1902.)

Einstein, Alfred, 'Music in the Romantic Era.' (London, 1947.)

Grout, Donald Jay, 'A Short History of Opera.' (London, 2nd ed., 1965.)

Hanslick, Eduard, 'The Beautiful in Music.' (New York, 1957.)

* *Kerman, Joseph,* 'Opera as Drama.' (New York, 1956.)

* *Kurth, Ernst,* 'Romantische Harmonik und ihre Krise in Wagners "Tristan."' (Berlin, 1923.)

Schuré, Edouard, 'Le Drame Musical.' 2 vols. (Paris, 1875.)

Miscellaneous

Du Moulin-Eckart, Richard, 'Cosima Wagner.' (Munich, 1929–1931.)

Bülow, Hans von, 'Letters.' Translated by Hannah Waller. (London, 1931.)

APPENDIX E

SELECTED LIST OF LITERARY WORKS

SINCE the importance of Wagner's literary works resides primarily in their bearing upon his art, the reader's interest will, it is believed, be better served by a selected list of the more significant of them, than by a comprehensive one including all the sundry articles, reviews, open letters, reports, addresses, programme notes, libretti, scraps of verse and reminiscence which Wagner wrote. A complete list is given on the contents page of Julius Kapp's edition of the *Gesammelte Schriften* (Leipzig, 1914). The greater proportion of them have been translated by W. Ashton Ellis (*The Prose Works of Richard Wagner.* London, 1892–9). Again the dates given are those of composition, not publication. Of the two works listed under the heading 'Collections', *Wagner on Music and Drama* is an anthology of significant excerpts and *Wagner Writes from Paris* a new translation of selected early Parisian stories and articles.

AUTOBIOGRAPHICAL WORKS

An End in Paris; The Artist and The Public (1840–1).
Autobiographical Sketch (1842).
A Communication to my Friends (1851).
My Life (1865–70).
The Work and Mission of my Life (1879).

SPECULATIVE, THEORETICAL WORKS

The German Opera (1834).
Pasticcio (1834).
On German Music (1840).
A Pilgrimage to Beethoven (1840).
On the Overture (1840).
The Wibelungs (1848).
Art and Revolution (1849).

Appendix E.—Selected List of Literary Works

The Art Work of the Future (1849).
Art and Climate (1850).
Judaism in Music (1850).
Opera and Drama (1850–1).
The Music of the Future (1860).
State and Religion (1864).
What is German? (1865).
German Art and German Policy (1867).
Beethoven (1870).
The Destiny of Opera (1871).
Actors and Singers (1872).
Modern (1878).
Public and Popularity (1878).
The Public in Time and Space (1878).
Shall we hope? (1879).
Open Letter to Herr E. von Weber (concerning vivisection) (1879).
Religion and Art (1880).
What boots this Knowledge? (1880).
Know Thyself (1881).
Hero-dom and Christianity (1881).
On the Human Womanly (1882).

Works concerning the Technics of his Art

The Virtuoso and the Artist (1840).
Concerning the Royal Orchestra (1844).
A Project for the Organization of a German National Theatre for the Kingdom of Saxony (1848).
A Theatre at Zürich (1851).
On the performing of 'Tannhäuser' (1852).
Remarks on performing 'The Flying Dutchman' (1853).
Gluck's Overture to 'Iphigenia in Aulis' (1854).
On Franz Liszt's Symphonic Poems (1857).
The Vienna Court Opera House (1863).
Report to His Majesty King Ludwig II of Bavaria upon a German Music-School to be founded in Munich (1865).
On Conducting (1869).

The rendering of Beethoven's Ninth Symphony (1873).
On Poetry and Composition (1879).
On Operatic Poetry and Composition (1879).
On the Application of Music to the Drama (1879).

REMINISCENCES

Recollections of Spontini (1851).
Recollections of Ludwig Schnorr von Carolsfeld (1868).
Recollections of Rossini (1868).
Recollections of Auber (1871).

COLLECTIONS

Albert Goldman and Evert Sprinchorn, *Wagner on Music and Drama.* (London, 1970).
Robert L. Jacobs and Geoffrey Skelton, *Wagner Writes from Paris* (London, 1973).

APPENDIX F

THE NIBELUNG'S RING

THE RHINEGOLD

THE Prelude tone-paints the flowing Rhine, and the curtain rises on the bed of the river. In the upper water three river nymphs, the Rhinemaidens, are playfully darting and diving. Their singing reveals, however, that they are guarding the Rhinegold embedded in the crest of one of the rocks jutting up from the murky bed of the river.

Presently there emerges from a dark cleft an ugly dwarf, Alberich, one of the tribe of Nibelungs who dwell under the earth. Stirred by the sight of the lovely frolicking maidens, he calls to them to let him join their play, to let him caress and love them. Then a sport begins. First one nymph, then another more boldly, then the third most boldly of all, dives down to this preposterous satyr to incite him with tender words and gestures, only to soar out of his reach. Gaily in chorus the three celebrate their game; gaily they evade the desperate pursuit of the maddened dwarf clambering through the wrack of the river-bed 'with terrible agility.'

Suddenly a strange glow illuminates the waters, arresting Alberich. It grows to a magical brilliance, at the heart of which shimmers the gold embedded here. Joyfully the Rhinemaidens circle the rock, singing of the 'laughing' radiance shedding its glory through the deep. 'What is it?' asks the spellbound dwarf, and they tell him: it is the gold to possess which were to inherit the earth; for a ring fashioned therefrom would give the wearer power unlimited. Then they prattle on, gaily contemptuous: since this ring can be fashioned only by one who forswears love, and since no man will do that—least of all this languishing dwarf—what harm in thus revealing their trust?

Listening, Alberich is seized by a fierce resolution. He climbs the rock and gains the summit; he shouts a curse on love; he grasps the gold, plunging the screaming Rhinemaidens into darkness; he makes off with his booty into the depths.

The scene changes to a spacious mountain height towering above the Rhine. Across the valley stands a lofty castle, its turrets and pinnacles sparkling in the light of a gathering dawn. Wotan, the Father of the Gods, and Fricka, his wife, are sleeping here; they wake with the dawn and beholding the castle—it is the newly completed home of the Gods—are deeply moved. Wotan, its architect, who has been dreaming of it, rejoices. But Fricka is filled with alarm and anger. She reminds her husband of the price he has promised to the builders of the castle, the giants Fafner and Fasolt: the award of Freya, her sister, pledged heedlessly, she complains, by Wotan in his blind greed for power. To her, she declares, this castle is a home to which she may bind the restless God, her husband. To Wotan—Wotan now admits, thereby angering her still further—it is a home from which to emerge to roam the world and win it. But faithless though he is, he reveres the honour of womanhood (did he not give his left eye to win her, Fricka, as his wife?) and he has no intention, nor ever had, of abandoning Freya.

Now Freya runs to them in terror, for the giants are pursuing her. 'Where is Loge?' Wotan asks in effect, thereby again incensing Fricka. For it was Loge, the God of Fire and Cunning—Loge, distrusted by her—who advised this bargain, promising to devise a means of redeeming Freya. And so where is he? (Where indeed? scoffs Fricka.) . . . Now come the giants, heavy-footed, demanding reward for labour performed, and roused to just indignation by Wotan's unabashed refusal to surrender Freya. Solemnly Fasolt reminds him that to betray them is to betray the whole social order of which he, the God and Lawgiver, is the pillar. Bitterly the poor giant resents the scorn which the God throws upon his love for the divine Freya. Fafner, the other giant, is cleverer: not for herself he values Freya, but for the fact that, deprived of the Golden Apples of Eternal Youth which she alone can tend, the Gods will fade away. The giants are only prevented from there and then dragging off Freya by the arrival of her brothers, Froh and Donner, whose efforts to save her, however, are thwarted by the Spear of Wotan, stretched forth—as stretch it forth he must at last, despite himself—to preserve the law.

At length the long-awaited Loge comes. At first he prevaricates, irritates. He has inspected the castle, he says, and found it well and truly built. . . . How to redeem Freya? . . . He has thought long thereon and cannot say. Wotan, who knows his Loge (Wotan it was who admitted the amoral, ubiquitous Fire Spirit to the ranks of the Gods), calms the others' wrath, and presses him. Loge reports that he has scoured the four corners of the globe, probed far and wide, only to find that the love of woman admits of no compensation. One man alone has renounced it, Alberich. Loge heard the lament of the Rhinemaidens for their stolen gold and promised to ask the Supreme Lawgiver to restore it. Impatiently Wotan brushes this aside. But when, in answer to Fafner's querying, Loge goes on to tell of the magic Ring and its promise of world power, the God's greed is awakened. How to obtain that Ring? he asks. Wilfully misunderstanding him, Loge replies that that would be easy, since it is Alberich who has paid the price; Wotan would merely have to steal from the thief his booty and restore it to its rightful owners. Before the God can decide the issue of his conflicting emotions, the giants, who have been taking counsel together, break in upon him with an offer to take this gold as Freya's ransom. At this, Wotan bursts into a rage: must he win the gold only in order to give it away, and to *them*? . . . But the giants are not to be shaken. They will go, taking Freya as their hostage, and return this evening for that ransom. Let Wotan find it, or Freya will be theirs for ever.

They go, and with their departure the stage becomes misty and the Gods wan and old—all save Loge, who mocks their plight, deprived of Freya's Golden Apples. . . . Wotan reaches a decision. He will deprive the Nibelung of his gold, not to restore it to the Rhinemaidens, but to ransom Freya. Loge shall assist him. At once, through a cleft in the mountain-side, the two of them descend, bound for Nibelheim, the home of the dwarfs.

The scene changes to Nibelheim, a dark and cavernous place.

Alberich enters, dragging with him another dwarf, Mime, a cunning goldsmith, now his recalcitrant slave. Writhing beneath the other's blows, Mime lets fall a piece of metal, which he had been working for Alberich and which he had planned to hide from him—the magic helmet, the Tarnhelm, of the Rhinegold, which gives its wearer the power to assume what shape he chooses. Alberich snatches it up, dons it, renders himself invisible, trounces the thief, and then departs in triumph to lord it over the other Nibelungs.

Wotan and Loge arrive, and they discover Mime, who sobs out his sad story. In the old days the gold which the Nibelungs had found and forged had been theirs with which to make toys and trinkets for their womenfolk; now they have to sweat for Alberich's profit. Soon the visitors see for themselves. Alberich returns, driving before him the horde of Nibelungs, whipping Mime into their midst, railing and threatening, spurred on by the sight of the strangers. . . . Their presence arouses his suspicion, nevertheless; soon he sends his victims packing and rounds on them: what do they want here? They have come to learn and admire, Wotan replies. Easily Loge draws out the simple dwarf (for that he is still). With this gold of his, Alberich proclaims, he will cause all men to renounce love as he did; he will corrupt and swing to his purpose all men, and women too; yes, the very Gods themselves. Duly impressed, Loge points, however, to the danger of theft: how will Alberich protect his treasure? Proudly the dwarf produces the Tarnhelm, and, Loge professing incredulity, there and then transforms himself into a dragon. Very fine, Loge exclaims, but would not greater safety lie in being tiny—as a toad, for instance? No sooner said than done. But no sooner done than caught, Wotan's foot across the squirming toad. Instantly Alberich becomes himself again, but it is too late. Bound hand and foot, his captors drag him off up to the mountain height whence they came.

The three reach the mountain height of the second scene and Alberich is ordered to disgorge his treasure. At his command the Nibelungs come to deliver up the gold and witness his humiliation. But this he can bear, even the loss of the Tarnhelm; it is not until

Wotan pitilessly wrests the guerdon of world power, the Ring, from his finger that despair possesses him. Released, he delivers a curse upon all who henceforward inherit the Ring without paying for it as he did—delivers it with a vehemence terrible and fearful, dwarf though he is.

Alberich departs. The giants, with Freya, at whose approach the mist dissolves, come to inspect her ransom. The other Gods assemble. Like Alberich before him Wotan can bear the ordeal up to a point. Fasolt insists upon a quantity of gold which piled up will hide Freya from his view, for only thus can he endure her loss. Piled up, the gold hides her, save only for a chink, to stop which the Tarnhelm is sacrificed. Fasolt peers again: alas, he cries, through the barrier of gold he has caught the flash of his beloved's eye! That Ring there on Wotan's finger, says Fafner, will serve to hide it.

Absolutely Wotan will not part with it. Loge's advice that he return it to the Rhinemaidens, the giants' threats, Freya's wails for help, Fricka's, Froh's and Donner's pleas, nothing can move him. . . . But suddenly at this critical moment there is an interruption: from a cleft in the mountain-side a figure rises, that of the all-knowing, eternal World-Mother, Erda, who delivers a message, solemn, mysterious and ominous. Let Wotan yield up the Ring, she sings, let him beware the Curse; for the days of the Gods are numbered, and their future dark. Before Wotan, hungry for more knowledge, can stay her she has sunk back into the depths. . . . Wotan yields up the Ring. At once, with fearful impact, the Curse descends upon the giants. Each claims the Ring, Fasolt because he loved the maid, whom he surrendered, the more, Fafner because he loved her less. In the ensuing quarrel Fafner smites Fasolt dead, thereafter to collect his treasure and make off with it alone, a murderer. . . . And so Freya is redeemed; but it is with a sense of guilt and fear, of one caught in the toils of his own actions and heading he knows not whither, that Wotan stands and counts the cost, Loge mocking, Fricka caressing him. Donner alone—Donner, the God of Thunder—is able to clear the charged air. Swinging his tremendous hammer he conjures a storm, and thereafter a rainbow, to form a bridge across the valley to the Gods' new home, now gleaming in the light of the setting sun. About to set forth, Wotan is seized by a momentous thought; as if acting thereon, he turns solemnly to Fricka and invites her to follow him now into their castle—into 'Walhall,' as he calls it for the first time. The name, born of his thought—it means 'Home of the Elect'—is strange to her and she inquires its significance. When the vision which upheld him in the moment of fear, he replies enigmatically, has been embodied in a victory, then, on that day, will he tell her.

And so they mount the rainbow. 'They are going to their doom,' muses Loge, who lingers behind. Shall he not revert to his own element, become a flame once more and consume them all one day? Perhaps. He is reckless, feckless. 'Who knows what I shall do?' he asks. Nonchalantly he wanders away from them.

As the Gods march across into their Valhalla, it is the Rhine-maidens who have the last word, their lament for the gold they played with, now stolen and bartered away, rising up from the river valley:

> 'Tender and true 'tis but in the waters,'

they sing,

> 'False and base are all who revel above.'

The Valkyrie

Act I

The scene is the forest dwelling of one Hunding. It is evening. Outside a terrific storm is raging.

The door opens and a wounded man, dishevelled, staggers in out of the storm, seeking refuge; he flings himself upon a rug by the hearth, too exhausted to care where he is or what will befall him here. At once Hunding's wife comes in; seeing the stranger, her astonishment soon gives way to pity for his plight. She succours him, brings water to quench his thirst and honey's mead for his wound, and as she does so they gaze upon each other with a strange intensity. Both are young and of heroic aspect.

Refreshed, he rises. He must continue on his way, he tells her, lest he bring upon her the ill fortune that has pursued him his life long. At this she breaks out impetuously that he cannot add to the ill fortune that is hers already in this house. And so he stays.

Now Hunding enters, a grim formidable figure, and at the sight of the pair is filled with suspicion. Nevertheless he invites the man to share his meal and asks for his story. . . . His father, the stranger tells, was Wolfe, a mighty hunter and warrior; when he was a child, enemies slew his mother and abducted his twin sister. Thereafter he roamed the forest with his father, hunting and fighting, until one day their foes separated them for ever. Then he left the forest and roamed among men; but their ways were not his ways; misfortune dogged him wherever he went—hence his name, Wehwalt, Bringer of Woe. . . . Finally the stranger tells of the affray which brought him to this door, of blood spilt by him in defence of a helpless woman, of a flight, weaponless, from a host of enemies lusting for revenge. . . . Hunding's ire is aroused now, for those enemies are his kinsmen, and their feud his feud. His guest may bide the night, he announces sternly, but by to-morrow let him find a weapon, for to-morrow Hunding will claim his life for the lives he has taken.

Hunding bids his wife prepare his night draught before they retire. She obeys slowly, her eye transfixed by the stranger, and by an object embedded in the tree around which the forest dwelling is built. He impatiently drives her before him.

Alone, the stranger vents his longing for the unhappy wife—but still more at this moment, his longing for a sword. It was a sword, he recalls, that his father promised he would find in his hour of direst need: where shall he find it? As he sings, the hilt of a sword embedded in the tree glows mysteriously in the flickering light of the fire from the hearth by which he is sitting.

Now the wife returns. She has drugged her husband's night draught; he is safely asleep. In her turn she tells a story—how at her loveless wedding feast an old man had appeared, wearing a hat of which the broad brim concealed one eye; how his majestic aspect filled all with fear save herself, upon whom he gazed with tenderness; how he plunged a sword into the trunk of this tree here, promising it to the man who could draw it forth. All tried, but none succeeded, and then she knew who that old man was, and for whom the sword was destined. Oh!—she cries out suddenly to the man before her—if it were he who would draw it forth, avenge her suffering and deliver her, then would she embrace her saviour! Released by her words, he pours out to her his pent-up passion. The door opens and moonlight floods in, for the wintry storm has passed and the night outside is clear—a glorious night in early spring, the season of hope and deliverance. Lovers now, they gaze upon each other with an intensity mounting to ecstasy, as gradually they reach through to the truth. Her image has haunted his dreams. She has beheld him mirrored in the brooks beneath her; heard his voice in her childhood; seen the glow of his eye in the look of that old man of the wedding feast. At length she questions him: Wehwalt is your name? No, not now that you love me. . . . Wolfe, your father was called? Yes, but his true name was Wälse. At this she is beside herself: Then you are of the line of heroes, of the Walsungs; for you the sword was destined; you are Siegmund! And now putting forth his strength, Siegmund draws the sword, naming it Nothung, and bids her fly with him under its protection. She proclaims herself Sieglinde, his twin sister. Be my bride, he cries, that the 'blood of the Walsungs' may bear fruit! Through the open door out into the moonlit forest they rush away.[1]

Act II

The stage represents a wild mountainous region. Wotan enters and with him his daughter Brynhilda, the Valkyrie, both fully armed. Summarily he commands her to protect Siegmund in his coming battle with Hunding, and she departs to do his bidding. Now comes Fricka in high rage with Wotan for his affront to her dignity—she is the Goddess-Guardian of Marriage—in championing the incestuous adulterer against the husband. Wotan defends his position: this marriage tie was loveless and therefore evil; the incestu-

[1] Wagner specified that the curtain should fall upon an embrace in Hunding's hut—but the music conveys the sense of a rush into the forest. It became customary to end the act thus; nowadays the custom is not always followed, more's the pity.

ous adultery was passionate, true, free and therefore good. She piles up further reproaches: wandering the world as Wälse, breeding these wild Walsungs of his, he has been dishonouring not only herself, his wife, but the laws which he created and which it is his obligation to preserve. He reproaches in his turn her lack of imagination; what is needed, he declares with strange emphasis, is a hero who will perform that 'deed' which is denied the Gods and which alone can save them—a hero, albeit, who will perform it unaided and of his own accord. If that is so, she retorts, then stop favouring Siegmund; withdraw the sword you have given him! . . . Thus unexpectedly hoist with his own petard, Wotan is confounded. He promises, writhing with reluctance, to abandon Siegmund, to revoke his command to Brynhilda. He pledges Fricka his oath. She departs in triumph.

Brynhilda has returned in time to witness her father's humiliation. Now, Fricka having gone, he gives way to an outburst of rage and anguish rising to frenzy. She, his most beloved daughter, his child who knows his inmost wishes (his 'Wish-Child,' he calls her), is shocked and bewildered. She begs him to explain the cause of his emotion. He does so. He tells a very long story: how in his greed for power he built Valhalla and paid for it by stealing another's booty; how thereafter, warned of impending doom by Erda and hungry for more knowledge, he sought out Erda, who conceived by him a daughter—Brynhilda—whom he raised with eight other warrior-maidens, Valkyries, to select heroes from among men and bring them to Valhalla to defend the Gods. . . . But we have done this, Brynhilda exclaims: what, then, do you fear? . . . That Alberich regain the Ring, he replies. Fafner, transformed by the Tarnhelm into a mighty dragon, possesses it now. He, Wotan, can never reclaim the treasure due to the builder of Valhalla. Only a hero can gain it—a hero unaided by the Gods, indeed in opposition to the Gods, bound by their own evil bargain. But how to find this hero? Wotan cries, his despair surging back. How to create him? I taint with myself whatever I touch. I raised Siegmund to lawlessness, to rebellion against the Gods. I bred him to heroism. Now I must abandon him to Fricka's revenge, him whom I loved, in whom I placed my hopes! . . . And so ruin stares Wotan in the face—the ruin for which Alberich is working. Erda has told him that should the Nibelung ever beget a son, then the doom of the Gods would not be far off, and this Alberich has done. Yes, the Nibelung will inherit the earth, Wotan concludes bitterly, and much good may it do him!

Hearing all this, Brynhilda is moved to eloquent protest at the violation to her father's feeling inflicted by the command that she obey Fricka now, and protect not Siegmund but Hunding. Inexorably, wrathfully, he insists, and storms off, leaving her sad and unwilling.

Siegmund and Sieglinde approach and Brynhilda retires to watch them. They enter in agitation, Sieglinde flying not only from danger, but from the memory of her loveless and therefore to her mind shameful marriage, Siegmund imploring her to stay here, to rest herself. His words of love serve only to aggravate her sense of unworthiness. She hears Hunding's horn and the baying of hounds. He is coming, she cries, he and his clan, lusting for Siegmund's blood; coming with their hounds to hunt him down and tear his flesh. The vision overcomes her and she faints in his arms. Siegmund draws her down, seats himself, rests her head on his lap, and as he caresses her, awaiting his enemies, Brynhilda solemnly steps forward and reveals herself to him as a Valkyrie, upon whom only a hero such as he is—a hero about to die and live on thereafter in Valhalla—may gaze. Never will he follow her there, he quietly says, unless Sieglinde accompany him. That she may not, the Valkyrie announces; and neither can Siegmund escape his destiny, for Wotan has withdrawn the spell cast upon his sword. At this Siegmund breaks out in anguish for the helpless woman he must leave—but not in order to join in Valhalla the father who betrayed him, no, but to depart to Hella! Then she is worth more to you even than Valhalla? Brynhilda asks, deeply moved by the spectacle of such a love. He turns upon her with scorn: Feast your cold eyes upon my misery if you must, but do not prate to me of the 'empty joys' of your Valhalla! Distressed beyond measure, she begs him to entrust Sieglinde to her care. He draws his sword:

rather will he kill himself and Sieglinde with this useless weapon! Beside herself, she stops him: Valkyrie or no Valkyrie, her shield she will use to protect him, not Hunding, that the lovers may live, not die!

Brynhilda disappears.

Dark thunderclouds press upon the mountain peaks as Siegmund turns once more to the still sleeping Sieglinde. Lovingly he caresses her, lays her down, kisses her forehead as if in farewell, before he departs into the darkness to meet the oncoming foe. Left alone, Sieglinde stirs restlessly, troubled by dreams of the flaming homestead of her childhood, of her absent father, her absent brother. With the cry 'Siegmund!' on her lips she wakes to a terrible reality. Siegmund and Hunding are shouting challenges as they seek each other in the mountain pass. She rushes between them as they meet at last—to stagger back, blinded by the light of Brynhilda's shield, stretched before Siegmund. Siegmund raises his sword to strike —but it is shattered, not by Hunding, but by a weapon, more formidable than Brynhilda's, protecting Hunding: Wotan's Spear. And so Hunding slays Siegmund.

In the darkness, which descends again, Brynhilda is glimpsed—Brynhilda, faithful to the memory of Siegmund, lifting the senseless Sieglinde upon her horse and hurrying away. But the last word is with Wotan. Having dismissed the victorious Hunding with a godlike contempt which withers and blasts him dead on the spot, he rages against Brynhilda, his disobedient vassal, and disappears amid thunder and lightning to find and punish her.

Act III

Upon a mountain peak Brynhilda's eight sisters, the Valkyries, are assembling. Four have arrived already and they call greetings to the others as they come, riding their horses through the clouds, each with a fallen hero across her saddle. Before they stride upon the peak they dismount and put their steeds to graze in a wood near by; as they watch these horses of theirs, fierce and mettlesome like the heroes they bear, push and kick against each other, they send out great peals of Valkyrie laughter. . . . All have arrived at last and they await only Brynhilda, that they may fare together with their heroes to Valhalla. But when Brynhilda comes it is with a strangely frantic haste and the body across her saddle is no hero's, but a woman's. Soon she is among them, leading Sieglinde, and the tale she tells arouses their astonishment and fear. None dares to grant her urgent plea—urgent, because Wotan will be upon her at any moment—to lend Sieglinde a horse, that she may escape him. . . . As for Sieglinde, it is death alone that she desires, she says; let the Valkyrie atone for having saved her by killing her here and now. But she must live, Brynhilda replies; she must live for the sake of Siegmund's child within her womb. Her despair transformed to courage, Sieglinde now in her turn beseeches aid of the Valkyries, but in vain. For Wotan is drawing nearer now, riding an approaching storm. Then fly alone, Brynhilda cries, and I will stay and, confronting Wotan's wrath, detain him; fly to the eastern forest, where Fafner guards Alberich's hoard, the region Wotan shuns; fly, enduring hunger and travail, knowing that you are destined to bear the most glorious hero in the world; fly, and take with you these fragments gathered by me, which once were Siegmund's sword. And let me name, she concludes, the hero who one day will forge them: Siegfried! Raised to the highest pitch of exaltation by this message, Sieglinde goes, embracing her destiny, blessings on her lips.

Wotan's voice is heard now and, cowering, Brynhilda seeks shelter among her sisters, retreating before him as he enters, angrily shouting for her. He scorns their 'womanish' appeal for mercy. Let this 'Wish-Child' of his who opposed his wish, who has turned against him the knowledge of his spirit, which he, her God and Father, breathed into her, come forward and hear her sentence. Humbly she comes, and he delivers it: her act speaks for itself; thereby she has disowned her daughterhood; his child no longer, a Valkyrie no longer, henceforth she will belong to the first man who wakes her from a magic sleep into which he will plunge her here upon this rock. Deaf to her sisters' anguished protest, he orders them off. The two are left alone, the father and the daughter, and a long silence falls between them.

At length Brynhilda speaks, and the case for her defence is strong. Was my offence really so shameful? she asks. Was I not only carrying out your real wish, despite yourself? Was it not Siegmund whom you loved, despite yourself? She goes on to tell of her meeting with Siegmund and of the knowledge of love she won from him—the knowledge in virtue of which she disobeyed her father. At this Wotan bursts out in raging self-pity again: fiercely though he may long for it, he, the God, may never enjoy this knowledge, and therefore their paths must separate. . . . Then she pleads against the form of her sentence: thus to dishonour his child is to dishonour himself. She tells of Sieglinde's destiny, of the child, Siegfried, within her womb, and the fragments of Nothung in her hand. Still he is inexorable; she must bear her punishment, and he pronounces it once more. She falls on her knees. One thing only she begs of him: let him not leave her the prey of the first intruder; let him conjure a fire around her that will daunt the approach of all save the bravest hero. And this he grants her, as he sings a grief-laden farewell. Kissing her eyes, 'kissing her Godhood away,' he sends her to sleep; then, summoning Loge, raises a protecting fire. 'Whosoever fears my Spear's point let him not cross this fire,' he proclaims before he turns away and disappears.

Siegfried

Act I

In his cavern Mime, the Nibelung, is hammering disconsolately at a sword upon his anvil. He sings of his troublesome foster-child, Siegfried, who is bound to break this sword, which Mime is forging for him, as he has broken all the others, so strong is he. One sword alone, Nothung, would resist Siegfried. Mime has the fragments, but all his skill notwithstanding, he cannot forge them.

Could he but do so he would incite Siegfried to turn it upon the mighty dragon, Fafner, guarding the Nibelung treasure in the forest outside. The dragon once slain, the treasure would then be his, Mime's.

Now in boisterous high spirits the foster-child appears. With him is a bear he had captured to frighten Mime with. When he has played out the joke and driven the bear away, he picks up the sword Mime has been working upon, tests it, smashes it and abuses the incompetent forger. . . . Loud and long is the dwarf's complaint: he has, he whines, nurtured Siegfried, warmed him, fed him, clothed him, sheltered him, taught him, he the 'poor old dwarf,' and this is his reward! Siegfried admits all this. And yet, he declares, he detests Mime—so intensely, indeed, that he cannot understand why he still treats this cavern as his home, why he returns here every day from the forest. (He brushes aside Mime's preposterous 'My child, that is because you really love me.') Out in the forest, Siegfried continues, like only consorts with like—fox with fox, deer with deer, bird with bird. Why then does he consort with Mime? Posing the question thus, he hits upon the answer: it is to find out from his foster-parent who his real parents were. The dwarf grows confused and angry; 'I am both your father and your mother!' he shrieks ridiculously. Only brute force wrings the truth from him: he took Siegfried, a babe, from a dying mother . . . nurtured him, he whines on, warmed him, fed him—— I've heard all that before, Siegfried breaks in; who was my mother? . . . She was Sieglinde, and his father died in combat. Siegfried demanding proof, Mime produces the fragments of Nothung, entrusted to him by Sieglinde. Forthwith Siegfried commands him to forge the sword. Then with it he will go out into the forest and into the world, free at last never to set eye on Mime again.

He rushes out leaving the dwarf in despair before a hopeless task. A stranger enters, a majestic figure in a broad-brimmed hat concealing one eye, and carrying a mighty spear as staff. He is known as the Wanderer, he announces; he is wise and can impart useful knowledge. He will wager his head upon his ability to answer any question the dwarf may put. Fear and suspicion prevent Mime from profiting by the offer. He asks only what he himself already knows: Who live beneath the earth's surface? who upon it? who above it? The Nibelungs, the Wanderer answers, the Giants, and the Gods. Then the Wanderer continues: Since Mime did not know what it would have profited him to ask, he will now wager Mime's head upon his ability to answer three questions. He asks the dwarf: Which is the race whom the Gods chastised, yet loved? The Walsungs, is the reply. What sword must Siegfried, the child of the Walsungs, wield to slay Fafner? Nothung, is the reply. Who will forge Nothung? Alas, Mime cannot reply. The Wanderer tells him: 'Only he who has never learnt fear' shall wield it, and to that man, whoever he is, shall Mime's head be forfeit. And so the Wanderer, who is Wotan, goes.

When Siegfried returns it is not only to find his sword unforged, but the dwarf in a state of panic, raving of one 'who has never learnt fear.' At length the hero's curiosity is aroused; at length also Mime's mother-wit reasserts itself. There is something of value he must teach Siegfried, he says, before he ventures out into the world, namely, the meaning of fear. He tries to teach Siegfried: has he never felt it, he asks, in the dark, sinister depths of the forest, in the mysterious rustling of twilight; has he never shivered and trembled, his limbs never failed him, his blood never run cold? But no, Siegfried has never felt any of this. Fafner could teach you, Mime continues, and he tells of the fearsome dragon. Agog for the adventure, Siegfried orders him back to the sword, and upon Mime's refusal, sets about forging it himself. . . . As he works on with a superb energy and strength Mime knows that he will forge it and that he will slay Fafner. As for Mime, he will brew a poisonous drink—will brew it now—and offer it to the victor after the battle. And so both of them work on—the one exultant, innocent, ignorant, riding to his triumph; the other exultant, too, but cunning and knowing, riding to his doom—until at last the sword is brandished aloft by Siegfried, whole and true once more.

Act II

It is night. Outside Fafner's cavern in the forest Alberich lurks, watching and waiting, sinister yet pathetic, consumed by the passion of his frustrated greed, and of his rankling grievance. Whereas the Wanderer, who presently joins him, is no longer the guilt-laden, troubled Wotan of old. Alberich's threats do not move, rather they amuse him. What must be, must be, he answers; quarrel not with me, but with Mime who is bringing here an ignorant boy who, he hopes, will slay Fafner and gain the Ring for him. As though to tease Alberich he there and then wakes Fafner to warn him. And when the impervious, possessive dragon refuses the Nibelung's over-eager offer to hold the Ring and so avert the danger, Wotan laughs aloud before he goes.

Alberich, riveted to the place, steals behind a rock. Dawn comes up and with it come Siegfried and Mime, who have been travelling through the night. Arrived, Mime tries to curdle Siegfried's blood with horrid details of the dragon close by, but Siegfried's only concern is to be rid of his abominable little foster-parent. Having driven him away (though only for the time being since Mime has promised to return with a drink to refresh him after the battle), the boy, free at last, stretches himself beneath a lime-tree and muses in the hush of the sunlit forest. What did his father look like? he wonders; why, like himself, of course!—like whom but himself? (least of all like that crooked, drivelling little hunchback of a Mime!) . . . But whom his mother resembled, that Siegfried cannot say, for he has never seen a female human being, only animals. Perhaps she was like a roe-deer, only far more beautiful! Ah, why must she have died? . . . As he muses the hush seems to deepen until suddenly he senses the swell of forest murmurs and within them the voice of a bird singing as if in answer to his question. Perhaps if he himself were to imitate the song he would learn to grasp it; he jumps up, plucks a reed, cuts it, blows—but the imitation is beyond him. Through the forest murmurs the bird sings on, and now Siegfried, quickened by the sound, takes up his horn and calls back to the bird with a ditty of his own, gay, fast, and loud.

The call is answered, not indeed by the bird, but by Fafner, lunging out of his cavern. Light-heartedly Siegfried challenges him to teach him fear. Fafner answers in another spirit: he has come out to drink and now he finds food. Easily Siegfried avoids the poisonous steam from the monster's nostrils and the dangerous lashings of his tail; easily he plunges Nothung into his heart. With his dying breath Fafner inquires the name of his fair slayer, so unaware of his momentous deed, and warns him of death in his turn at the hands of those who incited him to it. . . . Unimpressed, Siegfried draws his sword from the dead body; as he does so his hand becomes blood-stained; he sucks it, and at once, by virtue of a magic in the dragon's blood, is able to understand the song the bird is singing. She is telling of the Ring, the Tarnhelm, and of the gold hidden in the cavern. He goes to find them. His back turned, Alberich and Mime, like a pair of ravenous dogs nosing after the remains of a feast, creep in—and at the sight of each other set up a terrible yapping and snarling. They slip away when Siegfried returns, with the Ring on his finger and the Tarnhelm fastened to his girdle. Again the bird sings, this time to warn the hero of Mime. Since the blood he has tasted has given Siegfried the power to read Mime's thoughts, the plot which the dwarf returns to execute is foredoomed to ludicrous disaster. Obsequiously, ingratiatingly, he informs Siegfried that, Siegfried having served his purpose, he intends to poison him with this drink he is offering and thereafter cut off his head. Tittering with glee at the thought of the Ring within his grasp, he pours out the drink and presses it on Siegfried—who strikes him dead with his sword. . . . Siegfried carries the dwarf into the cavern to lie amidst the gold he coveted, and pushes the huge body of his other victim into the entrance to seal the tomb. Then, hot and tired after the exertion, he stretches himself once more beneath the lime-tree, rejoicing in its shade. Once more, too, he falls musing in the forest hush, but now there is a note of sadness in his voice as he gazes up at the medley of birds chirping in the branches. He is so alone, he sings; his one companion, a wretched dwarf, he has just killed; will not the bird, his friend, now tell him where he may find another, a true companion? The bird will indeed; she sings of a lovely woman asleep upon a fire-girt mountain peak, his, if he but awaken her. A joy of desire beyond his comprehension grips Siegfried as he hears this. I sing of love, the bird continues, of the raptures and the pangs that only lovers may understand. . . . But can I penetrate the fire, can I awaken her? Siegfried cries. Only he who has never learnt fear can do that, the bird answers, and Siegfried is filled with jubilation. But how to find the rock? This time the bird answers not in song, but by leaving her tree, hovering above Siegfried and then flying off that he may follow her. And follow her he does.

Act III

To the base of Brynhilda's mountain strides Wotan, the Wanderer, to summon from the depths the slumbering World-Mother, Erda, and ask of her how he may stem the destiny which he sees rolling towards him. But in her message this time there is no enlightenment, only protest. Men's ways have clouded her spirit and she desires only the sleep which Wotan has disturbed. Justifying his ways to her, it is he who in the event enlightens: the downfall of the Gods no longer troubles him, since through Siegfried his crime can be absolved and the Curse of the Ring negated. For this child of the Walsungs came to being despite Wotan, won the Ring unaided, won it furthermore without coveting it, fearlessly and innocently. The Curse cannot touch him therefore. Soon the hero will awaken Erda's wise daughter, the Valkyrie, and gladly the God will yield the future of the world to them in the glory of their youth.

And so Wotan returns Erda to her sleep and calmly faces the approaching Siegfried, whom the bird guides to this spot and then leaves. Siegfried turns to climb the mountain forthwith. Hailed by Wotan, he inquires the way. Instead of telling him, this garrulous, inquisitive passer-by—as he seems to Siegfried—questions him and elicits his story, which he laughs with pleasure to hear. Siegfried is impatient, irritated. Rudely he comments upon the other's strange, broad-brimmed hat and missing eye; roughly he bids him begone, lest he share Mime's fate. . . . The Wanderer answers gently, captivated by the proud, radiant youth, yet affronted nevertheless, answering threat with counter-threat, until finally he breaks out in anger and forbids Siegfried's progress into the furnace, of which the glow fringing the mountain-top becomes visible as he speaks. Undeterred, Siegfried moves on, but now it is Wotan's Spear which bars his way. With a single stroke of Nothung he shatters it. Quietly Wotan bends and gathers the fragments: 'Fare on: I cannot withstand thee,' he says, and passes from Siegfried.

Siegfried climbs through the fire to the summit of the mountain and stands in wonder at what he sees: Brynhilda's horse, Grane, sleeping; Brynhilda herself sleeping as Wotan left her, a long shield covering her body, armed and helmeted. His wonder grows when, having removed the shield, he loosens the helmet, and long curling strands of hair fall free—grows still greater when, having untied the breastplate, he beholds a woman. Now at last the fearless hero is to learn the meaning of fear; helpless as a child, he is swept by the power of his emotion to her bosom, crying for the mother he never knew. . . . But she sleeps. Pondering how to awaken her, contemplating her loveliness, he forgets his fear and abandons himself to the joy of kissing her.

His kiss awakens her. With solemn thanksgiving she greets the sun, greets her renewal of life. Joyfully she hails Siegfried—hails the realization of her vision, the fulfilment of Sieglinde's mission, the fulfilment of Wotan's wish despite himself. But these intimations of the past are lost on Siegfried, filled with desire for her—a desire which she now resists. She looks around to her horse grazing in the field, awakened with her; to her helmet and breastplate removed by her lover. She is exposed. Fear seizes her. All her inheritance of knowledge and wisdom, she feels, is slipping away; she is a Valkyrie no longer, sacred no longer, but a forlorn, defenceless woman. . . . In another mood—a mood of almost maternal pride and tenderness—she contemplates the radiant world-conqueror and begs him to guard himself from the onslaught of love, to remain as he is, intact and glorious. But her words serve only to fire his ardour. Be mine, he cries. I was always yours, I will ever be yours, she replies. But be mine now, he urges. At the end she yields with an ardour answering his. Laughing, I love you, she sings in the ecstasy of her passion, and she adds: laughing, perish with you in the bliss of love; laughing, bid farewell to Valhalla; laughing, await the Dusk of the Gods.

The Dusk of the Gods

Act I

Upon Brynhilda's rock sit the World-Mother's three daughters of the night, the Norns, through whose hands flows the Thread of Destiny, of which their Mother alone has foreknowledge. As they spin the Thread, they speak of the history which it embodies, of the rise and fall of Wotan, whose Spear, the shaft of mankind, wrought by him from a branch of the World Ash Tree, has now been shattered and who now awaits his end. But what of the Ring? they ask. What of Alberich's curse? At these words the Thread snaps in their hands and they vanish.

Dawn rises upon the rock and the light of the fire, flickering in the night, subsides. Siegfried and Brynhilda come to bid each other farewell, for he must now return to the world to perform new deeds of heroism. With pride she bids him go; her sole regret, she declares, is for her maidenhood's wisdom dispelled by his love, lost therefore not only to herself, but to him too. Her love will do duty for her wisdom, he answers. He gives her the Ring itself, not (for she has not imparted her wisdom) in trust for the awful power entailed therein, but as a simple love token. In return she gives him her horse, Grane, the living symbol of her lost Valkyriehood. And so they part.

The curtain falls, but the music continues, depicting Siegfried's descent to the Rhineland. When the curtain rises again it is upon the residence of one Gunther, the ruler of the Gibichungs, a clan of river-dwellers. Gunther is seated in his hall with Gutrune, his sister, and Hagen, his half-brother, whose mother is Gunther's mother, Grimhild, but whose father is Alberich. . . . Gunther, a weak man aware of his weakness, asks of the stronger, cleverer Hagen how he may increase his glory. In reply Hagen tells of Siegfried, the dragon-killer and inheritor of the Nibelung's Ring, and of a Valkyrie upon a fire-girt mountain. Concealing the fact that the hero has scaled the mountain and won the Valkyrie, he advises Gunther to marry her. Unmoved by Gunther's astonishment, he insists: Gunther could win Brynhilda were Siegfried to penetrate the flames and bring her to him. Siegfried, once he had drained the love-potion Hagen gave to Gunther's sister and married her, would do this for him. Thus, through Siegfried and Brynhilda could Gunther increase his glory.

Siegfried meanwhile has been sailing the Rhine in search of adventure, and now the sound of his horn reaches the hall of Gunther's dwelling open to the river. Gunther welcomes him, and the hero, for his part, pledges friendship—the friendship, he calls it, of one whose sole birthright is a sword. Questioned by Hagen, he declares that the Nibelung's treasure means nothing to him; thereof he has retained only the Tarnhelm, fastened to his girdle, and the Ring, which he has bestowed upon a 'fair woman' (whom Hagen, but not Gunther, surmises to be Brynhilda). Gutrune, who had withdrawn, now returns bearing a drinking-horn. (Alas for Siegfried that he cannot read their minds as once he could read Mime's! Having heard the songs that women sing he no longer heeds the birds—so he will tell us himself one day. From his ordeal of fire he learnt nothing but the bliss of love and the glory of adventure; emerged not the baptized hero of mankind, of whom Wotan dreamt, but merely a hero among men.)

Whoever drinks the potion Gutrune offers Siegfried will betray his past, will fall in love with the first woman to cross his vision and forget all others. So, having drained the horn, Siegfried becomes enamoured of Gutrune and woos and wins her. Hearing of the bride coveted by Gunther, the woman upon the fire-girt mountain, he readily undertakes to bring her to him. Disguised by the Tarnhelm he will approach in Gunther's form, bear her to the river bank and there change places with Gunther, who will conduct her down the Rhine to his home as bride-elect. Having sworn blood-brotherhood, the two set off, leaving Gutrune overwhelmed by her undreamt-of happiness, and Hagen to watch through the night—to watch, even as his father before him did, and wait for the Ring, now on Brynhilda's finger.

The scene changes; once again we are transported to Brynhilda's rock. She is sitting, contemplating Siegfried's love-token, covering it with kisses. Storm-clouds roll up and presently she hears through them the once familiar sound of an approaching Valkyrie. A voice, that of her sister Waltraute, calls her name; soon Waltraute enters. That she is wildly agitated Brynhilda does not observe, so possessed is she by the hope of Wotan's forgiveness, so eager to impart her happiness. Violently Waltraute disabuses her, repels her. She has come to bring ominous tidings of Wotan and the Gods. . . . After their father parted from Brynhilda he no longer sent his Valkyries to battle, but wandered through the world alone. Not long ago he returned holding in his hand the shattered fragments of his Spear. At his command his heroes cut down the World Ash Tree, piled up its remains in great layers around the Hall of Valhalla, and then assembled there with all the Gods. To them Wotan came, still holding the fragments of his Spear. He seated himself upon his throne. Not one word did he deliver to the expectant, anxious throng. Gravely, silently he sat there awaiting the tidings of his two ravens he had sent out over the earth. At his knees crouched the Valkyries, embracing, beseeching. Once only, to Waltraute weeping on his bosom, he uttered Brynhilda's name in loving remembrance: were she to give back the Ring to the daughters of the Rhine, he had murmured, then might the Curse be lifted and the Gods saved. . . . Unknown to Wotan, Waltraute has fled here to deliver this message; yes, to implore her sister—for she sees the Ring upon her finger—to yield it up. Are you mad? is Brynhilda's reply. I give up this Ring, Siegfried's love-token? Do you know what it means to me (no, how can you know)? It means Siegfried's love, worth more to me than Valhalla itself and all its eternal glory! And she drives away the lamenting Waltraute.

Luridly the fire burns up again around the mountain and through it a figure approaches, strange to Brynhilda, to wreak upon her, albeit unknowingly, a terrible vengeance. Gunther, the Gibichung, he proclaims himself. He commands her to wed him within her cave here; then follow him. She holds aloft the Ring, her protection—but he wrests it from her. Overpowered, she enters the cave.

Before he joins her Siegfried swears upon his sword that he has not betrayed and that he will not betray his brother, Gunther, with the bride that he is wooing for him.

Act II

On the bank of the Rhine outside Gunther's dwelling Hagen is keeping his vigil through the night. At his knees, exhorting and haranguing, crouches the dwarf whose purpose he serves, his father, Alberich. Grim, immobile, Hagen answers the Nibelung as though in a trance he were addressing the figment of an old and evil dream. He owes no gratitude, he declares, to a father who raised him to a life of sad and joyless hatred. Yet Alberich need have no fear, for the Nibelung's purpose is Hagen's own: he will gain the Ring. Satisfied, the father takes leave of his son—of his 'hero,' as he calls Hagen before his voice dies away and he disappears into the darkness.

Another dawn comes up, and with it Siegfried arrives, gay and untired, to report the success of his mission and the approach down the river of Gunther and Brynhilda. Gutrune appears to greet him, and to her, his bride, he delivers his account of the story. The sword Nothung had separated him from Brynhilda in the cave; having followed him down the valley to the river bank, it was to Gunther, with whom he there changed places, that she finally yielded. Reassured, yet still fearful of the hero she is about to wed, Gutrune retires with Siegfried to prepare a festal greeting to the approaching couple, while Hagen remains to summon the Gibich vassals to the marriage.

Raising a cowhorn to his lips Hagen delivers a summons, not to marriage, but to arms—a strange, sinister summons, gloomy and yet charged with a sense of inexorable, fierce triumph. Alarmed, the vassals gather: Where is the enemy? they ask. Grimly he tells them of the approach of their ruler and his bride, wooed for him by Siegfried, the dragon-killer; grimly he bids them sacrifice to the Gods and make merry for the wedding. They laugh at his grimness, and turning to Gunther and Brynhilda, whose boat is now drawing near, deliver a ringing chorus of welcome. . . . Pale, her head bowed, Brynhilda steps ashore, to be presented by Gunther to his vassals. Siegfried and Gutrune come down from the dwelling; presented to this other happy couple, to be united beside Gunther and herself, Brynhilda raises her head—and sees Siegfried.

Now Hagen's purpose is to be fulfilled and richly so. Recovering from her astonishment, Brynhilda perceives on Siegfried's finger the Ring wrested from her; she accuses him of stealing it from Gunther, who denies having possessed it. The truth dawns upon her and she is seized by a passion of rage and more than rage. In wild hysteria she invokes the Gods. If to break her heart be their revenge, she shrieks, then let this man who has broken it be destroyed! Waving back the horrified Gunther she turns to the assembly and charges Siegfried with treachery. 'He forced delight and love from me,' she cries piteously—yet deceitfully, for she is aware that they know nothing of her relation with Siegfried save the occasion of his wooing on behalf of Gunther. Siegfried repudiates the charge of betraying a blood-brother; solemnly over the point of Hagen's outstretched spear he gives his oath. Brynhilda strides through the ring of witnesses, snatches the spear and with a fervour surpassing his swears across it that his oath was a perjury. Siegfried laughs off the charge. He tries to console Gunther. Radiating merriment and good cheer, he draws the vassals away with Gutrune and himself to their wedding feast within the dwelling.

Brynhilda remains with Hagen and Gunther. For a while she stands brooding over her tragedy, bewildered by it. Soon her grief wells up and she is wailing—wailing at this expense of her spirit in this waste of shame, this bondage of her love and wisdom to a traitor. Again the thought of revenge seizes her and Hagen is swift to take advantage of it. How can he assist her cause? Not in open combat, she tells him contemptuously; but were he to strike Siegfried from behind. . . . Now Hagen turns to rally Gunther, mourning his disgrace and the treachery of the man he trusted. Goaded by Brynhilda's reproaches he seeks once more the aid of his cleverer half-brother. One thing alone, Hagen pronounces, can wipe out your disgrace: *Siegfried's death!* . . . Gunther recoils. Remorselessly Hagen and Brynhilda remind him (since, loving Siegfried, he needs must be reminded) of the damning facts. But what of Gutrune? Gunther protests. Hold a hunt to-morrow, Hagen advises, and give out that Siegfried has been slain by a boar. . . . At length Gunther is prevailed upon and they swear revenge in a dark and terrible trio. Then they turn to join the throng within the dwelling—but at that moment, as if to meet them, Siegfried and Gutrune's bridal procession emerges and the three are swept up and borne away to the altars of the Gods, where the double wedding is to be celebrated.

Act III

The scene is the Rhine again—not the depths this time, but the surface of the river winding through a rocky, wooded valley. Here in the sunlight swim the Rhinemaidens, for in the water below it is dark now their shining gold is stolen. In the distance the horns of a passing hunt are heard. Soon a huntsman appears in pursuit of a bear among these rocks. It is Siegfried. Gaily the maidens proceed to coax and wheedle the hero: if they find his bear for him, will he give them that golden Ring upon his finger? They mock his hesitation as he thinks of Gutrune: 'So fair,' they laugh, 'so strong . . . what a pity he is such a miser!' Stung by the words, Siegfried calls to the maidens, who have dived below the surface, to come up again and he will give them the Ring. . . . They emerge, but they have not heard his offer; playful no longer they warn him of the Curse of the Ring. So doing, alas, they defeat their end, for a hero may be coaxed, but not intimidated. Siegfried will die to-day, they insist. Were the Ring worth no more than a finger's weight, he would never yield it to a threat, is his reply. And as for his life, he values it as lightly as a clod of earth—and suiting an action to his words he picks up such a clod and throws it away behind him. . . . The Rhinemaidens sing on for a while —sing of a hero, valiant, but faithless, foolish and blind—before they swim away into the distance and out of sight.

The sounds of the hunt are heard again. Siegfried blows his horn and very soon Gunther, Hagen and some vassals come clambering down into the valley. Since it is late afternoon and they are hot and tired after the day's sport, Hagen proposes that they rest here among the shady rocks and refresh themselves, and so they bring out their wine-skins and drinking-horns, stretch themselves upon the ground and, as it were, chat. Lightly Siegfried tells of his encounter with the Rhinemaidens, of their prophecy that he will meet his death that day. He is thirsty, he says, and Hagen pours him out a drink. As though to draw him out, Hagen asks whether it be true that he can understand the songs of birds. Once he could, Siegfried replies, but since he has heard the songs that women sing he no longer heeds the birds.

Hagen's question, though, would seem to have struck a chord, for now Siegfried offers to enliven Gunther, lying beside him, depressed and gloomy, by telling the story of his youth. All gather round to hear. Siegfried tells of Mime and the forging of Nothung, of the slaying of Fafner and the tasting of the blood. Word for word he repeats the songs the bird sang of the treasure in the cavern and of the treachery of Mime. He describes Mime's end, and Hagen breaks into grim laughter. 'What else did the bird tell you?' the vassals ask. Hagen offers Siegfried a drink to refresh his memory— a drink into which he pours the sap of a herb that will remove the spell of the love-potion. Word for word Siegfried repeats the song the bird sang of the woman upon the fire-girt mountain, of Brynhilda. Transported, carried away by the flood of his returning memory, he sings on, oblivious of his hearers, oblivious of Gunther's consternation—sings of his journey to the mountain, of his ascent through the fire, of his kiss and Brynhilda's awakening.

At that moment two ravens fly out of a bush, circle above Siegfried and soar away over the Rhine. 'Can you read the speech of those ravens?' Hagen asks. Siegfried stands and gazes after them, and it is then that the Nibelung's son drives his spear into the back of the hero. . . . Still Siegfried's thoughts are with Brynhilda. The music of that awakening, the music of the dawn of love, is upon his lips as he dies.

The scene changes to the hall of Gunther's residence. Night has fallen and Gutrune, whose sleep has been troubled by evil dreams, is awaiting the hunters who have not yet returned. Restlessly she moves through the hall. She saw a woman go down to the river bank; was it Brynhilda? . . . She fears Brynhilda. . . She approaches the door of Brynhilda's room, listens, calls her name. There is no reply. Nervously she peeps in. The room is empty. Now, through the bare, dark hall Hagen's call rings, still gloomy, fierce, triumphant. We are home, laden with hunting spoils, he cries grimly; we are home, with the body of Siegfried slain by a wild boar. The hunting party enters and mourners come crowding in. Very soon a quarrel breaks out between the half-brothers and the bereaved Gutrune. She accuses Gunther of murder; Gunther denounces Hagen, who defiantly acknowledges the deed: he has avenged a perjury, one sworn upon his spear—and therefore now he claims this Ring on Siegfried's finger! Gunther resists this shameless attempt, as he calls it, to rob Gutrune of her inheritance, and in the resulting struggle is slain.

At last the Ring is within the son of the Nibelung's grasp. But as he steps forward, the dead hand that wears it raises itself threateningly, and Hagen shrinks back in terror.

Brynhilda enters. She is beyond laments, beyond recriminations; with the stern and solemn composure of one about to deliver a funeral oration she approaches the corpse. It is as though the tears shed for her dead lover had made fertile again the wisdom of which her passion had drained her—the wisdom of the Valkyrie, who was Erda's daughter and Wotan's 'Wish-Child.' With pity rather than bitterness she silences Gutrune's vain reproaches. With the majestic pride of a daughter of Valhalla she commands the vassals to build a funeral pyre of logs upon the edge of the Rhine and to lead to her her horse Grane, that she may ride him into the flames and share the death of a hero.

But now as she stands contemplating the corpse her sternness melts. How true he was, she mourns, and yet how faithless! Gazing upwards she sings her protest to the Gods, but also her resignation. She has loved, she has lost and she has learned. Now she knows all. She has heard the rustling of Wotan's ravens; soon they will wing home with the longed-for tidings; soon she will yield up the Ring.

She takes the Ring from the dead hand and puts it on her finger. She takes also a flaming torch and beckons with it to the ravens still soaring above the river outside; she calls to them to fly home past Brynhilda's rock where Loge still burns and bid him pass up to Valhalla.

Then, casting the torch into Siegfried's funeral pyre, she rides in ecstasy to her death. And when the fire has subsided the waters of the Rhine well up and swimming over the waves are the Rhine-maidens, who joyously recover their Ring from Brynhilda's ashes and draw down with them into the depths the Nibelung's son who sought to keep it from them. . . . A glow is seen in the sky, the glow of Valhalla ablaze, the glow of the Dusk of the Gods. Its brilliance illumines for a last fleeting moment the great hall itself and Wotan within upon his throne, silently facing the throng of Gods and Heroes, the Valkyries at his knees. As the flames sweep over them, blotting them out, the curtain falls and the drama ends.

INDEX